Holly FitzGerald

Ruthless River

Holly Conklin FitzGerald was born in Seattle, Washington, and grew up in Woodbridge, Connecticut. She graduated from Lake Erie College and received a master's degree in counseling from Suffolk University. FitzGerald was a therapist for adults, children, and families for many years before teaching and counseling at Bristol Community College, New Bedford, Massachusetts. She lives with her husband in South Dartmouth, Massachusetts.

Ruthless River

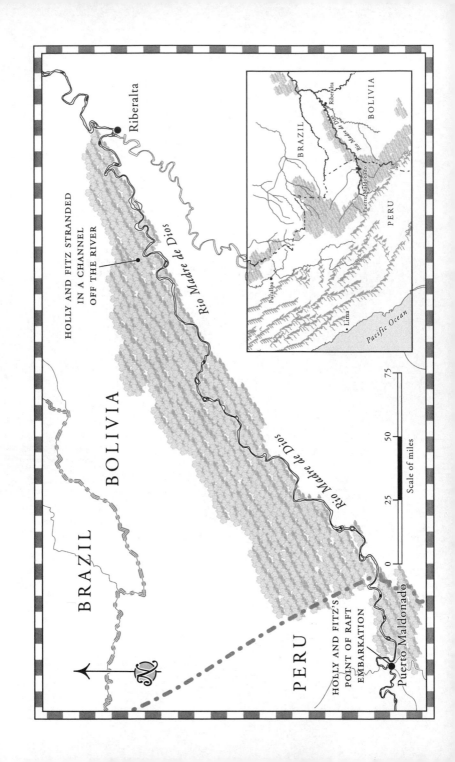

Ruthless

River

Love and Survival by Raft on the
Amazon's Relentless Madre de Dios

Holly FitzGerald

Vintage Departures · *Vintage Books*
A Division of Penguin Random House LLC · New York

A VINTAGE DEPARTURES ORIGINAL, JUNE 2017

Copyright © 2017 by Margaret A. FitzGerald

All rights reserved. Published in the United States by Vintage Books, a division of Penguin Random House LLC, New York, and distributed in Canada by Random House of Canada, a division of Penguin Random House Canada Limited, Toronto.

Vintage is a registered trademark and Vintage Departures and colophon are trademarks of Penguin Random House LLC.

Library of Congress Cataloging-in-Publication Data
Names: FitzGerald, Holly Conklin.
Title: Ruthless river / Holly Conklin FitzGerald.
Description: New York : Vintage, 2017.
Identifiers: LCCN 2016037102
Subjects: LCSH: FitzGerald, Holly Conklin—Travel—Amazon River Region. | Amazon River Region—Description and travel. | Amazon River—Description and travel.
Classification: LCC F2546 .F559 2017 | DDC 918. 1/104—dc23
LC record available at https://lccn.loc.gov/2016037102

**Vintage Departures Trade Paperback ISBN: 978-0-525-43277-7
eBook ISBN: 978-0-525-43278-4**

*Map by Robert Bull
Book design by Jaclyn Whalen*

www.vintagebooks.com

Printed in the United States of America
10 9 8 7 6 5 4 3 2 1

To my beloved Fitz
and to our family

Many waters cannot quench love, neither can the floods drown it . . .

Song of Solomon 8:7 (KJV)

Contents

Ruthless River

Prologue

The thumping wakes me. Small, dark shapes bump against the faded sheeting of the pink plastic tent on our balsa log raft. It's the bees again. They want in.

It's only about nine in the morning, but already our tent is sweltering. The tropical sun casts an intense circle of light halfway up the thin plastic. I want to open the flap for air, but when I do, hundreds of bees will swarm inside to cover our emaciated bodies like hot moving blankets. They will lap the sweat off our sunburned tissue-paper skin, stinging constantly at our slightest movement.

Slowly, the Bolivian jungle is swallowing us alive.

Struggling to sit up on the maroon nylon sleeping bag, I lean over Fitz. He lies on his side, his back to me. I touch him to see if he's breathing. He does the same to me when he wakes first, I think, though I've never dared to ask.

Last night we held each other, as we do every night after the bees leave and the heat and humidity drop sufficiently for our sticky skin to dry. I listened to my husband's soft breath as we slipped into unconsciousness, curled in each other's arms, wondering if both of us would live to see morning.

Fitz's gaunt face makes him look much older than his twenty-six years. Half hidden by a raggedy beard and mustache, bronzed matted curls spilling around his head, he is still beautiful to me. Whiskers hide his jaw, but I can feel bone, the cavernous hollow of his cheek. Once a stentorian-voiced, tall, and muscular man, Fitz has become a stooped skeleton with sagging skin and a whisper that I must lean in to hear. Not long ago, his walk was so striding I had to skip to keep up. Now we only crawl along our raft, for fear of falling and breaking a leg.

The raft we call the Pink Palace is perhaps eight feet by sixteen feet, hardly bigger than the Toyota we left on blocks in a garage back home. She has no motor. She barely bobs on the muddy water that floods deep into the jungle as far as we can see. Parrots cackle high in the canopy above us, like guests chatting over one another at a party. But Fitz and I are very much alone, trapped in a dead-end channel of the piranha-infested Rio Madre de Dios.

Spaced three to five inches apart, the balsa's four logs are the only support we have in this landless place. When I sit on them—or the deck, as we call it—looking around me, I see only water rising high up tree trunks. It has spilled, perhaps for miles, in every direction. There is no land anywhere.

In my journal I record our constant ache for food. We have all but surrendered hope on this, our twenty-sixth day of starvation.

Tears well in my eyes. With no fleshy padding, my bones jar against the unforgiving floorboards. I stroke Fitz's back, still silky under his blue T-shirt, down to his hip and buttock, where muscle used to be. Nothing is left but skin falling loosely over his pelvic bone; his vertebrae protrude like the spine of a gutted fish. Brushing my hand across his body I will him to stay alive. Our time on Earth is flickering. When Fitz looks at me, he must feel as frightened as I do when I look at him. From what I can see of myself, my stick limbs and fingers, my concave stomach, I am excruciatingly thin.

"Please, Fitz, wake up."

He doesn't stir.

"Fitz." I shake him gently, but there is no movement, and his arm flops when I let it go. A trickle of sweat slips down my back; my heart begins to race. Until this moment, I hadn't dared imagine that Fitz might leave me here, alone. I thought if we died, we'd die together. I don't want to face life without him, never again to feel his bear-hug embrace or hear his gravelly "I love you." I want desperately to believe we have more time.

We'd been on our dream honeymoon in South America months longer than expected. Mesmerized by all we'd encountered, we'd traveled through the Andes by buses, trucks, and trains. Then came the jungle.

"Fitz," I whisper, watching for breath. "We're going to make it out of here. I just know it."

Hundreds of bees continue to knock against the tent, seeking a way in.

Where did we go so disastrously wrong?

I know where the fault lies.

Chapter 1

Waiting

ABOUT SEVEN WEEKS EARLIER

If there is a true beginning to our story, it emerges on the rain-soaked unpaved streets of Pucallpa, Peru—a town meant for leaving.

"Hol, remind me why we're in South America?" Fitz asked, wiping mud from his cheek.

"For the adventure of a lifetime!" I laughed, adjusting the camera bag on my shoulder. I could barely hear myself talk over the hammering rain.

We'd just spent two hours trying to get a stranger's pickup truck out of a muddy ditch. The truck had been our best hope to reach the rustic airport to buy tickets for a plane south to Puerto Maldonado. We had ten days to get there in time to take the scheduled commercial vessel into Bolivia on the first step of our journey east across the continent. If we missed the boat, there wouldn't be another for at least three months. We'd been in Pucallpa for three days and were impatient to leave.

Fitz and I held hands as we sloshed through ankle-deep

puddles to our hotel, forlorn as puppies in a rain barrel. Sludge and sewage flowed down the street to the swollen Rio Ucayali, a river bordered by rickety wooden huts on stilts. The water had risen up the stilts, making the homes appear to be floating amongst the garbage and rainbow streaks of motor oil swirling on the surface. Vessels huddled together, rain drumming on their metal or drooping palm-thatched roofs.

Other than a few missionaries, Fitz and I were the only gringos in this jungle town. A day downriver were two American anthropologists we'd met while knocking around the Andes. Fitz and I had accepted their invitation to spend a week visiting them and the Iscabacabu tribe they were studying, but we were now back in Pucallpa, ready to fly to our next stop, Puerto Maldonado.

At the cinder-block hotel we changed out of our wet clothes and quickly dressed for dinner. With no screen on the barred window and no mosquito netting for the beds, insects flew in and out as if we were the featured buffet.

The restaurant D'Ono Frio was a short walk from our hotel. The chicken soup seemed a safe bet, but it arrived with rooster feet sticking up from the bowl. I stared at Fitz. "How do I eat these?"

"You don't," he said, eyes wide. "Just spoon the broth. Glad I didn't stray from my usual." He dug into his favorite, lomo saltado, a simple dish of stir-fried chopped meat and red peppers. Dinner for two came to $2.24.

Fitz was used to shoestring adventure. He'd hitchhiked across the States three times, with little cash in his pocket, before and after Vietnam. Once, he and a friend had clung for hours, screaming, to ropes on the steel bed of a tractor-trailer bouncing through the darkness across New Mexico and Arizona. He could act foolishly, but he sure was lucky.

He'd come out fine, not even a bruise. When I had suggested traveling around the world, I wanted a plan and savings to carry us, not just luck. So we worked two jobs each until we'd banked $10,000. By September 1972, we were ready to go, three months earlier than expected, with a rough itinerary in our hands.

I slurped the broth and continued to push the rooster feet around the bowl, not knowing how to hide them, feeling sure they were considered a delicacy.

"That was delicious." Fitz sighed with satisfaction when he was done with his meal. He set his fork down and stretched back in his chair.

"Hey, don't rub it in," I said with a grumbling kind of laugh. I furtively wrapped the rooster feet in a napkin and stuck them in my bag, hoping the cook would think I'd eaten them and not be insulted.

Upon returning to the hotel after supper, and wrapped in a towel from showering in the shared bathroom down the hall, Fitz sat on our bed made of two cots pushed together. Using a chair as a table, he bent over his typewriter, fingers flying. Under the light of a single bulb that dangled mid-ceiling, he wrote about the night downriver when we had encountered the Iscabacabu tribal chief named Morecada. A reporter at the *News-Times* in Danbury, Connecticut, Fitz had made a deal with his editor to contribute weekly columns during our year of travel. He carried his portable Corona and a stack of foolscap everywhere. The idea was for readers to follow a young local married couple's low-budget trip across the globe. I was documenting our travels in my journal and with my 35mm Pentax, supplying photos for Fitz's readers. We'd already spent four months in South America, carefree, still craving adventure.

Fitz pulled out the page, reading aloud: "From the corner of our tent where he crouched, the old Indian leapt to his feet with a shout, grabbed his tribal war club, and lunged toward us.

" 'Ya! Ya! Ya!' shrieked Morecada between the verses of an ancient song of battle, jumping forward and back, forward and back, eyes red with fury, taut bare chest running in sweat, body shaking with violence, hard breath snorting through holes cut in his nose for feathers."

Morecada had been more than a little frightening in his private performance for us. His tribe had been decimated by the white man. Only twenty-seven members were left.

I brushed my long auburn-brown hair. "I like it. Readers back home will be scared stiff."

Fitz smiled. "Good. I'm writing Mr. Palmer that this may be the last story for a while. After we leave Pucallpa, communication will be nil. I doubt we'll find a post office along the river."

Even in large jungle towns like Pucallpa, communication with the outside world was limited to letters and emergency ham radio. From my pack I took a thin blue aerogram paper that folded into its own envelope, then sat next to Fitz. "I better write my parents, too. I don't want them worrying if they don't hear from us for a few weeks."

Two nights later, our mail posted, Fitz and I learned that the road to the airport had dried sufficiently for use in the morning. We woke before dawn, keen to catch the first bus to the airport and be at the ticket counter before it opened. With flights delayed a week because of the rains, we figured tickets would be at a premium—and we needed to make that boat.

We were first in line. Eventually the line lengthened

with men and women—handsome, short, dark-skinned, dark-haired. The barefoot women wore long, colorful hand-loomed fabric skirts and beaded jewelry. I wore my wash-and-dry synthetic dress. Fitz and I, light-haired with blue eyes, looked out of place. At six foot one, Fitz was at least a head taller than everyone else who waited quietly in line. Then chaos erupted when the clerk in his crisp khaki uniform appeared behind the counter. Burly men and women dove between our legs and under our arms, cutting in front of us, shoving us aside. In seconds we were dead last.

"This is crazy," Fitz yelled, trying to push his way forward.

Within minutes the tickets were sold out. The clerk closed his window, telling us stragglers to return tomorrow for a plane next week.

"We started out first in line!" I wailed. "I can't believe this!"

I kicked a pebble with my sandal as we waited for the bus back to Pucallpa.

While eating dinner at D'Ono Frio that evening, Fitz coached me. "Look, if someone pushes you aside, you have to stop them. Stand firm."

I chewed on tough, nameless meat, served without gravy. "It's like rugby out there," I complained. "I feel like a football."

He worked his lower jaw. "Yeah. You're light as a feather, Monkey-face, and they're rough. Let me handle this." His unusual endearment for me was picked up from Eugene O'Neill's *The Iceman Cometh*, one of his favorite plays.

Despite being a brusque New Yorker, Fitz had been the only man to give up his seat to women traveling on South American buses and trains. I was proud of his chivalry. Now we both realized that if we were ever to escape Pucallpa, he'd have to drop his manners. "It doesn't feel right," he said.

Come morning, Fitz was fifth in line for tickets. When the clerk entered, two muscular women, wearing geometric-patterned skirts stuffed with petticoats, came at Fitz from behind, trying to slide past him. He lowered himself to their height and extended his arms to stop them.

They tried again but couldn't get by him.

A third woman came in from the left, with cloth bundles on her back that she shook from side to side. She hurled herself against Fitz, bouncing off him. He stretched and blocked her using his legs and my camera bag as he closed in on the counter. Gasping, he reached it and clung to it as if it were a lifeboat. When he relaxed just long enough to wipe his brow, a woman came up between his legs. He squeezed his long legs around her torso and kept her where she was.

"*Quiero dos entradas, por favor, para Puerto Maldonado*," he blurted to the clerk, resolute and standing as tall as he could while scissor-holding the woman. He received the coveted tickets for a plane leaving in five days.

We killed time borrowing books from the North American Mennonite mission library, shuffling back and forth through dripping humidity. Reading most of the day in our tiny room, we waited for the sun to go down. Sometimes Fitz and I trekked to the central plaza marked by a cement tower with a broken clock overlooking the harbor. There we saw children jump into the river from shaky porches or tool around in dugout canoes, oblivious to the dangers lurking below the surface.

We found a small movie house, too. The whole town seemed to cram into the smoky theater that offered lawn chairs for seats; noisy fans pushed hot air from one corner to another. Fifteen cents bought admission for scratchy third-rate American films like *What's the Matter with Helen?* and *The Landlord*, with Spanish subtitles. We didn't care how bad they were; we went anyway. The cinema was the local social hour, where everyone chattered loudly over the barely audible English.

Departure day came at last.

We would fly to Puerto Maldonado, where we would catch a commercial riverboat across Bolivia to Riberalta and then hitch a ride into Brazil. From there we'd hang a hard left north by taking another commercial boat to Manaus, midpoint of the Amazon, "the River Sea." With luck, we might make the coast in time for Carnaval on March 6.

Or so we thought.

Chapter 2

The Plane

FEBRUARY 7

Early that morning, Fitz and I eagerly handed our tickets to the military airline clerk.

"We have seats, right?" Fitz asked in rudimentary Spanish.

"Maybe," the man said.

As we clasped the counter while people pushed against our backs, the clerk explained that the small twin-engine prop plane could take only thirteen passengers. There were at least twenty people waiting behind us with tickets in hand.

"But we just gave you our tickets," Fitz said.

The clerk shook his head and told us to wait by the exit door. The crowd followed and began pushing us and each other.

Through the window I caught a look at the ancient US army surplus DC-3 on the dirt runway. Officials were loading cargo. A bright red bull's-eye was painted on the plane's white side.

"That doesn't give me a lot of confidence," I joked.

Fitz told me it was the kind of plane he'd parachuted from while he was in the service.

"Let's hope we won't be jumping out of this one," I said. Fitz's jaw tightened; we weren't on the plane yet. Within a few minutes the clerk left his post and walked over to us. He told us the flight would make two stops in the jungle on its way to Puerto Maldonado. Then he opened the door. There was a rush of people around us.

"Hold on!" Fitz seized my hand.

We raced across the red dirt, bags banging against our sides. We were nearly last to board, but we made it.

Fitz and I plunked down on a long army-green metal bench that was bolted to the side of the plane, our backs leaning against the bare metal fuselage, small windows to either side of us. We buckled in, trying to find a comfortable position on the hard seat. Ropes strapped down a pile of luggage and cargo toward the rear of the plane. On top of the pile a treadle sewing machine teetered despite the ropes.

Seven of us passengers sat on one side of the aisle facing six on the other. Fitz and I were the only gringos. The plane filled with a lively combination of Spanish and Quechua, the indigenous language. Once the propellers started humming everyone fell silent.

I squeezed Fitz's hand. He leaned sideways and grazed my nose with a kiss.

"Seeing the Amazon is a dream come true," I said, watching the propellers spin. "This whole trip is!" I'd fantasized about it since I was a child.

Fitz hugged me then adjusted the glasses that constantly slipped down his nose. The plane started along the dirt runway and accelerated to a lurching takeoff.

We flew low, jouncing over the jungle. Out the window a dense canopy of lush vegetation reached to the horizon.

This web of tightly knit tropical trees of varying heights and hues rolled and swelled under the plane like a green ocean. No open land, no farms, no roads, no huts, just vast verdant wilderness.

From my subscription to *National Geographic* I knew that primitive tribes still inhabited Amazonia, some as yet untouched by Western society. What did they think of our plane speeding across the sky? Below us lived slithering boa constrictors and skulking jaguars. Caiman, the South American alligator, feasted in the rivers alongside piranha. Vampire bats, scorpions, monkeys, ocelots—all called this home. I couldn't wait to experience the secrets of the jungle.

Occasionally, the glint of a brown ribbon appeared and disappeared as if the rivers were winking at me. Lakes, too, swept by, jewels in the sun, breaking up the hypnotic landscape. Depending on the shadows and reflections of the sky, the rivers were chocolate, red-brown, blue, or green. Rarely we glimpsed small clearings like sandbars with huts. We were flying farther away from civilization, pushing deeper into the unknown, where even missionaries and oil rigs did not venture.

The plane dipped below the trees, landing shakily on a grass runway to drop cargo near a village. The takeoff was rocky, the plane leaning to the side, one wheel off the ground before the other. Once fully in the air it jerked up and down, and so did my stomach. No one from home knew exactly where we were going or how long we would be there. I almost wished that I hadn't prepared my parents to expect no word from us for quite a while. Our travels along the Madre de Dios River would take us even deeper into the jungle, beyond the reach of communication. My chest constricted at the thought of our being so out of touch.

A little boy sat across from me. He had a bowl-shaped haircut and wore oddly formal trousers, a button-down shirt, and plastic sandals. He looked shyly down at his comic book, avoiding my smile. His parents and an older boy were next to him.

In the seat across from Fitz sat a heavy middle-aged woman wearing a tight, shiny polka-dot dress with a scooped neckline. Four strands of faux pearls and a gold cross hung around her neck. Black Grecian-style curls were pinned high on her head and toppled down around her ears. Although she looked out of place, I was encouraged that she appeared to be dressed for a party. Perhaps there was civilization where we were headed.

Several young men wore straw hats and short-sleeved shirts of subdued shades, a stark contrast to the brilliantly colorful clothing of the women whose tied bundles of food and gifts sat at their bare feet. Clearly, this was not a tourist route.

A few more minutes of turbulence and the little boy retched. His mother leaned over him with her purse so he could vomit into it. She wiped his face with a handkerchief and stuffed it into the bag.

The plane bounced and rattled then began to turn, shuddering as the engines roared louder. Peering through the window I saw that we were circling above trees and a brown river. I didn't see a town.

The wobbly plane began to descend very fast, pushing me sideways, causing me to grasp the bench. I looked at Fitz, who was studying the *National Geographic* map he'd marked with the route we'd taken through Colombia, Ecuador, Peru, Bolivia, and now again in Peru. He didn't seem to notice our rapid descent. Across the aisle the young boy clutched his mother. His brother clutched his dad. The woman with the polka-dot dress held her gold cross close to her chest. Her eyes were closed, her lips moving.

Below us the jungle opened up to reveal a field. It looked like the grassy runway we'd landed on earlier, with no airport building. The river curved around two sides of this field, making it a near-peninsula adjacent to the trees. We flew through unsettling winds, crossed the river, then nose-dived toward one end of the field.

"We're coming in pretty fast, aren't we?" I asked. My stomach heaved as we dropped below the canopy, emerald jungle slashing past us on the left. The river was to the right; its bend must be in front of us now.

Fitz raised his head to look out the window between us.

"Fitz, what's happening?" I yelled above the machine-gun roar of the engines.

"What the hell's going on?" He grabbed my hand.

We swooped down to just feet above the field, flying parallel to the river. As the water whizzed by us I saw small whitecaps. The engines screamed in my ears. Bags piled in the aisle shifted, loosening. The plane was flying way too fast to land safely. I assumed the pilot would pull up and circle again, but the plane's landing gear hit the ground hard, bouncing the plane, still speeding, toward the river bend.

"He's not braking!" Fitz squeezed my hand tighter.

I pressed my feet into the floor as if to help the pilot. A sharp, metallic zing seared the air.

"Was that a wheel?" I yelped.

Fitz's eyes darted left and right. "We're going too damned fast."

Passengers screamed as the plane skidded toward the river. The two boys started to cry. Green jungle whipped by, then water, then jungle again. The smell of vomit hit my nostrils. I gripped Fitz's arm, pulling us together.

Suddenly the plane pitched left into the forest. We were thrown back and forth, held by our wide seat belts; a sharp, metallic sound coincided with the one wing and propeller dropping from view; the remaining propeller screeched like ice in a blender until we slammed to a hard stop. On impact, the sewing machine burst its ropes and shot past our heads, like a missile, bashing into the cabin door. A man was flung from his seat and landed facedown in the aisle.

Everyone's eyes and mouths opened wide. The boys clung to their parents, sobbing.

The plane slumped to the right, turning its interior into a slide. The polka-dot lady and the family with two kids were on the bottom of the chute. Fitz and I were on the top. I caught sight of the plane's right wing and engine out the window. They'd snapped off entirely. Nobody moved. Then, like a flock of swallows, the thirteen of us leapt up as one and rushed toward the exit.

Fitz grabbed our basket with the handloomed Indian blanket ponchos and slung both backpacks onto his right shoulder. I seized the camera bag and Fitz's typewriter.

"Stay in front of me so I can see you," Fitz urged, keeping a hand on my back. Everyone shoved like they had in the airport. As we reached the door, there was no ladder; we had about five feet to drop. A uniformed man called up to us, "*Vamos.*"

"I'll go first and then catch you," Fitz said. He landed squarely then stood to lift me down.

We paused ten feet from the plane to get our bearings. Four or five khaki-uniformed men in dark green legionnaire-type hats were running around, intently examining the plane. Fitz took my hand. He seemed dazed and overburdened by the two packs and the ponchos. One side of his shirt collar was flipped over his lapel. His gray suit jacket looked odd against the backdrop of the steamy jungle, but it was the only jacket he'd brought on the trip.

"You okay?" he asked.

"I think so." I was shaken, but more concerned for him and the startled look in his eyes. "Here, let me help. I'll take my backpack."

"No way, Hol. You already have the other stuff. Let's just get out of here. This thing could blow anytime."

We stumbled away from the plane and across the mucky field, the odor of fuel and burnt rubber overpowering the dank smell of mud and rain forest.

Finding strength, I bounded forward, but within fifty feet I was panting, slowed by the camera bag and typewriter. Twenty yards ahead, passengers were walking through the cropped field. I didn't know where we were going, just that it was away from the plane, in the direction of the river.

When I turned to Fitz behind me, I caught full view of the aircraft. The right wheel had, indeed, snapped off. The rear landing gear, twisted sideways, was bent nearly perpendicular to the ground. The entire right wing, with engine, had sheared off when the plane smashed into the forest, chewing trees like celery. It lay on the ground, an amputated limb.

The river ran along the right side of the grass strip then curled in front of it. The pilot must have been traveling too fast to stop without hitting the river and too slowly to try a second pass. It looked like he'd cut the gas and hung a hard left into the trees. I pulled out my camera.

"They'll never believe this at home. Stand right there, Fitz."

"Jesus, Holly, this isn't a time for pictures. The plane could blow!"

But Fitz did pose for me. As recording photographer for our journey I couldn't resist a couple of action shots.

We trudged on, following the others. Wondering where we'd landed, I asked a fellow passenger walking near us, "*¿Esto es Puerto Maldonado?*"

"*No, no hay,*" he replied.

I couldn't tell who was leading us. No one had seen the pilot since he'd rushed into the thicket beyond the nose of the plane. We'd all escaped; the plane hadn't exploded. "Wow, we were lucky, Fitz," I said. "I can't believe we all made it."

"Yeah," he said, sweat pouring from his brow.

"Do you want to take that jacket off? You must be dying."

"Nice choice of words." His ear for wit was quick, even now, which told me he was all right. Then his manner shifted, his voice edgy. "I'm fine, Holly. Let's just get to wherever the hell they're going. I really don't feel like getting lost out here."

Up ahead, people were crossing the grass landing strip to the river. The scrub was so soggy that when my sandals slapped the ground mud splashed up my legs and squished under my toes. As we got closer to the river, the mud was calf deep. I didn't want to go barefoot for fear of ringworm, so I continued gripping the wooden soles hard with my toes, making little progress.

"Come on, Holly," Fitz called. "What's wrong?"

"It's the sandals."

"Again? What's with those damn things?"

"They're not the right shoes for mud."

"Don't you have something else?" Fitz asked, starting back toward me.

"Heels."

"Jesus!"

I couldn't have agreed with him more, but I was too tired to say so.

We at last arrived at the river—not a big one, perhaps only twenty yards across. The parents of the two boys along with three women stood at the muddy edge mumbling a little and shaking their heads. The two children were quiet.

We dropped what we carried onto the ground. I stretched my arms. It felt good to be free of the weight. A few passengers were struggling behind us, lugging heavy bags, wilting from the midafternoon sun and the humidity. We were all mud splattered and wet with sweat, but there was no shade or breeze to cool us.

The heavyset woman in the polka-dot dress dragged a huge suitcase behind her. Her once lightly bobbing curls were flopping heavily at her neck. Her white pumps sank into the mud with each step as she approached the riverbank. With a small cotton handkerchief she wiped perspiration from her face. She was muttering loudly to herself and to a teenage boy who was walking with her. The teenager rolled his eyes, saying nothing.

The man who'd been flung forward when the plane crashed hobbled up next and dropped his luggage. He was about nineteen or twenty. When he swept off his straw hat I noticed he'd been scratched up pretty badly on his cheeks. He slumped down, rubbing his swollen right ankle. I searched in my bag for a compress. Another man, huge sunglasses on his smooth, wide face, came to his side, peered at the ankle, and admonished him, probably for not wearing a seat belt.

I offered him an ACE bandage I'd found at the bottom of my backpack.

He said, "*Gracias*," and wrapped it around his foot.

When he began to rise, part of the bank, saturated with rain, collapsed under him, toppling him into the water. His friend grabbed his hands and pulled him back onto land. They shook their heads, laughed a little. We all gave a collective sigh, backing away from the bank.

Turning around, I stared again at the plane that lay like a broken bird, its beak pressed into the jungle. I caught myself jabbing my nails into my palms. How easily we all might have been killed by the crash, the hurtling sewing machine, the leaking fuel lines of the lost wing, the gas tanks that could have exploded.

My mind flashed back to the packed buses traveling steep, narrow roads without guardrails in the Andes and to the frequent crosses marking places where vehicles had gone over cliffs. On one leg of our trip Fitz and I had stood together, looking into a ravine at the carcass of a bus a thousand feet below. Was it all random? Sudden death seemed prevalent here.

I turned from the plane back to the swollen river.

"Fitz, where's your hand?" I asked. Fitz placed his hand in mine. It felt warm and firm. As I looked up at his wan face our eyes met. Mine glazed with tears. He wrapped his arms around me. I leaned into his chest and shuddered at what might have been.

Like statues, we stood staring at the river, wondering what to do next.

Chapter 3

Jungle Trail

I don't know exactly how long we stood there, nor did I notice the man steering a small motorboat until it was practically under our feet. He told us to get in, four at a time, so he could take us across the river. Seeing no one else in charge, we stepped on board, hoping to meet an airline official on the other side.

Clambering up the opposite steep bank, Fitz and I followed the others along a mud path into the jungle. We entered a dark tunnel of long, drooping leaves and hanging vines. Birds were calling loudly to each other overhead.

At a curve, we came across a man dressed in ragged clothes, too big for his thin frame, hacking at the thicket with a machete. The others had walked by him without noticing, but we nodded *hola*. He beckoned to us, asking in Spanish if we'd like to put our bags in his wheelbarrow. His wide smile revealed missing teeth.

"*Sí, gracias,*" we said, relieved to plop our luggage down.

"What a nice man," I said to Fitz. "Maybe he came to help when he saw the plane go down."

"Yeah, he probably farms around here since he's cutting brush."

The man didn't appear strong enough to be a farmer. His back was too bent and he looked emaciated. I felt perhaps we should be pushing the wheelbarrow. Before I could suggest that, the man lifted the handles and took off down the path with our luggage. Fitz and I stumbled behind him. Other passengers were no longer in sight.

"What's the name of this place?" Fitz called out in Spanish.

"Sepa," the man called back without turning his head.

"Is it far?" I asked. "I didn't see it from the air." The man didn't seem to understand the question, probably because of my rudimentary Spanish.

"I live here." He stopped to face us.

He began talking so excitedly that saliva flew through the holes where his teeth should have been. He made swirling gestures with his arms, but we couldn't make out what he was saying.

"*Por favor*," Fitz told him, "*no comprendo.*"

"*Sí, sí.*" He put down the wheelbarrow and spoke more slowly. I caught the words for sister, tree, and seven. Fitz began to look in his pocket dictionary.

The meanings of some words were clarified by the man's mimicry. He spread his legs apart, made a fist in front of him, then pulled his other arm way back, held it there for a second, then lunged it forward again before repeating the motion.

"He's doing a bow and arrow!" I laughed at the incongruity of playing charades in the jungle with this Indian.

"*Siete fleches.*" His words flew out of his mouth on a stream of spittle.

Fitz stared at the dictionary, translating, "That means seven arrows."

"Which goes with his charade," I replied, "but what's his sister got to do with seven arrows?"

Fitz flipped pages again. "Oh," he said, looking up, his eyes large. "I think he's saying he tied his sister to a tree and killed her with seven arrows."

"You're kidding? Here, let me see that."

"Suit yourself," Fitz said, eyeing me with a grim look of surprise.

I searched the pages for the words I didn't know: *tie, kill, arrows*. Sweat rose on my forehead. "Could some of these words have second meanings?"

"I don't think they would all have second meanings."

I looked at the man now swinging his machete wide across the path as he hacked at new growth in front of us. His lithe body was wiry, his sunken jaw making him seem older than he probably was. With his exuberant speech and fiery eyes, either he was a lot younger than he looked, or he was delusional.

"We're walking with a murderer?" I whispered, slogging through thick mud with mosquitoes nipping at my ankles and flying up my skirt.

"It looks that way." Fitz wiped his neck.

After we had been following the man along the winding trail for some time, my throat felt parched. Spots began to dance in front of my eyes. "I need water."

We didn't have any. Fitz stepped back to my side and touched my shoulder. "Take some deep breaths. Wherever we're going, I'm sure we'll be there soon."

I stopped to inhale heavy air but felt like I was sinking into the mud.

"Sepa, Sepa," the man said, pointing up the trail.

"Where are the others?" I asked, more wary than before.

Fitz and I looked up the muddy path into a maze of dense brambles on each side. They arched out and upward, darkening the jungle around us.

"Here, sit down for a minute," Fitz suggested.

"No, we better keep going."

"*Vamos*," the man replied, as if he understood us.

He dropped his machete over our packs in his wheelbarrow so that he could move more easily. His feet barely touched the slippery ground as Fitz and I struggled over roots jutting up from the trail. We slid and crashed into the mud but pulled ourselves up and continued on. My lungs were on fire. The man disappeared around a bend. Then Fitz disappeared, too. Vines seemed to loop out just to slow me down. It took time to snap them back. My heart began to pound as I fell behind.

Slipping over a gnarled root, I stubbed my toe. Grabbing that foot, I hopped for a second before skidding out of my sandals altogether. Darn these Dr. Scholl's! I pushed them on my feet and looked up. "Fitz?"

No response. I hobbled forward as panic rose in my chest. Glancing ahead toward minuscule movement in the bushes, I spotted a brown-and-tan snake, dappled like sun and shadows, maybe four feet long, slithering across my path. It vanished into the brush on the other side. My eyes followed it and caught sight of another snake curled up like a tire in the low crotch of a tree. I lunged forward, feet slapping mud against the wooden soles of my sandals.

"Fitz!" I yelled.

Silence. I was way behind now.

A spiny vine caught my hair. "Let go!" I hissed as I jerked myself forward, finally entering a fork in the trail. Staring up each path I had no idea which one to take. Perspiration slid down my back. Damn, it's hot! Damn, I'm thirsty! Damn, where is Fitz? I couldn't believe he hadn't looked back for me.

I searched for footprints and threads from his clothing

along the start of both paths but found no clues to indicate which path he'd followed. I didn't dare choose. When Fitz noticed I was missing he would come back to this spot. I had to stay calm and wait.

Dusk was lengthening the shadows through the vines; I strained to hear voices. Underbrush rustled. I stood taut, watching. Not another snake, please! I wanted to run, but to where?

It seemed like half an hour—but maybe not—when Fitz finally reappeared.

"Where've you been?"

"I thought you were right behind me!"

"Well, I wasn't!" I snapped, too rattled to feel relieved. "Why didn't you look back to check on me?"

"I got caught up staying with our bags."

He put his arm around me, but I twisted away.

"Well, that's important," I said, shifting my uplifted hands as if I were weighing scales. "Bags . . . wife . . . so hard to choose." Sometimes he was so dense I could spit.

"That's not fair." A grin broadened across his face. "You know the bags always come first."

"Yeah!" I snorted, startled. Despite myself, an edge of laughter crept in. That was his way: deflect anger or fear with humor. "Look, I was scared. I was out here all by myself. I . . ."

"I'm sorry . . . really. I got scared, too, when I looked back and couldn't see you. I could swear it had been only a couple of minutes."

"It sure felt a lot longer to me." I was going to add that it didn't take that long for a snake to bite, but Fitz leaned in for a kiss. I didn't pull away this time.

The Indian was waiting behind us.

"Come on," Fitz said. "I think we're almost there." He took my hand and guided me back the way he'd come.

We could be lost in here forever, I thought, but I let it go. After all, he did apologize.

"Sepa," the Indian pointed.

As if by magic, the jungle opened to a meadow full of sunlight, like the city of Oz. The huge rectangular field had long, low buildings on either side. A village! The buildings were gray, not the usual cheery colors of houses we'd seen in other communities. At the edge of the path was a large sign cemented into the ground. I assumed it welcomed us to the town, so I barely glanced at it, too busy feasting on the sight of civilization. Across the grounds I saw some of the passengers from the plane.

"Look!" Fitz stared at the plaque.

In bold, carved letters it read in Spanish: WELCOME TO SEPA, NATIONAL PENAL COLONY OF PERU.

I read the words a couple of times to take them in. Our plane had crash-landed on the grassy airstrip of a federal prison.

A guard waited for us near the sign. "*Vamos*," he said. "Take your things." He nodded toward the wheelbarrow.

Evidently, our wheelbarrow man was not coming with us. We hoisted our packs onto our shoulders, and then Fitz reached into his pocket and took out Peruvian currency. He thanked the man for helping us with our load.

"It's not much," Fitz said to me. "Perhaps he can buy cigarettes or something."

"Don't give him money," the guard reprimanded Fitz. "He's a prisoner."

Fitz and I looked at each other as the guard confirmed

exactly what the Indian man had told us. He had, indeed, executed his sister.

The man giggled and pocketed the money. The guard shrugged then escorted us across the field toward the building where the other passengers were milling around.

"But he's outside," I remarked. "He's walking around, like he's a free man."

The guard scowled at me. "The jungle is the prison. No one escapes."

"But he has a machete," I persisted.

The guard shrugged again. "The prisoners work. They need the machetes to keep back the jungle."

He told us there were no roads out of Sepa, and the field was too muddy to bring in another plane. Only little motorized dugouts traveled back and forth from the colony to the landing strip. With the rainy season still upon us, no one knew when the landing strip would be ready again.

Deep in the dense and unforgiving thicket, prison walls were not necessary. The inmates could wander wherever they wished. They could never escape. It dawned on me that now we were imprisoned, too.

Chapter 4

Sepa

The line curved into the office of the *comandante*, where our passports were to be checked.

"Why are you here?" he asked.

"*Touristas*," Fitz replied.

The *comandante* raised an eyebrow. "This place is not in the tourist books." He smiled bleakly.

Along with the other passengers we were then taken to the guards' barracks, to a huge room with bunk beds. The walls and floor were cement, making the room cooler than outside.

A guard pointed to the bunk closest to the door. Mine, the bottom bunk, had a heart-shaped pillow leaning against the regular pillow and bearing a hand-crocheted "I love you" in Spanish. It was a simple touch that reminded me that these men had lives, too.

The guards disappeared, leaving their barracks to us. They had relocated their personal items so smoothly that we hadn't noticed. I wondered where they would sleep. Two guards remained standing near a wall by the door to help us settle in. They told us dinner would soon be served in the canteen. Fitz and I wondered if our bags would be safe left out in the open. An observing guard saw us mumbling and guessed our concern.

"Your things are safe," he assured us. "You can leave them here."

Since we were the only gringos and didn't know the language well, we did what the other eleven passengers did. We changed our muddy clothes and followed them to the mess hall where we all sat down at rows of long tables.

A young man came around with plates of rice topped with bits of what could have been canned tuna. It was unappealingly dry. We all fell upon it, eating feverishly. Fitz, a cautious eater, was so famished he gulped it down without a mutter. No one talked during the meal. When we were finished, one passenger asked, "What happened to the pilot?"

No one had an answer.

"When will the next plane arrive to take us to Maldonado?" the lady in the polka-dot dress demanded.

The guards just chuckled.

The boat we had planned to take to Riberalta would be leaving Maldonado soon. I began to worry that we might miss it.

After dinner, four of the guards pulled out some playing cards at a table in a corner of the mess hall. One of the men gestured to Fitz and me, asking if we'd like to join them. We pulled up a bench.

At first, we concentrated on learning the rules, but as we relaxed, the guards, curious about us, our trip, and life in the United States, peppered us with questions. They were proud and excited when they recalled President and Mrs. Kennedy's visit to South America. We asked them about themselves and learned that they signed up for guard duty for five years at a time. They told us that Sepa held the most dangerous prisoners in all of Peru: murderers, rapists, and armed robbers, and they warned us not to walk anywhere alone. They assured us, however, that the prisoners' huts were on the other side of a field, a safe distance away from us. I would have felt better if there were at least barbed wire between us. I decided to focus on the game. Fitz, a good cardplayer, was playing it cool. He would usually win whenever we played with our friends in Boston. I smiled at him, thinking back to the night he had walked into my life.

BOSTON, SUMMER, 1969

It was the day before Woodstock. I met Fitz at my twenty-fourth birthday party, hosted by our mutual good friend Jane, who had been a roommate of mine in college. She was so happy to see Fitz safely returned from the war that she insisted he come to the party, knowing he'd have stories to tell. Prior to his war experience, he had flunked out of college and moved to the East Village, where he'd worked as a messenger then news clerk at the *New York Times*. He'd spent his evenings writing poetry at McSorley's Old Ale House. When the draft loomed near, Fitz quit the *Times* and hitchhiked to San Francisco a few months before the 1967 "Summer of Love." By mid-August he'd been drafted and would serve eight months in combat in Vietnam.

"He's the best storyteller there is and smart as anything," another college friend, Olivia, had raved. As promised, Fitz had us all at the edge of our seats, laughing at him laughing, waiting for the punch line. He also recited poems that he pulled from his head and relayed in a bold, captivating tone.

When I said that was impressive, he told me he always carried a book of poetry with him and that memorized poems helped him get through the service. He complimented me on my yellow dress and worked hard to get my attention all night.

Fitz had registered for the upcoming fall at Suffolk University, where I was taking my master's in counseling. He seemed more mature than the rest of us, though he was actually a year younger. He fit right in with our group and spent the rest of the summer going to restaurants, cafés, and parties with us. Sometimes I would notice a pensiveness cross his face, but I didn't ask him about it. Fitz insisted on paying our tabs, saying he was glad to be home. By summer's end, however, I learned that his generosity had left him broke. Worried that he might be hungry, I went to the grocery store and bought a steak, chicken breasts, some vegetables, potatoes, and bread.

Forty Anderson Street was a brick apartment house on the cheap side of Beacon Hill, only a few blocks from the gold-domed State House. I rang the front doorbell then stepped back out to the sidewalk, knowing the bell could be heard in the apartment but the buzzer could no longer unlock the door.

Fitz came to a window on the top floor and leaned out to drop me the key. "Hi," he called out, grinning, his mop of brown curls catching the sunlight. "Coming up?"

I could see the long dimples in his cheeks even from that distance. I'd never been to his fifth-floor studio without the others and was nervous because this was our first conversation alone. The brown bag of groceries was heavy in my arms. I looked at it, suddenly feeling awkward. "Hey, man," I tried to sound casual. "I thought you might like these. I'll leave them here." I set the groceries on the step and turned quickly to go.

"Wait, Holly! I'll be right down."

"Oh, I can't. I'm . . . I'm on my way to class."

I actually had a half hour before class started, but it hadn't occurred to me that Fitz might want to talk. I felt speechless—worse than when I'd sat next to Paul Newman in my dad's seat at the 1968 Democratic Convention in Chicago. I could barely nod hello to the stunning blue-eyed actor who'd smiled as he chewed gum. Fitz was more handsome and charismatic to me. I wanted to run, but my legs were spaghetti. What if I tripped on the broken brick sidewalk in my sling-back magenta heels? I'd make a fool of myself in front of him. Just let me get around the corner. Finally, I escaped up the hill before Fitz made it down the stairs.

Later that afternoon, he phoned me at my apartment in Cambridge.

"Would you like to come to dinner?" he asked. "I've got plenty of great food!"

Although I'd been hoping he'd call, my stomach did cartwheels. Dinner with him, alone?

He'd been so entertaining in the group. Now I wondered if I'd be amusing enough. "Well, sure." I laughed hesitantly. "That sounds like fun."

The September night was cool. I wore a linen jacket that reached just below the belt of my Marimekko black-and-white-print miniskirt. A guy coming out the front door of 40 Anderson Street let me in so I didn't have to buzz Fitz to throw down the key. I climbed the four flights of stairs, readjusting bobby pins to keep my long hair in place.

Outside Fitz's door I took a deep breath before I knocked. What was there to worry about? I felt good, for heaven's sake. My hair glistened after I'd washed it. I'd even put on mascara to enhance my blue-green eyes under my dark eyebrows. As I waited for the door to open, I glanced at the silver rings on each of my fingers. One was decorated with royal blue cloisonné; another was a poison ring with a little box under a turquoise lid. It seemed to be taking some time for Fitz to answer. I readjusted the bobby pins again. Oh, yes, I'd forgotten to knock.

Fitz stood tall as he opened the door, but not overbearing, unlike the first time I ever saw him, when he'd looked intimidating until he'd smiled.

"Hi," I said to his bright blue eyes behind his glasses. "Someone let me in the front door so I just came up."

He looked handsome in a pale blue button-down shirt, open at the collar, a tea towel flung over his shoulder. "Well, I'm glad you did. Here, let me help you with that."

As he eased me out of my jacket he caught his hand in my hair. "Oh, Jesus, I'm sorry," he said, untwisting the strands from his fingers. "Not a good way to start!"

We both began to laugh, lightening the moment.

Fitz chatted about the Boston we both loved and how he'd wanted to live on Beacon Hill since he was a little kid. Now he couldn't believe his good fortune.

His studio's bay window let plenty of light into the sparsely furnished apartment, with its table, two chairs, and a bed covered in black sheets. In the center of the white horsehair-plaster wall above the bed Fitz had hung a three-foot wooden crucifix with a bronze Christ. The effect was monastic and, frankly, strange, but somehow appealing. He'd bought the cross at Goodwill Industries, but when I asked about it, he couldn't really say why he had brought it home, other than that "it looked good."

Before dinner, he took me up to the roof through a trap-door in the outer hall ceiling. He opened two folding chairs and placed them close to each other. Though we didn't touch, I felt his heat. The Charles River was practically at our feet, just a few blocks away. Small sailboats tacked grace-fully, flooded pink by the lowering sun. I lost myself in the ripples of light and shadow on the water and the salt-shaker contours of Longfellow Bridge. The early autumn evening air was soft on my skin. The sounds of subdued laughter and of sultry music blended with honking cars and distant sirens. I could not recall when I'd ever felt so relaxed with a guy.

Our chairs were near the edge of the roof. On the street below us people walked up and down the hill in small groups, or alone, some silent, some talking. I wondered what stories they had to tell, what desires and dreams they would either embrace or push away. I wanted a future filled with adventure and imagined that Fitz did, too.

I admired the old brick buildings, their inset doors with brass knockers, sun sparkling off the glass of bay windows, framed by embossed green copper, and window boxes filled with red and pink geraniums.

"I love it," I turned to Fitz. "I feel like I'm on top of the world!"

"We are." He smiled at me.

I got flustered when I felt he was looking at me for too long. "What?"

"Sorry. I was just noticing the sun on your hair. It's pretty." He had his hands folded in his lap and looked down at his feet. "I'm glad you came."

"Me too," I quickly remarked. "And I'm so glad you got your wish to be on Beacon Hill." I was happy for him, and happy that he was sharing it with me.

After we climbed down the ladder from the roof, Fitz broiled the steak and mashed the potatoes.

"Thanks for the groceries, Holly." He turned from the stove. "It's a welcome change from what I've been eating!" He pointed to an open fifty-pound burlap sack of onions, about three feet tall, in the corner of the kitchen. I had smelled it even before he'd opened the door to the apartment. His sun-bronzed curls fell forward on his forehead as he leaned down to take the steak from the broiler.

"I bought it for a dollar at Haymarket. A dollar for fifty pounds of onions!" He stood up, his eyes sparkling. "Can you believe it? What a bargain."

I hadn't the heart to tell him the onions were sold cheaply because they were spoiling. I just agreed, charmed by his optimism in the midst of bleak reality.

As Fitz gave me platters to bring to the table, his fingers brushed my hand. Goose bumps immediately raised on my neck. Quickly, I turned my attention to the hot, juicy steak and carried it to the table.

He finished mashing the potatoes, but he wasn't finished with his story. He told me the train attendant wouldn't let him on the T with the onions because they stank. Fitz's shoulders heaved up and down as he burst into a roar. "I couldn't give up such a good deal, so I lugged that damned thing all the way from Haymarket, down Cambridge Street, and up Beacon Hill. Then up the stairs. People were sidestepping every which way to get away from me!"

My sides ached, I was giggling so hard. I began to hiccup and looked at Fitz. We both doubled over, catching the giddiness from each other, like a ball thrown back and forth. I felt free, as if flying, or dancing with a really good partner.

"How could you carry something so heavy so far?"

"Used to the weight, I guess. In 'Nam I humped the platoon radio, a six-pound spare battery, plus my rifle and everything else the other guys carried. That's why the radioman gets an extra ration of warm beer—on the rare occasions when there is beer."

The last of the evening sun fell on Fitz's face like warm fire, magenta rays cascading through the windows. He pulled out a chair for me and we sat down to eat. I complimented his cooking, which segued into stories of food and family and people we both knew. The conversation took off into unknown corners. Fitz told funny stories, and I told some of my own.

But Fitz's first story was still on my mind.

"You can make anything funny. But, really, what are you going to do? You can't just eat onions."

We looked at each other and guffawed again.

"This is a temporary situation," Fitz explained. "I'm a writer. To make a living I'll write for newspapers . . . only tomorrow I have to go to the pawnshop. I'm down to zero. Would you like to come?"

"Sure. Why not? I've never been to a pawnshop."

I was a little concerned that Fitz was so strapped, but I was intrigued by him.

After we'd stuffed ourselves, Fitz looked me in the eyes. "You know, I always wait outside your classroom. I look in the window of the door to see if you're there, but the minute the bell rings and the door opens, I take off."

"You're kidding!" I was as delighted as I was astonished. He looked down at the floor and smiled sheepishly.

"Well, why don't you stay until I come out?"

Pushing his chair back, he stretched his legs. A small nervous cough came from his throat.

"I don't know. Tongue-tied, I guess."

"You? I can't believe that!"

"Well, it's been known to happen to guys, you know, around a beautiful girl."

He looked up and his eyes, deep azure, met mine. I wanted to glance away but his gaze held me. I couldn't help but smile.

"Do you mean to say that if I hadn't brought you groceries, you never would have said anything?"

"Well, I hope I would have . . . I don't know. I guess I never thought you'd be interested, a classy girl like you." His elbow brushed against his fork and it crashed to the floor.

"Gee," I said, reaching to pick it up, thankful for something to do to hide my blushing face. "You're giving me all kinds of compliments, but I never would have known . . ." I bumped Fitz's head as he leaned down at the same time.

"Are you all right? I'll get some ice."

"I'm fine." I had to laugh. He'd set me at ease from the start, though my stomach remained fluttery the entire night.

Next day we met on Beacon Street to walk over to the pawnshop. It was a warm Saturday morning, and we took our time, peering over glossy black iron fences into little gardens, admiring the shiny door knockers and crisp, newly painted doors and shutters that ran along the charming brick sidewalks.

I pointed to a hydrangea vine climbing a trellis against a brick row house. As my hand fell back to my side it brushed Fitz's. Silently, he took my hand. We continued on down colonial Beacon Hill. Nothing had changed but the beating of my heart. Fitz's hand felt natural in mine, like it should have been there all along. We crossed the grassy Boston Common to Park Square, pausing to look back at the gold State House dome glittering in the sunlight. Then, dodging traffic, we turned left on Stuart Street, finding ourselves immersed in the peculiar urban mix known as the Combat Zone.

Fitz and I hurried past strip clubs and pornographic theaters to reach Chinatown, where even public telephones were shaped like pagodas. We strode past the *Boston Herald Traveler* newspaper building and into a gritty neighborhood of bars, army-and-navy surplus stores, and laborers lined up at Manpower hoping for a day's work. Next door was a business that cashed checks for large fees in the shadow of the elevated train. Fitz joked that a homeless shelter was down the street—just in case.

I had only been involved with Fitz for a day, but already we were lifting the veil on Boston together.

We reached the pawnshop in the South End. The pawnbroker was protected in his glass cage with metal bars. Fitz had brought a silver-plated goblet to swap for cash, and he immediately started to charm the man into giving him a good price. I looked around the dingy shelves of clocks and camera equipment. The floor was covered in chipped linoleum. Scratched glass-topped counters displayed bangles, trinkets, and a couple of guns. This was a very different part of life staring me in the face. I supposed it was good for me to see it firsthand, but it startled me to see Fitz enter this world so easily. I wasn't sure if this was his personality, or if his time in Vietnam had led to an "eat, drink, and be merry" attitude, resulting in him spending his very last penny.

Undaunted, he handed over the goblet.

"Five bucks," the man in the cage grunted through a hole, a cigar hanging out of his mouth, smoke swirling around his head.

Fitz nodded then pocketed the money and the receipt that shot out from a bin under the counter. As we left the shop, I noticed a spring in his gait. He would live on those five dollars for another few days.

Once we started dating more seriously, Fitz found a regular job in the bowels of Massachusetts General Hospital. We finished up our year of classes and I received my master's of education in counseling. Fitz began sending résumés out to New England newspapers and was hired as a reporter. We weren't able to afford much back then, but he proposed to me with a gorgeous blue enamel and coral bracelet and a puppy I named Zelda. Two months later, we were married in Connecticut, where I began my career in counseling. When we started saving for our worldwide trip we called it our delayed honeymoon.

A loud roar brought me back to the canteen and the jungle. When I looked around, I noticed we cardplayers were the only people still in the mess hall.

"I've got it," one of the Sepa prison guards announced in Spanish. He laid his cards on the table and counted his points. The generator sputtered, signaling that it needed more gas.

"Good game," Fitz said, stretching. "Want to call it a night, Hol? We've had a hell of a day."

A guard accompanied us to our bunks in the darkness. As we followed the beam from his flashlight a guttural growl came out of the trees to the right of us.

"What's that?" I grabbed Fitz's arm.

"Jaguar!" the guard hissed. "*¡Vamos!*" A branch snapped. "Hurry, Fitz!"

We rushed into the barracks and climbed into our bunks in the dark. The lights from the generator were already out, and the other passengers were asleep.

Pulling the sheets over my face, I listened beyond my own heavy breathing for the jaguar outside. "Fitz, do you hear that?"

Fitz, who could fall asleep quickly, was already lightly snoring. I couldn't believe how he did it. I reminded myself that at least we had cement walls and a guard outside.

Chapter 5

Prisoners

FEBRUARY 8

I awoke to the sound of rain on the metal roof. Too muddy for a plane to land. Another day of waiting. My sleep had been fitful, the jungle noises meshing with dreams of the plane's engines chewing up the trees. I also dreamt that Fitz and I couldn't find each other. Rubbing my eyes, I saw Fitz's bump in the bunk above me. He was still sleeping, but the rest of the barracks was empty. The others must have gone off for breakfast. Needing to go to the outhouse, I remembered the guard had told us not to walk outside alone.

"Fitz, wake up." I gently pushed at the lump. It moved.

"What?"

"Will you take me on an outhouse date?"

"I'll have to check my calendar," Fitz said, yawning.

"Ha!" I laughed and began to search for the toilet paper roll in my backpack.

When we appeared in the doorway, a guard who had been sitting there all night stopped us. "Take a big stick. Bang it on the ground as you walk. The snakes will know you're coming and won't come out."

We obediently took up sticks and thumped down the sopping path toward a line of guards and plane passengers also waiting at the outhouse. I could smell pancakes and coffee as we passed the mess hall. A toucan called out from a nearby tree, as if in response to the prisoners who were yelling at each other. Small rodents scurried by me into the brush.

We'd learned from the guards that one of the prisoners baked and sold bread. Fitz pointed to a hut on the prisoners' side, just as the sun came out. "I wonder if that's the bakery."

I peered across the field and sniffed the air. "I don't smell anything."

As the only baker in the penal colony, the prisoner had a monopoly on the bread market. He was, however, disgruntled about something and had gone on strike. The guards had assured us that things would soon be worked out and there should be bread by lunchtime.

We walked past outbuildings where prisoners chopped back jungle paths with machetes. Some of the men leered at us as we passed. I told Fitz I hoped he would always accompany me to the outhouse and stand guard.

"I wouldn't want you going alone," he said, catching the eye of a prisoner as we banged our sticks on the muddy trail.

When we closed in on the outhouse, its smell hung heavy in the damp air. After waiting in line for several minutes I gingerly stepped inside to find a hole had been cut into a wooden box for a toilet seat. I didn't dare look down. Flies flew up from the hole as I fumbled with the hook on the inside of the door. The narrow wooden hut had a small diamond-shaped screened window, but the smell still left me gasping. I tried to hurry, sweat rimming my face.

When I leaned in to open the door again it wouldn't budge. "Fitz, please pull the door!" It gave way immediately and I stumbled out into the exquisite fresh air. "Next time I'm finding some bushes; that was awful."

"Not with all the snakes and prisoners around here," Fitz said. "It can't be that bad."

"Sure it can," I said, grimacing, and held the door for him to enter. "Good luck!"

While I waited for him, I stared across the soccer field at the adobe-and-cement prison huts. Their corrugated metal roofs looked just like the ones in Pucallpa. There was also a reed hut with a thatched roof. The guards had told us that the prisoners ran a shop for cigarettes, soap, and other necessities, adding that we could go over there for supplies if we wanted to. I was mystified at where the prisoners got the items. Even in the middle of nowhere, in their constricted circumstances, these men had a social system that seemed to work.

As I watched them I couldn't help but wonder at the differences between the prisoners and us. Fitz and I were young suburban Americans, raised in families who had enjoyed a level of privilege and freedom that these men would never know. My dad was an architect who'd attended Ivy League schools. My mom's dad had been in shipping, senior vice president of what became United States Lines, having worked his way up by reading law. Mom graduated from Chapin School in Manhattan then went on to Bennington College. Her career as a sculptress was interrupted for a few years when she moved with her best friend to Stowe, Vermont, to open a ski lodge.

I was the first of two daughters; Fitz was the second of four brothers and sisters. His father, Brian, had emigrated from Ireland to New York at age eleven. Brian never attended high school but read constantly and valued education above all things. After an apprenticeship to a plasterer, he became a New York City police officer. Following the war, he was admitted to Columbia University, graduating after nine years of night classes. Fitz's mother had been raised by her grandmother then sent from Ohio at fourteen to find her own way in New York. She supported herself while attending night school and learned to fly an airplane before she learned to drive. Until this trip, I hadn't fully fathomed how fortunate we'd been to live in a country of opportunities. I'd taken so much for granted.

On our first sunny morning in Sepa we were all told at breakfast to ready our bags and bring them outside to depart. We cheered then took leave of our gracious hosts with vigorous good-byes.

Fitz and I dragged our packs across the field and along the memorable jungle trail. Wheelbarrow man was nowhere in sight. We took the boat to the grass landing strip and waited in the heat for three hours, our backs turned to the old plane's mangled carcass. Eventually a guard appeared. "No plane today. Not dry enough." He guided us back across the river and up the trail to Sepa.

The line for the lunch of tuna and rice was quiet. I sniffed the air for bread. "*No hay*," the server said. We were all served Jell-O instead.

Fitz and I resumed our routine of playing cards and reading books as we counted down the hours to make our boat. We had just three days to reach Puerto Maldonado before it left.

Later that afternoon Fitz looked across the field. "Want to go over there and see if the baker's back to work yet?"

"It creeps me out," I said, but I didn't want him to go alone. Besides, we didn't have anything else to do. Four thin prisoners and a rotund one watched us approach.

"No bread," they told us.

The bull-like man came forward, eyeing Fitz. "You have cigarettes?"

Fitz pulled his pack out of his pocket and handed him one. The other men quickly moved around us. "More," they said. Fitz handed each one a cigarette then began to shove the pack into his pocket. "More," the big man insisted.

Fitz hesitated. He was taller than any of them, but it was five against two (if you counted me), and they had shovels.

I stood beside Fitz, holding my breath and looking at the prisoners' severe, haunted faces, hoping Fitz wouldn't try to slug one of them. He offered the cigarette pack to the bull-like prisoner just as a soldier appeared behind us, rifle slung over his shoulder and a stick in his hand.

"Take your cigarettes," he ordered, standing tall in his starched, neatly pressed uniform. "Don't come back here."

We fled across the field, hearing the yelling but not looking back to witness the strong thwacks from the guard's stick.

Some of the South American travelers were becoming seriously aggravated, making it clear to the guards that they had work and families to get home to. They complained that they were missing birthdays and weddings. The woman with the sagging curls was particularly snarly. "I have to get back. My husband will have your heads if you don't get me home soon," she warned, reciting his credentials as she stomped in circles across the mess hall floor. Her white-and-green polka-dotted dress was wrinkled and mud stained, and her pumps would never be white again.

The guards wagged their heads. "The weather's not in our hands."

All Fitz and I could think about was bread. When we didn't see it for dinner I began to suspect the baker and the bread were nonexistent. I wondered how long we would be stranded inside this forbidding jungle. Part of me was still hopeful we would make it to Carnaval.

Chapter 6

Puerto Maldonado

On the morning of February 10, we plodded back down the jungle path then ferried across the river to the landing strip. Everyone watched in silence as a plane circled overhead before descending. When it taxied across the grass success-fully, we all applauded in a burst of relief. Ominously, the plane looked exactly like the first one, the fuselage bearing the same red bull's-eye. The carcass of the original still lay lopsided off the strip like a shamed contestant.

Fitz and I settled onto the bench, once again staring at a mound of luggage tied down in the middle of the aisle. The sewing machine was absent. Everyone fell silent as the plane revved its twin engines, began its scream across the grass, then rolled slightly as it cleared the river.

I don't recall anyone speaking for the entire two-hour trip to Puerto Maldonado. I, for one, was mostly praying as I gripped Fitz's hand.

We continued to clasp hands as we descended into the airport, both of us making a point of not looking out the window until the plane had come to a complete stop. The tension inside the plane was matched by the suffocating heat outside. There was no fleet of taxi drivers waiting to haggle over fares into town. We said good-bye to the other passengers, who were met with embraces by family and friends. Briefly, I wanted that, too.

The curve of the road wound up a gradual hill to meet the horizon, like a vanishing point in a painting. Rio Madre de Dios lay just a mile away. We would ride her through the jungle toward the Amazon River.

Lugging our packs, we flagged a ride with a passing truck. In back were five young girls riding home from school. The presence of gringos always was a source of jubilant curiosity for children. We exchanged names and pointed out the English word for everything we passed. Giggling, the girls shouted the Spanish equivalents.

One girl, Margarita, with lovely brown eyes, led us to a cheap tavern in town with three inexpensive rooms at the rear. Rustic but clean, it cost only one dollar a night. Grateful to have a room to ourselves after three nights in the barracks, we were pleased to see that the half walls were screened to receive the tropical breeze. Behind our room was a patio rimmed by flush toilets and outdoor sinks. There was even a shade tree.

As soon as we stowed our bags, Fitz and I set out to book passage on the boat to Riberalta. Puerto Maldonado, population thirty-five hundred, was a frontier town. Capital of the Peruvian department of Madre de Dios, it was by far the least inhabited capital in the nation. Cut from the jungle, it looked to be about six square blocks of homes and shops, unpaved roads, and a small sawmill for Amazonian timber that was sent from upriver. A tall cement tower with a broken clock stood in the center of the town square. Open sewers ran down the sides of the roads to the harbor, where children swam and bathed, and where women washed clothes.

The chief port officer, the *aduana*, was an easy man to

find in his office by the harbor. I stared at his neatly mustached lip in disbelief as he calmly informed us that no boat would sail to Riberalta for at least three months. He leaned back in his chair behind his desk as he explained there was practically no traffic between Peru and Bolivia through this frontier. Only one man, who had relatives in Riberalta, was known to make the trip every few months. He would take passengers aboard, for a minimal sum, if they were traveling in the same direction. He'd just left recently.

"But what about the commercial boats? When do they leave?" Fitz asked, shocked.

"Commercial boats?" The *aduana* stood up, his posture now ironing-board straight. "There are no commercial boats."

Apparently the commercial boat route that was displayed on our map with dots did not exist. Obviously, commercial boat departure dates, written in the travel guide, did not exist either. We showed the map and the book to the port officer. He handed it to his men. They muttered and shook their heads. No one knew why the route was printed on the map, or why the dates were in the book. "A mistake," the *aduana* said, shrugging, his hands uplifted. "There are no boats."

When we remained standing in his office, not knowing what to do, the officer finally said, "Perhaps there is a plane going there sometime. Check at the airport." He shuffled some papers to show he was a busy man.

Fitz and I looked at each other. Since no phones existed to call for an airline schedule, we would have to return to the airport.

I thanked the *aduana* for his time and asked how to get back to the airport.

"Go to the Plaza de Armas and wait. There will be a truck sometime today."

At the airport we learned that no flights were scheduled out of Maldonado in any direction for three weeks, and then only back to Pucallpa. We told the officer that we were desperate to get to the Amazon River.

He shook his head. "I'm sorry. No flights to Riberalta. No one goes. It's a small place, smaller than here, and we are small. Not many people come or go at all."

During our four and a half months traveling in South America, we'd never been so disappointed. Unless we waited three months, until someone might take a boat down the river, we would have to abandon our dream of seeing the Amazon River. Riberalta was our gateway to Brazil. From Riberalta it was only two days' ride by truck to Puerto Velho, where all the guidebooks agreed that boats could be found to take us down Rio Madeira north to "the River Sea." We had no sure way to go but backward, and we would need to wait weeks to do that.

We decided to go back to the hotel to think about it.

In the evening, some friendly people in the streets directed us to a café called La Genovesa. It had four tables, a corrugated metal roof, and a dirt floor. Low half walls of thin, plaited wooden straps allowed outside air to supplement the sulking ceiling fan.

The smell of Italian spices softened our mood. The owners' petite teenage daughter, Eamara, had glossy black hair and smiled as she showed us to a table. She served plates of steak, boiled potatoes, fried tomatoes, and bananas. The food was not much different from the usual South American fare, but the herbs transported us to Boston's North End, or to Julio's, the small Italian place Fitz had taken me to in a basement near Gramercy Park.

"We would have made that man's boat if it hadn't been for the damn plane crash," Fitz grumbled.

"What about the commercial boat that was supposed to leave tomorrow? We would have made that if it existed."

"Ha!" Fitz grunted.

"Well, what are we going to do now? We're stuck here with no boat and no plane."

Fitz began scraping his dish. "That was damn good. I could have another."

I laughed, agreeing and enjoying his pleasure. I watched his curly head ponder his plate as his fork stabbed a small red pepper. "Be careful of those brutal seeds," I warned, recalling that Fitz had eaten some red pepper seeds in La Paz. They'd been so hot he'd jumped onto the table between the dishes then leapt off the other side to run around the block, his jaws open, trying to cool his mouth.

"You can bet I won't forget those!" he said, rolling his eyes. We both started laughing.

When there was nothing left on his plate but the pepper seeds, Fitz leaned back in his chair, lit a cigarette, and shook his head as he inhaled. He exhaled slowly then rubbed his neck.

"So what else can we do but wait for a plane back to Pucallpa?" It seemed he was posing a rhetorical question, but a scowl crossed his face as what he'd just said seemed to sink in. "No way." He lowered his voice. "So here we are, stuck again."

"I think we can forget Carnaval." I paused for a minute. We were right back to complaining. "We were lucky, you know. We could have been killed in that plane crash."

"Yeah, we're lucky all right," Fitz said, sighing. "But I don't see what that has to do with this."

"Nothing. I'm just trying to look at the bright side. I can't think of what to do. I don't want to stay here forever, but I don't want to go backward either." I swirled the last of my Coke in the bottom of the glass.

"Want some more?" Fitz stubbed his cigarette out and turned to look for Eamara.

"Excuse me, please," a voice came from behind me. I turned to see a distinguished man with salt-and-pepper hair getting up from a table nearby. "My name is Juan Nevanschwander. I am Peruvian, but I understand English well. I can't help but overhear your difficulty."

The man appeared to be in his fifties, with an air of well-polished Europe about him. He approached us, his white tailored suit in startling juxtaposition to the mud and sewers of Maldonado. A statement of hope, I thought, civilization in the frontier.

Fitz and I looked from him to each other, surprised that we'd been overheard. We had been so immersed in our conversation, we hadn't noticed anyone was listening.

"We rarely see travelers here," Juan continued. "Unless you're exploring for gold, I can understand why you want to move on."

"Well . . . ," I said, my mind whirling, wondering what we'd said about feeling stuck in Maldonado. "It's a nice town. It's just that we had plans to get to the Amazon River, and now no boats are going there for months."

Juan asked the other patrons in Spanish if they knew of any boats going to Bolivia. "It's true," he said. "There are no boats." He nodded to an empty seat at our table. "Perhaps I can help you. May I?"

"Sure," said Fitz, popping up to pull out the chair.

Juan called Eamara for three glasses and a quart of beer. "I learned English when I worked in a Chicago bank for three years. I'm a mining engineer."

"Really? What brings you here?" I asked.

"Gold."

"You're a prospector? That sounds like the old days. They still do that kind of thing here?"

"I work for a Bolivian bank that hired me to explore precious metal deposits." He pulled a tobacco pouch and pipe from his suit pocket and smiled at them. "It's nice to get back to civilization. I just returned from two months upriver. Have to go out again next week, after I get more supplies."

My eyes widened. He thought this town was civilization? After living in Chicago?

"This place has had booms in its past—rubber, timber—but nothing for a long time. It's poor," Juan said, taking a sip of beer. "People leave. There's no work. Just prospecting for the next thing the jungle may have to offer."

"This really is the frontier," I said.

"Yes. You've come a long way to see it."

He wanted to hear our story. We told him about our plan to travel around the world. "Ambitious," he said, nodding, "but how did you pick here? There's nothing to see that you haven't already seen in Pucallpa and other river towns."

We explained about trying to meet a boat to Riberalta via Puerto Maldonado and the crash landing that had thrown us off.

Juan raised his eyebrow. "You still want to keep going?"

Fitz and I looked at each other. "Why, yes," we both said, surprised that he had asked.

Juan tapped tobacco into his pipe as he observed us curiously. His right eyebrow arched higher than his left.

Fitz said, "You mentioned you might be able to help. Do you know of a way?"

"To tell you the truth, there's not much traffic between Peru and Bolivia at any time of year. It's just not a popular place to visit." He sipped his beer then rubbed his bronze jaw back and forth as if it ached. "But you know . . . ," he said, pausing to place his glass back on the table.

I leaned forward in my chair. "Yes?"

"Have you thought of taking a raft? People here use rafts more than boats. We call them balsas. That's the real means of transportation."

I looked at Fitz. We had noticed a number of log rafts, both large and small, coming downriver into the harbor. A lightbulb clicked on behind my eyes. I knew Fitz saw the light in my eyes, too, because he shook his head quickly.

"You can only go downriver," Juan continued, "but there's plenty of wood, so people take rafts as far down as they wish then leave them for others."

I wondered how people got back upriver, but since we were only going downriver I didn't want to get off track by asking.

"I just came on a raft from upriver myself," Juan said. "I do it all the time." His black eyes snapped.

"Are you saying that we should take one of those banana-laden rafts?" Fitz asked. "They don't look very sturdy." A frown played on his forehead.

"No. I'm suggesting you make a raft to fit your needs. There are lots of people who have big ones that you can use. You don't want it so big that you can't handle it, or too small either. You can make it comfortable. Put a tent on it . . . and a cookstove." He smiled. "A floating home."

"Wait a minute," Fitz said. "We take it down the river ourselves? We know nothing about rafts . . ."

"There's nothing to it. A raft just goes with the current once you get started, until you want to pull in."

This was beyond my wildest imaginings. It was a way to get out of here and move on to the Amazon. It could be fun. I began asking Juan every question I could think of without looking at Fitz to see his reaction. "Is it safe for people like us, who don't know the river or the jungle?"

"Absolutely. It's the same for anyone. You go with the river."

It sounded preposterous. "Are you sure people do this for long trips?"

"Of course. That is how they do it. I've traveled these rivers many times. People use rafts. That's why there are so few boats."

"But we've never done it before." My heart was skipping. I wanted to believe, but I needed reassurance.

Even though I asked the same questions over and over, our new friend assured us that the river would do the work. Juan lit his pipe again.

"How far to Riberalta?" I asked.

"As the river turns, perhaps eight hundred kilometers."

I glanced at Fitz. "That's about five hundred miles." I turned back to Juan. "How many days would it take to get there?"

"The river is high and fast right now." Juan exhaled a swirl of blue smoke. "No more than ten days. If you go night and day you should make it in five."

"Go at night? We'd crash into something we couldn't see!"

"No, there'll be nothing as big as you on the river. No harm can come to you."

"Could we get lost?" I persisted. "What about tributaries?"

"There are no rivers flowing off the Madre between here and Riberalta." Juan puffed on his pipe thoughtfully. "Just stay in the main current and you won't go off on a detour. Such detours always return to the main channel, but they take you longer. If you stay in the middle of the river, you'll get there faster."

I paused, trying to think of other questions. "How will we know when we're at Riberalta? Don't the towns look the same on the river?"

"No towns. Only *fincas*"—farms—"and the compounds at the border crossing. That's it, jungle all the way." He smiled. "You'll see the real thing, no fake setup for tourists."

After a minute of silence Juan said, "Another thing. You don't need to worry about fresh fruit and bread. Just call out and people from the *fincas* will boat out and bring it to you."

Fitz, who hadn't said anything while I'd fired off my questions, finally spoke up. "Say we were to do it, how do we go about building a raft?"

"Best thing is to find one already built. Go down to the river and ask around. I can't go with you tomorrow, but if you don't find one, I'll go with you the next day."

"Well, what do you think?" I asked on our way back to our room.

"I think he's crazy." Fitz kicked the dirt in the road.

"But what else can we do? Wait here in this godforsaken town for three months for a boat? It could be a real adventure! Juan said nothing could go wrong . . ." My mood was flying as I talked, my feet barely touching the earth.

"And you believe him? We just met him for God's sake. We don't know him from a hole in the wall. Do you think because he sounds like he has all the answers that he couldn't be wrong?"

"Oh, Fitz, he says he's rafted hundreds of times. You even asked him how to make a raft. You're interested, too." I saw no risks.

"Look, we can stay right here for three months and wait for a boat," Fitz said. "In fact, I'm surprised after what we've been through that you're not voting for that, or even to turn back."

"Oh, come on. You don't think I'd want that, do you? You need to let loose and not be so cautious. We'll be Huck and Jim. You just want me to talk you into it."

Fitz didn't say anything. Now I'd done it.

"I just don't want to be foolish," he finally said.

I saw there was an opening. He might really want to do it. I pushed the limit.

By the time we reached the hotel Fitz was talking about looking for a raft.

Chapter 7

Finding a Raft

At breakfast the next morning everyone at La Genovesa was excited about our expedition and was offering us advice about where to find a raft. Juan, who ate every meal there when he was in town, said he'd show us the path leading to the Tambopata River, a tributary feeding the Madre de Dios. I swallowed the last of my toast and downed my coffee. Fitz paid the bill then pinned his jeans pocket closed so he couldn't lose his wallet to chance or thieves.

We followed Juan through town to where a narrow path paralleled the river and a bank dense with vegetation. Banana trees rose around us, the individual leaves up to six or seven feet long. There Juan left us, agreeing to meet for lunch.

The path took us to a clearing where a shack on stilts was surrounded by a small field of corn. A little raft was moored to a stake in the bank, too small for us. No one was around.

"Let's keep going." I noticed how prettily the morning light played on the banana leaves and corn. Plunging back down the path, we discovered that it wound through similar clearings, spaced fifty or sixty yards apart.

Encountering people working their *chacras*—small farms—we bade them good morning, asking, "¿*Tiene balsas aquí?*" Have you rafts here?

The people were all good-natured. Rafts or no, they asked where we were from and where we were going. At the mention of Riberalta they nodded and smiled, then wished us good luck.

Eventually, we came to a clearing where a bare-chested young man chopped wood with a machete while his wife played with two children on a stilt shack's porch.

He introduced himself as Ernesto Rivera and his wife, Guillermina. They were interested to know all about us and said they were both schoolteachers. The shack wasn't their home, just a shelter they used while farming. They lived in town and came to the river when school was out of session. Neither spoke English, but they were very helpful as we struggled with Spanish. Ernesto had no raft but was happy to take us across the river in his canoe to his friend's plantation. There we found a raft measuring about sixteen by fourteen feet. Much too big for us, it had huge gaps between the logs.

Without a word, Ernesto's slashing machete quickly severed the crosspieces of the first four logs, leaving the best four for us. Ernesto explained we should build a platform over half the raft and cover it with a tent for shelter and comfort. Ernesto's friend gave us the raft, even volunteering to tow it to a convenient spot for outfitting. He wouldn't accept payment. Within minutes, Ernesto, his friend, Fitz, and I were chugging across the Tambopata River in his pecky-pecky, a long, narrow boat with a lawn-mower-sized engine.

"We depend upon the kindness of strangers!" Fitz shouted to me over the clatter of the engine.

I smiled at his bastardization of Blanche's line in *A Street-*

car Named Desire and called back, "Everyone's so nice. It almost makes me want to stay."

We tied up on the bank of the Tambopata River, a few yards from where it flowed into the Madre de Dios River, and not far from the sawmill where we could buy boards to make the platform for the tent. Our closest neighbor was a slaughterhouse just above us on the bank. It was nothing more than a cement floor pitched to a drain with a thatched roof and no walls. Large steel hooks dangled from a beam beneath the roof. Four tethered beef cattle munched grass nearby.

In the morning, we returned to work on the raft to find one cow gone. A carcass of fat-streaked flesh hung on hooks. I smelled the bloody stench and presumed that the three other cows did, too.

Fitz stared at the remaining cattle, which continued to graze indifferently, flicking their tails in the sun. "It's like 'Nam," he said, "death is all around but you can't believe it will happen to you."

Ernesto helped us with our raft after working his *chacra* each day. Word spread quickly through the jungle town about the two gringos. Soon it seemed everyone knew of our plan. Children hung around the raft all day while we worked. Their parents came in shifts to watch us, a few at a time, before continuing down the path to their plots. When the children became bored they would splash in the water or play tag. There were times when I joined them. Three young men who'd been lounging idly on the bank helped us carry lumber from the sawmill. All day long people came to the riverbank, stared awhile, and then left. Sometimes they sat watching quietly. Other times they asked questions about the trip, or about building the platform for the tent over the widely spaced balsa logs, listening carefully to our broken Spanish answers. They corrected us when we made mistakes, and we would laugh at our linguistic clumsiness.

When I gathered sticks on the bank for our cookstove, the children followed me. I laid the kindling on the raft. Soon the kids fell into doing the same. Grins in their round, brown faces exploded with pride as they placed piles of sticks onto the stern of the raft.

"You're wonderful," I said. "Thank you so much."

They shifted and wiggled then ran off to find more.

As we walked through town, carrying nails or rolls of plastic sheeting, borrowed hammers or saws, people waved and smiled at us. Sometimes they gawked. I felt like a celebrity. We were busy and the time passed quickly. By evening we were famished, eager for La Genovesa's food and company. En route, villagers stepped out of open-fronted shops and cafés to greet us warmly and inquire about our progress. It was the most sociable town we'd ever visited. These people made their own entertainment. They loved to share stories and became immersed in the making of ours.

On our third day, when we had finished hammering the last board of the tent floor, Juan and a friend from the bank, Jim, helped us to construct the tent over it, using poles cut from trees and sheets of pink and blue plastic we'd purchased in town. We stretched the plastic over the poles and borrowed a large stapler from the bank to secure it in place. The plastic was thinner than a tarp but much thicker than a trash bag.

Fitz made a stove by cutting open one side of an empty five-gallon canola oilcan and covering the opening with chicken wire for a grill, as instructed by the hardware shop owner. Then he nailed the bottom of the metal can to a log on the raft, equidistant between the tent and where the tiller would go. This would be our outdoor kitchen where we would burn the kindling inside the can to boil water, heat Spam, or fry eggs in a pan on top of the chicken wire. Many used these same stoves like barbecue grills back home. The grill was safe enough, but our "deck" would never pass inspection in Connecticut because of its ankle-snapping gaps.

We purchased oranges, bread, canned sausages, tuna, sardines, and cheese, as well as a drop line and two fishhooks. The hooks were huge, but they were the only size carried by the store.

"What kind of fish could this be for?" I pulled a four-inch curved hook out of the brown paper bag. "You'd have to be awfully strong to pull it in."

"Looks like it's for the fish from *The Old Man and the Sea*," Fitz said, laughing.

I thought about the story of the hungry Cuban's perseverance with the great fish at the end of his line. "I hope we'll have better luck than he did."

We left the open-fronted hardware store and walked toward the raft with our supplies.

"Everything's bigger here in the jungle than it is at home," I noted, "the trees, the reptiles, the fish. They're all bigger than life, even the mosquitoes . . ."

"That reminds me," Fitz interrupted. "Juan said to get a *mosquitero*. Oh, and a machete. I'm not sure what for."

"Maybe we have to cut back limbs or vines on the river," I said.

"Maybe. I asked him why we needed it, but he was ambiguous. Probably thinks it's obvious," Fitz replied.

The only explicit advice Juan had actually given us was "Don't ever swim in the water."

"Why?" I had asked, taken aback. We'd watched the children splashing in the harbor, enjoying it with high squeals. "I thought the caiman are dormant during the rainy season."

"They are. It's the candiru you have to watch out for," he'd said solemnly.

"The who?" Fitz had asked.

"A minuscule saw-toothed fish, downriver. They'll swim up your butt and latch on to your intestines, suck your blood until you die."

Fitz and I had stared at each other and then at him.

"You're kidding?" I'd gasped. We'd seen piranha and knew that when in a frenzy they could strip prey to the bone within minutes, but mainly if the prey were already bleeding.

"You don't have to be bleeding. Candiru are parasitic. They'll find you if you're swimming."

"Okay, we definitely won't be swimming," Fitz had agreed.

Each evening, we would meet up with Juan at La Genovesa to discuss the day's work or to draw up lists of provisions we would need for our trip. One night, Juan suggested that Fitz buy a rifle.

"What for?" Fitz asked, his voice rising.

"You never know . . . ," Juan replied.

"Are the people on the river unfriendly?" Fitz took a cigarette out of his pack and pushed his hand around his pocket for matches. "Would the Indians or animals attack us?"

"No, nothing like that." Juan looked into the distance as if he were seeing into the wild. "You won't have any trouble with the indigenous people. And as long as you keep by the river, you won't meet any fierce animals."

"Then why bring a rifle?"

Juan shrugged his shoulders. "You never know. It's just something useful to have with you."

Fitz hated guns. Two years as an infantry rifleman had convinced him that having a rifle as a civilian was a bad idea. "I'm not going to get one," he said after Juan left. "It's just an invitation to trouble."

I understood his reluctance to carry a gun. He'd never said much about the war, but I did know of one experience that had affected him deeply. On his first day carrying his lieutenant's radio in Vietnam, the lieutenant was shot dead trying to save another friend who also died in the ambush.

After Fitz returned to the United States, the lieutenant's family asked him to visit in Darien, Connecticut, to talk about their son's death and to provide details concerning rolls of film he had mailed home from Vietnam. When I put Fitz on a bus to go, he was not looking forward to the visit but felt it was the least he could do for the lieutenant. He looked somber upon his return. The visit apparently helped the family reach closure, but it had compelled Fitz to relive the horrors of war.

On our last afternoon in Puerto Maldonado, after buying all our supplies, I tallied the costs in my budget log.

All totaled, we'd spent $19.37 on goods, including four boxes of food—mostly Spam, beans, cheese, and rice. We'd bought two Panama straw hats ($2.34 each); a flashlight and batteries ($1.23); the mosquito netting, the chicken wire, the recycled five-gallon canola oilcan (without the oil), the rolls of plastic to build the tent, a hammer and nails, and a fifteen-foot rope (cost lumped in with general supplies). The steel machete was $1.34; for the workers who used machetes, that was equal to a month's salary.

We already owned a sleeping bag, a sheet, and the two handwoven blanket ponchos we'd bought at a market in the Andes. I doubted we'd need wool blankets in the jungle, but they'd be good padding to put under us for sleeping on the hard floor.

Ernesto had made a rudder from a piece of wood he'd found in the scrap pile behind his house. We'd watched him wield his machete, shaping the wood as if it were clay. The base of the machete's wide blade was used like a hammer, its edge sharp as a knife.

Fitz and I nailed the rudder to a long pole and then slid it through two crossed sticks at the stern of the raft. We then tied a thirty-foot vine that Ernesto had given us onto the stern to use as a painter.

After four days, the raft was set to go. We would sleep on her tonight and leave in the morning.

Fitz and I made our rounds that evening, saying good-bye to the shopkeepers who'd given us their time and helpful advice. We strolled, hand in hand, to La Genovesa for our last dinner, where we were to meet up with Juan and Jim. They were leaving at first light for an expedition up the Madre, so they would miss our grand launching.

Jim handed me a brown paper bag. "For the christening," he said. "There's no champagne in the jungle, but you've got to have something."

I opened the bag and pulled out a quart bottle of local beer. "How nice of you!"

"You have that tradition, too, right?" he asked. "For the launching of a new boat? It's good luck."

"Yes. And we could use all the luck we can get!" I laughed. We all laughed. I was excited about the trip but nervous, too.

"I wish you could be at the launching," I said, sad to think we would probably never see these kind men again.

"I'm sorry to miss it," Juan agreed.

Our paths were going in different directions—he was headed west, in search of gold, and we were going northeast. Part of traveling was leaving behind people you liked.

"We won't forget you," Fitz said as he shook the men's hands gratefully.

"And we won't forget you," they said in unison, looking at the two of us.

"You'll have the time of your life," Juan said, smiling, bowing, and kissing my hand.

The Genovesa family came over to our table. It was our last good-bye to them as well. They gave us letters they'd written to relatives in Riberalta, which we promised to deliver. Mr. Genovesa's wild, spiraling gestures, his sky-high exuberance, his wife's smiling, sun-shaped face and soft voice had been as much a part of our meals as lomo saltado, Italian style. We felt as if we'd just finished dinner at one of our parents' homes, so comfortable at La Genovesa that we sometimes forgot to pay. They never gave us dinner checks or told us how much we owed. We had to pry it out of them.

After hugging the Genovesas, Fitz and I wandered along the riverbank to the hotel to collect our things. The fragrance of flowers floated on the night's river breeze. It seemed as if we, too, were floating, heads full of jungle-rafting dreams. The bright moon suffused this world in a silver bath and splashed the river almost white.

In anticipation, we carried all our supplies to the raft. That night we would be trading screened windows and a bed at the Chavez Hotel for hard boards and mosquito netting in the tent. Even the almost-full moon seemed jovial, like a lantern beckoning us onward. My step quickened as the light illuminated our path to the river. A few clouds moved across the sky, crisscrossed the moon, and then passed on. One lingered long enough to shadow the light. I did not see this as an omen as I skipped down the dirt road to the raft. I felt nothing but joy and a sense of adventure ahead.

Too hot to crawl inside, we settled on top of our sleeping bag—the blankets placed beneath it for padding—with a sheet pulled over us. Fitz untied my braids, smoothing my hair down my back. Soon I was lulled to sleep by water lapping against our raft and soft summer voices drifting along the river.

Chapter 8

Launch Day

FEBRUARY 15

I bolted upright from our makeshift bed. It had been surprisingly restful. Inhaling the fresh morning air, I felt a rush. "Wake up, Fitz! It's launch day!" I kissed his cheek and ruffled his hair.

When I stepped outside, everything was wet, but not a drop of rain had seeped into the tent. It was watertight. The *mosquitero* had kept us safe from the buzzing mosquitoes. "This is unbelievable," I called to Fitz. "We're really ready to go!"

I looked past the Tambopata riverbank to where it merged with the Madre de Dios River. The Madre was maybe half a mile wide at this point. The early morning sun sparkled on her surface as she lazily meandered. Trees speckled our bank with shadow, but the shade didn't reach the Tambopata's water. Our raft, tied with its long vine to one of those trees, was floating in bright sunlight. Beyond us, where we were headed, the Madre widened to the east and curved. What beckons around that bend? I wondered.

I darted inside and smacked a kiss on Fitz's mouth. "Are you ready for the time of your life?"

"Yes," he said, opening his eyes.

I pulled his arms up while he tried to wind them around me and pull me down. "Come see. You're going to love it." I wriggled free. "The sun's out. It's a glorious day for the raft trip!"

"The hell with that. I like it right here." He reached for me again.

"Fitz, come on," I said, giggling while trying to ignore him. "We have lots to do."

"Okay, Hol. I'm awake!" He wiped his eyes and stretched out his long legs.

"Hungry?" I ducked out of the tent to put kindling in the stove.

High in the trees, birds were in full song, flying back and forth across the Madre. The fragrance of oranges drifted toward us on the dawn's dewy air. I took a deep breath. The air was cool and sharp, early morning, when everything begins again. Two small bright green birds perched briefly on the tent's peak then flew away. They're just like us, I thought, flying free.

"I'll make coffee." Fitz yawned. As he pushed aside the tent's flap he bumped his head on one of the framing poles. The tent's opening was six inches shorter than he was.

Fitz boiled river water from a water bottle we'd treated with halazone tablets to make the water safe to drink. He prepared our first breakfast using the frying and saucepans from my Girl Scout mess kit. I'd carried it for the past few months in my backpack but had never used it until now. Fitz fried two eggs for me. Loathing eggs himself, he decided on cheese, bread, and jam.

By the time we sat down to eat, the tropical sun had dried the logs. Some locals crouched on the riverbank, watching us. I didn't want to leave these friendly people who'd helped us get the raft ready to launch. My stomach knotted. Were we crazy to head out alone, into a jungle river we knew nothing about? It was what we'd wanted to do, and had planned to do ever since we'd sought out the balsa raft. No second-guessing now.

"Let's make sure we haven't forgotten anything," Fitz said as we finished our coffee and rinsed the dishes in the river water.

I took out a pad and pencil and checked off the items as Fitz called out each one, down to malaria pills, a sewing kit, and two now unneeded rope hammocks that we'd planned to sleep in on the boat we'd missed.

When we were done I picked up a fan made of shimmering blue-and-green parrot feathers, a gift from an Ecuadorian Indian chief. "This will be good to swipe at the heat," I said.

"For sure," Fitz agreed.

"Wait, we have to christen the raft! We need a name."

After staring at our pink-and-blue plastic tent for a moment, Fitz suggested the Pink Palace, alluding to the totally pink Lima mansion of America's ambassador to Peru. A month earlier, Fitz and I had accepted a last-minute invitation to the plush palace from Ambassador Taylor Belcher. Fitz had arrived at the fancy soiree with big, wet splotches still remaining on his hand-washed gray sport coat. He'd self-consciously explained them away, claiming that we'd been caught in the rain on the other side of the city. The ambassador drew his wife and guests around to marvel at Fitz's tale. Evidently, it hadn't rained in Lima for twenty years. Fitz's luck held. When we left the residence a few hours later, it was pouring down buckets.

I laughed now. "The Pink Palace it is—just the name for a lucky voyage!"

Villagers gathered on the riverbank to see us off. I glanced up the path to see two police officers approaching. Khaki-smooth and manicured, their necks were wrapped in ties and tight collars. They looked like mannequins. How were they not sweating? I wondered. People stepped aside to let them pass. All conversation ceased.

"*Buenos días, señor y señora.* Where are you going?" the taller officer asked in Spanish. Perhaps in his forties, he had a trim black mustache, piercing black eyes, and an unnaturally erect posture.

Fitz explained we were going to Riberalta, Bolivia.

"On this?" the shorter, older officer nodded to the Pink Palace, his bushy brows hiding his eyes.

"*Sí,*" Fitz and I both said, proud to show off our vessel.

The men looked skeptically, not at the balsa, but at us.

"Do you know rafts?" the taller man asked, his hands now resting on his hips.

"No, but a friend told us 'just go with the river.' He said there'd be no problem." Fitz paused. "Is there a problem?"

The officers looked at each other, shrugged, and said, "*No, no problema.*"

"But a license is necessary," added the shorter officer. "All *comandantes* must have a license to go down the river. Come with us."

I looked at Fitz, then at them. "Where are you taking him?"

"To get the license. We must have a record in the *aduana*'s office," the tall officer replied. "Your husband won't be long. Anyone can take a raft. There's nothing to it."

Why did we need a license for a raft? I thought back to the plane crash. Maybe it was good to document where we were going. Still, I felt intimidated by the police officers' serious demeanor. I turned to Fitz. "I'll go with you." I was afraid that Fitz was going to be carted off, never to be seen again.

"Stay at the raft to watch your things," the second officer suggested, his mouth turning downward as he spoke.

"It's funny that we never heard about a license before now," I mentioned to Fitz in English. "It's so casual around here. I never would have thought they'd be so official." I slapped at a couple of annoying mosquitoes hovering around my ear. "I suppose they wouldn't give us a license if they didn't think the raft was seaworthy."

Fitz nodded. "I'm all for a record. It makes sense to have the captain of the port know when we left." He rubbed his neck. "It makes me feel better about this whole thing."

The officers explained that once they issued the license they would radio ahead to Riberalta to say that we would be arriving there within a few days. If we didn't arrive, the Riberalta port authority would radio back to Puerto Maldonado.

"If necessary, we could radio a commercial plane from Lima," the first officer assured us. "Planes pass over the area two or three times a week."

He made a license sound like very good insurance.

"How many days to Riberalta?" asked Fitz.

They conferred. "About ten, unless you go day and night, then five."

"Is that what people do?" I asked. "They go day and night?"

"*Sí, señora,*" the taller, more commanding officer answered. "Your raft is big. Safe." We'd heard this from Juan.

It was confirmation that the Pink Palace could stay afloat should the river get choppy.

The men watched us digest this information. When we had no more questions they said, "Let's go, *señor*. It won't take long."

Fitz squeezed my hand. "I'll be back soon."

I watched him walk over the dusty hill between the two officers. He was taller than both of them, and in at least as good a shape. I didn't like that they had guns, but I felt sure Fitz could handle himself.

I puttered around the balsa, organizing our backpacks and boxes of supplies along the wall that faced the stern at the foot of the sleeping bag. There was just enough room to fit everything and keep the sleeping bag open, as a luxurious rug to lounge on in the day. Then I lined our books alongside the length of the sleeping bag. I felt pleased with our cozy little home as if it were an exotic Bedouin tent. When Fitz had been gone two hours, I began wondering what was keeping him. I wanted to go find him, but didn't want to leave our belongings unattended. Everything takes a while here, I reminded myself. I had better stay put.

The kids waiting along the shore looked bored. "Hey, you want to play charades?" I called, pantomiming a horse.

They got right into it, each one taking a turn, acting out an animal, dancer, or soccer player. One boy climbed onto the shoulders of another and pretended to smoke a cigarette. "Ah, a tall man . . . the gringo, the gringo!" they all laughed, imitating Fitz.

I cheered when I saw Fitz walking down the hill waving some papers high in the air.

"Here it is!" he called. "Our license! We're official!"

He showed me our much-stamped license. He was now recorded as the vessel's indisputable *comandante*. The police had typed in Fitz's occupation as a newspaper reporter. "I tried to tell them you're a social worker, but I couldn't get it across," Fitz said, leaping onto the raft. "They listed you as a housewife, *su casa*." He shook his head as he chortled.

I was so relieved to see him that my wild hug pitched us toward the water.

"Whoa!" he said as we wobbled back and forth then steadied ourselves.

Our audience on the shore began to clap when we didn't fall in. I'd forgotten we were on display. I turned to wave in acknowledgment.

"Take a look, Hol," Fitz said, one hand still on my waist, the other clutching the documents.

I leafed through the sheets of paper, amazed. All these official stamps on every page and we didn't need to know a thing about rafting.

"And listen to this!" Fitz's tone was light as he explained that the captain had a new ham radio that he was itching to use. "He showed it to me—it's beautiful. He's actually looking forward to radioing ahead so Riberalta will be on the lookout for us."

I placed the documents in the camera bag and stuffed our passports back inside the money belts around our waists.

Fitz took a deep breath. "And get this—the captain has a Mark Twain calendar in his office, a gift from another traveler. That's got to be a good omen."

I was delighted to see Fitz so exuberant. He tied a cord to the paper-bagged quart bottle of beer Jim had given us and handed it to me. It felt loose inside the paper bag. I hoped it wouldn't slip as I grasped the cord to let the bottle dangle. Just swing the cord hard and the bottle will follow, I told myself.

Pronounce our raft's new name and smash the bottle on the raft; it should be easy. After all, my mom, when only ten, had christened *Virginia*, then the largest passenger ship on the seas.

More people arrived, waiting to see what would happen next. Youngsters climbed onto the raft to get a better look.

Fitz held the camera to catch the moment. "Okay, Hol!" he urged.

I wound up my arm and, with all the strength I had in me, swung the cord tied to the bottle as I called out the raft's name.

Fitz clicked the camera as the bottle was in midair. He clicked the camera again as it hit the balsa's outermost log. He clicked one more time as the bottle bounced off and slid, unbroken, into the brown water.

"Ooooh," I heard the villagers lament, like a Greek chorus on the bank and on the raft. Then silence swelled around me as the bottle disappeared, swallowed by the murky river.

"It didn't break!" I cried, slapping my hands to my face, feeling responsible for any bad luck that might result from the unbroken bottle.

"It doesn't matter," Fitz said. "It's just a superstition."

We could have walked back to town and bought another bottle. But it was now near noon and we had to get going. I told myself that christening bottles that didn't break were like cracked mirrors and spilled salt, black cats crossing your path: I didn't believe in them.

"Come on, Hol, we've got to focus on reaching the border before dark. We're not even sure how long it'll take."

He came down the bank, where he'd been taking photos.

I was still mad at myself. How could I have not broken that bottle? I thought about bottles breaking all the time when you didn't want them to.

Fitz put his arm on my shoulder. "It's not the real thing anyway," he said. "It's supposed to be champagne."

No one could tell us how many hours the journey from Puerto Maldonado to the border post at Puerto Pardo would take. On the map it was about forty miles as the crow flies, but we could double that to account for the twists and turns of the river.

I began to wonder if perhaps people didn't come down this river at all. Maybe they only went west. We definitely didn't want to float unknowingly across an invisible line between Peru and Bolivia. With no motor we would just glide with the current. The Madre looked slow right now, but looks could be deceiving. The border is only a few hours away, I assured myself. We would make it before dusk.

The villagers and Fitz shoved us off. With the last push, Fitz hopped on and we waved good-bye. I took a photo of the kids waving back. Glancing up the bank at the slaughter shed, I saw there was only a single cow left alive, flicking her tail.

The raft floated out twenty feet then started back to the bank along the Tambopata.

"Holly, the current's too strong to get in it, help me!" Fitz pressed his pole in the water against the bottom, trying to push us out again.

I threw my camera into the bag and grabbed the paddle.

Fitz poled and I paddled. The raft bounced around the bend and hit the bank of the Madre. We pushed off. My hands were slippery with sweat as I paddled toward the center. We sidled along the main current struggling hard to enter her, but she wouldn't take us. Other currents grabbed us, whisked us back to shore. We fought our way out once more, renegade currents swirling us in circles as we headed toward the center.

"This is it, this time!" Fitz said as we again glided next to the main current.

"Yes, this is it for sure!"

But at the last moment eddies yanked us away. We tried again and again. I began to doubt the river would ever accept us. Assurance dissolving, I was hit with a memory: In high school I'd stood in a long line to audition for the elite choral group. I loved to sing. As my turn came closer I heard each girl's melodic voice accompanied by the teacher on piano behind the door. They sounded so beautiful, so professional. My underarms began to pool. A few girls were still in front of me. Wet leaked through my shirt. Two girls. My heart thumped. Only one girl left. The pure notes soared. I bolted into the nearby bathroom. Leaning against the wall, I heard the bell ring: auditions over. Girls were giggling in the hall. I bit the index finger on my fisted hand, knowing I'd given up without even trying. Never again.

So I kept paddling. Eventually, the main current received us capriciously, like a moody nightclub bouncer. We were out in the middle now, standing tall in the noonday sun. Wiping our faces, we looked back to see how far we'd come. We had rounded a bend—or several. Puerto Maldonado was gone.

We were both heaving deep breaths. "Wow, we're really moving fast!" I gasped, astonished at the raft floating smoothly on the river, relieved that we could stop fighting the current. I brushed Fitz's hand and smiled. "The two rivers had to become one. That had to make it extra hard to get into the current."

"I think so." Fitz leaned down and kissed me. "Well, we did it, Hol! There's no going back now."

We stood with our arms around each other, my body wilting into his. "Even a boat would be hard to navigate against this current," I said.

The river now looked at least three-quarters of a mile wide, flowing fast and full. A little shiver passed between my shoulders. The Rio Madre de Dios was stunning, but her power scared me.

Yet the Pink Palace floated easily, and I, assured by her steadiness and size, decided to sit down at the stern and take in the view. Fitz remained standing, watchful for a while longer. I swept my eyes over the river on either side of the tent, shielding them with my hand from the white sun flashing off the water. The Madre was vast and so was the jungle on both her banks. Farmlands of grasses and crops stretched up high hills, and small wooden houses with porches, like Ernesto's, were nestled among miles of jungle. After a few more bends the river grew wider. Fitz and I saw no houses on either bank, only dense, steep rain forest interrupted by sporadic plots of plowed land. Soon we saw no open land at all, just hills of thick canopy rising to the horizon.

"There's no one else here," I murmured. "I've never been this far from people before."

My interest intensified at such virgin beauty, at the river's freedom to go where she wished. Yet a curl of apprehension crept into me as we traveled deeper and deeper into the unknown.

Chapter 9

First Day on the River

The jungle softly undulated alongside the river, perhaps a half mile away on either side of us. We were so far out that the forest looked like tiny clouds of green moss and Brillo pads. Our Rio Madre de Dios was ever changing but somehow always the same. She was a snake that carried us on her back.

The logs of the Pink Palace rode two or three inches above the main current that carried us forward, usually near the center of the river. Occasionally the current swirled us toward one shore or the other. The trees looked very different close up. Wild, gnarly branches with waving slim leaves looked like long, unbrushed hair. Other trees were stately and tall, with wide, handlike leaves. Thick vines strangled tree limbs. The Madre would jerk us back to her center again without warning.

It was a quiet, sultry day. We could hear every small bird, each splash from a fish. Red-and-blue macaws flew above us, squawking to each other in a full blue sky. We were the only craft on the river, and we made no sound at all, traveling like a feather, barely aware that we were moving. Yet when I looked out at branches and logs floating nearby, I saw how swiftly the river took them. Lighter than us, they sailed toward the horizon, disappearing around a bend. The river was faster than a galloping horse. Unlike a horse, the Madre never had to rest.

I smiled at Fitz and he grinned back. We'd done it! We were actually floating down the Madre on our jungle queen headed for the Amazon. We joked about which of us was Huck Finn. We both wore straw hats, but Fitz was *comandante*. I guessed I'd be Jim, or maybe Becky, but Becky hadn't gone down the river.

Were there any stories about a girl riding a raft? Perhaps one day I would write one. We bantered for hours now that we had nothing else to do. I teased Fitz, the "*comandante*," and he teased me about "*su casa*." I took photos of him at the helm, wearing his straw hat, navy-blue-and-white-striped shirt, and jeans—my river boy.

Juan was right—we didn't need a guide. We lazed along, letting the river carry us. The Madre's playful currents relaxed me into a trance. I rested my head on Fitz's lap as he held the tiller. From far off I heard birds cry out, smelled the drifting scent of ripe mangos and something like gardenia. My eyelids closed.

"Holly, look!" Fitz called out, making me laugh with surprise as I opened my eyes to see iridescent butterflies—red, yellow, orange, purple—fluttering around me. Then they darted off.

I dangled my hand in the water, then finally sat up and stretched my arms out like a bird. "I don't know when I've ever felt so liberated," I said. I squinted at Fitz in the sunlight that jumped off the river.

He swept strands of my windblown hair from my face, coming closer for a kiss.

Had I ever felt so happy? How fortunate we were to have each other to adventure with.

The Pink Palace's plastic tent sparkled at the bow. The rest of her round logs, about two feet in diameter, spread seven feet to the stern and served as our deck, on which we spent the afternoon sitting, or walking back and forth, splashing our faces with the cool river.

"Hey, I guess we have time to relax now," I said. "The fort won't be coming up for hours."

Fitz grinned, his dimples going deep. He put his arms around me. "The Pink Palace can take care of herself," he agreed.

"The scenery can, too," I replied.

"You're my scenery," Fitz said, smiling as he guided me inside.

An hour or two later, we sat by the tiller feeling the heat of the late afternoon sun. We ate the last of the bread and became thirsty for fruit. Juan had advised against bringing much bread and fruit because it would only rot in the humidity. He'd said there would be plenty of farms along the way. "Just call out and people will boat out and bring it to you."

We floated down the center of the widening river, seeing no signs of human life.

"Gee, we still haven't seen anybody," I said, feeling a little unsure.

"Hol, we've been preoccupied!"

"True." I agreed, laughing, my anxiety ebbing away.

We continued to glide down the Madre, far from anything we'd ever known. As the afternoon sun began to glow orange, we started looking more carefully for signs of civilization. Eventually we saw six thatched-roof houses set high on a hill in an open area of red dirt and green scrub grass.

So far away from us, they appeared small, like a doll village. Then I spotted three figures walking near the river. One wore a red sash.

"Oh, Fitz, there are people! They'll come out!" We called out, "*¡Hola!*"

The people waved.

"Have you bread? Oranges?"

"*Sí.*"

No one paddled or motored out to make a sale. This happened twice more with the same result: friendly waves, children and dogs running along the bank, but no one boated out with bread and fruit.

Uneasiness settled into my gut. We had passed only two slim dugout canoes all afternoon, about a mile from us, hugging the shoreline. Their motors putted as they made their way up the swollen river. Perhaps there was a reason there was such little traffic? Maybe even indigenous people couldn't break easily into the current and found it difficult to boat at this time of the year. I began to wonder about Juan's advice. Had he even been on this part of the river, especially during the rainy season? He'd said he was going back upriver by pecky-pecky, but had he ever gone downriver this far?

We assumed the border post at Puerto Pardo should be coming up in the next couple of hours, but it could be earlier or later, for we weren't sure of the raft's speed. We began watching intently, having no idea what the fort might look like. It might be hidden in trees as Sepa had been. There were no landmarks to guide us—nothing but trees and entangled vines. The fading sun cast shadows on the rain forest, making it appear dark and dense.

Pink dusk splashed across the sky and over the river,

a splendid view before nightfall. I heard the far-off cry of some beast, then a loud sound like whistling from across the water, clear and sad, following us. It made me shiver.

"Fitz, is that a bird or a person?"

"Sounds like a man!" Fitz stood at the bow, his eyes searching.

"It's amazing that a whistle can carry so far."

"Why would he be whistling so loudly in the jungle?"

"It's spooky. Maybe it's a signal." I remembered a story I'd heard a few months earlier about five missionaries who had been killed by Indians. But that was in another part of the Amazon basin, a couple hundred miles away. Still, my head began to throb, thinking of people who might not want us around, who might be watching us from behind the trees.

"Juan said there weren't any unfriendly people along here," Fitz said firmly, but he stared toward the darkening jungle, his arm above his eyes to cut the dropping sun's glare.

I stared, too. Then dogs began to bark. It reminded me of Zelda, our Keeshond, and of my parents' and sister's dogs. Was a man walking his dogs in this wilderness?

Fitz called out, "¡Hola!"

The whistle and barks immediately stopped. After a minute, as our raft continued down the river, the whistle and barks resumed. Fitz and I both called out. Each time we did, the sounds ceased. Goose bumps rose on my neck. "Why do they go silent when we call?"

Perhaps the sounds weren't from men or dogs at all, but from mimicking birds that had once heard men pass this way. We could be passing virgin landscape that no human had ever crossed. I wasn't sure which was worse: hostile people or no people.

The sun was dropping with no sign of Puerto Pardo, Peru.

"It's going to be dark soon," I noted. "We won't be able to see the fort."

"We'd better put in."

"But is it safe to land?" I listened for the weird whistles.

"If Juan is right, it should be safe." Fitz sighed. "This whole venture is based on trusting what he told us. So we might as well trust him now."

I guessed Fitz was right. We had nothing else to go on. In a while the whistles and the barking began to disappear.

"We'll see the border better in daylight," Fitz continued.

"Okay. When the current moves toward the bank, let's try to pull in."

Now that we'd been on the river for half a day, we hoped that we were more adept at handling the raft than when we'd started. When the Pink Palace surged toward the shore Fitz steered and I paddled hard. As we got within inches of the bank we grabbed for the bowed branches, but the powerful current wouldn't cooperate, wrenching us back to the middle of the river.

We neared the shore repeatedly, touching the trees, then pulling at them to bring ourselves in. Each time the current yanked the raft, and the boughs were ripped from our hands. The Madre teased us again and again.

"We're coming close!" Fitz called from the helm.

I stroked and stroked, and as we neared shore I reached out and grasped a limb. "I think I've got this one!"

"Hold on, hold on, Hol!"

The limb skidded through my fingers.

The Rio Madre de Dios, her cunning strength serenely masked, flicked a finger and twisted the cumbersome Pink

Palace back into deeper water. "This rudder is for the birds! It's too small." Fitz threw the tiller aside, grabbed the paddle, and stroked hard toward the shore.

I pushed with the pole as it touched the bottom close to the bank. I grabbed a tree limb and so did Fitz. We wrestled to hold them. Sweat crept across my brow. I fought and lost. Fitz did, too. Tears filled my eyes and my throat burned. "Let's try again," I implored. I clutched another branch. "I've got it this time!"

But the branch slipped my hold like an unruly child, throwing me off balance—almost into the menacing river.

Fitz threw his arms up. "This is impossible! We can't get to land! We have no control! No goddamn control at all!"

The Pink Palace was too big to follow anyone's lead but the Madre's. I stared at Fitz and at the receding trees. At that moment, it dawned on me that we were totally at the mercy of a dangerous river. She was stronger than we'd realized. We couldn't paddle the Pink Palace to shore alone. We would have to call out at the border and hope the border guards could dock her.

There were no roads out of here. If the guards didn't see us and we drifted past the border, the river would only get wider as it wound inexorably toward Riberalta, five hundred miles away.

We'd been warned to avoid the crashing rapids just beyond Riberalta. Fitz and I had been assured we could easily pull in at the town, but now I saw that we would be helpless, were helpless now. I raised my swollen hands to my cheeks and gasped for air as the river took us back toward her center. Looking at Fitz I expected to see determination. What I saw was fear.

"It's getting dark," I said, wanting my voice to be calm

but feeling it rise. "If we pass the border without knowing it, we won't be legal!"

"What else can we do? We can't stop the goddamn raft." He swiped his hair with his hand. "We'll just have to keep going through the night then call out for help when we spot the border—if we spot it."

"How will we see it in the dark? There's no electricity out here."

"We'll just have to get lucky," Fitz said, his voice now resolute. "It's probably on the top of a hill."

We stood on opposite sides of the raft to view both banks of the Madre. I tried to stare without blinking, for fear of missing a border post that was perhaps no bigger than a single hut and that had no lights.

Chapter 10

The Border

I was comforted by the emergence of a nearly full moon rising into an endless panorama of stars. Our raft glided silently through the light reflected on the water. In the shadowed jungle there was not a single man-made flicker from farm or hut, but we occasionally saw tiny glints of light moving through the trees. We both suspected them to be the wary eyes of creatures following us closely. All was quiet around us, except for intermittent shrieks that made the back of my neck cold.

"That's the same noise we heard at Sepa."

"Yes," Fitz replied, carefully navigating the curved logs to reach me in the moonlight. He pressed his arm around me. Was he trembling?

The commanding screeches reverberated across the water. I was almost glad we weren't on land.

"Do you think we missed the border?" I asked, leaning into him. "Wouldn't they have a light to show boaters where to pull in?"

"What boaters?"

My eyelids were drooping from the strain of staring into

the shadows. Fitz must have seen this because he suggested I go lie down in the tent.

"I'll watch for the border," he said. "I'm sure there'll be a clearing and some kind of outline of a building."

"No. I'll stay up with you."

He stepped to the bow and looked toward shore. "There's no point in both of us waiting up." His cigarette glow illuminated his determined face.

"Don't you want company, babe?"

"No, Hol. I'll keep watch better on my own. I need to stay focused." His posture was taut. Maybe he'd developed jungle eyes while watching for the enemy in Vietnam.

When my head hit the sleeping bag I crashed like a baby. I trusted my husband, the *comandante*, with my life.

I woke to Fitz shouting for help: "*¡Socorro!*"

"Fitz?" I yelled through the plastic tent walls, scrambling to get up.

"We're here! A guy just lit a cigarette. I could see his face in the flare of the match."

"Where?" I stumbled through the tent flap.

"Up there!" Fitz was pointing to the right bank of the river, clicking our flashlight toward the tiny glow in the dark. He called out, "*¡Socorro!*" over and over. I followed suit.

We heard abrupt, muffled voices, then men shouting. We continued to yell, "*¡Socorro!*" amid banging doors, running and yelling now coming from the riverbank. A rifle exploded with fire.

"Get down!" Fitz screamed.

Several more shots rang out.

Backing into the tent, I flattened myself to the floor. Help us, please! I prayed as bullets whizzed over our heads.

"The fucking idiots think we're smugglers running the border!" Fitz hissed.

A bullet tore through the tent just above me as we continued to drift down the river in the dark. The men were now at the water's edge, the shooting replaced by revving pecky-pecky motors. A beam of light splashed through the tent as small boats banged alongside the Palace. The motors were idled, puttering while harsh voices boomed over each other. The men poked at the tent. "Come out!" they insisted in Spanish.

The tent siding was going to rip so I pulled back the flap and saw men in two motorboats, their rifles aimed directly at us. Some were in uniform; others were wearing only jockey shorts that shone white in the moonlight and looked ludicrously out of place. Fitz was prostrate on the balsa logs, his hands on the back of his head. The men commanded us to get into the boat nearest us as more boats surrounded the raft.

Although it was a calm evening, the current was so strong it took several boats to push the raft to shore. The men muttered impatiently, shaking their flashlights at each other to signal where to land, evidently farther downriver than they wanted to be. They told us to take our backpacks and get out of the boat. Some of them leapt onto our raft and rummaged through our things.

With rifles still on us, we were led along the bank and finally up a steep, winding path. Fitz was in front of me, moving as quickly as he could, but the trees blocked the moonlight so we tripped on roots and rocks underfoot.

After a few minutes, we entered a dark hut, the only illumination coming from a flashlight throwing long shadows onto the guards' faces and the walls. Several soldiers surrounded us. We were ordered to sit on the floor. They opened our bags and dumped everything at their feet.

"¿*Qué es?*" One soldier held a skirt up as he stared at me. His right incisor was missing. Shadows crossed his face, making him appear devilish.

"A skirt," I answered, disturbed by the way he was looking at me.

"¿*Qué es?*" another man demanded. Spit flew through the gaps in his teeth and sprayed me in the face.

"That's a shirt," Fitz said, directing the man to look at him.

The guard would not remove his eyes from me. He laughed when he saw me wipe my cheek, then muttered something to the guard next to him. They both laughed.

A guard wearing only his underpants stood to the far left of us. He picked up a bra and dangled it by the strap in our faces. "¿*Qué es?*"

I turned to Fitz. He stayed calm as he stared at the man.

The guard laughed as he caught the eyes of his friends. He wiggled his hips and twirled the bra in the air. The others guffawed. A man with a long face and hollow cheeks reached down and grabbed a pair of my nylon underpants. I felt my cheeks burn.

The smirking man looked at the others for validation. They all grinned. He rubbed the underwear in his hands then held them up in front of his face.

"Put that down," Fitz said coolly, his eyes snapping. Silence.

A round-bellied man whose chest hairs burst from his rumpled shirt reached for my box of Tampax. "¡*Ay!*" He glared at Fitz as he shook the box and tipped the white cylinders to the floor.

The other men snatched them up then tossed them to each other. We didn't say a word.

The men leered, poked at more of my underwear, and dangled it for the new guards, who were now coming in to see what all the laughter was about.

These men might not have seen a woman in ages, I thought, panic creeping into my chest.

I sank my fingernails into my palms to distract myself from fear. Nobody seemed to be in charge.

At last, an officially dressed *aduana* opened the door. He was lean and neat in his pressed uniform with his rank on his sleeve. The guards stood to attention. The *aduana* barked orders and commanded everyone to go to bed. He told us to set our sleeping bag on the dusty floor of the hut, then left us alone among a few stored boxes.

We lay down with nothing over us, trying to draw solace in each other's arms. "Are you okay, Hol?"

"I'm fine, but those men were scary."

"They were jerks. The bastards could come back anytime. Don't worry, Hol, I'm not sleeping tonight." He hugged me to him.

I doubted I could sleep either, especially with the animal sounds that felt ominously closer on land. But I hoped I would. I nestled into Fitz's chest and squeezed my eyes shut.

FEBRUARY 16

We heard the guards approach the hut at dawn. I sucked in my breath as the door opened, bringing with it the smell of freshly made coffee. One guard handed us each a cup. Another gave Fitz our passports. We couldn't believe it when they explained that they were going to escort us across the border to Puerto Heath. No one apologized for last night's behavior, but we weren't going to stick around any longer than required.

Two men motored us the short distance to the Bolivian border post, which was tiny, with just a few pecky-peckies pulled up to shore. The Pink Palace was tied to a thick tree trunk farther downriver.

The Peruvian guards took off again as the Bolivian *aduana* strode toward us along a path leading from his log house. He introduced himself as Sergeant. Still shaken from our Peruvian reception, I felt immediately reassured by his kind eyes, and the sight of young children scampering after a ball up the hill behind him.

Sergeant explained that he lived at the post with his wife, three children, and a few other men. He said he'd heard the gunfire in the night and was relieved to see that we were all right. He went on to apologize for the attack of the border guards. "We get smugglers back here sometimes. The Peruvian guards can get crazy."

"We were calling out for help, not trying to hide," I said.

"*Sí, señora*, it doesn't make sense. We don't shoot like that on our side, I can assure you. We are civilized here."

He led us up the path, where trees shaded the house. There were no flowers, gardens, or feminine touches, but it felt like a home. The contrast to Puerto Pardo was remarkable.

Sergeant welcomed us into a sparse dining room that was filled with sunlight. Motioning to the table and chairs, he beckoned us to sit down. He explained that he'd not had visitors for a long time, then asked us what we were doing at the border. We told him our story and why we were on the raft. "Ah!" he exclaimed, looking into our faces more intently now.

Sergeant introduced us to his wife, a trim woman, perhaps in her thirties, with dark shoulder-length hair and an inquisitive smile. She offered us a shower from the rain barrel on their roof, and a hot midday meal of fish and rice. We could not resist either.

Over lunch, they pressed us for news of the outside world and stories of our travels. We shared a languid afternoon with them, but beneath our gaiety we were wary about getting back on the raft. We admitted to Sergeant that we couldn't control the Pink Palace and that we couldn't bring her in.

"All rafts can be difficult," he agreed, "but you should have no problem if you just carry on down the Madre and call out again in a few days' time. Someone will help to bring you in at Riberalta."

Fitz and I looked at each other.

"But what if they don't?" Fitz asked.

"And what about the rapids?" I added. "We can't go over those."

"Really, there's no problem," Sergeant replied in his easy South American way. "You barely see the rapids in the flood season. The port authority will notice you before you reach them." He grinned. "Without guns this time, I guarantee."

"How can you be so sure?" Fitz scowled.

"You won't be near a border so there will be no armed guards."

I wanted to be absolutely certain we wouldn't run into more trouble. "So we should be okay to ride the river day and night?"

"That is all you can do with this raft. You will be fine."

"What do you think?" Fitz asked me, when we were alone after lunch.

"What other option do we have? I'm scared, but it seems a normal thing to do here."

"They might not have enough food to feed us. They probably want us to get out of here."

I liked the *aduana* and didn't believe he'd steer us wrong. At 3:00 p.m. we clambered back onto the raft. Sergeant ordered two guards in pecky-peckies to pull the Pink Palace out to the main current. We waved and called "*¡Gracias!*" over their motors as we continued down the vast Madre. We felt like children leaving their parents. It didn't occur to us that Sergeant and his family might be the last people we ever saw.

"Here we are again," I announced as the Pink Palace caught the current in the center of the river, "completely on our own."

"Well, Hol, you heard the *aduana*. It's a straight run to Riberalta."

I didn't know if his confidence was real or bravado, but I wanted to believe him. I lifted my face toward the sun and felt the air brush my cheeks. As we flew over the waves, water sprayed up between the logs, cooling our legs. Although we couldn't see below the surface of the murky brown water, we knew it was deep. Our pole never touched bottom. We were a mile or more from either bank, too far out to worry about jungle animals. Jagged-edged logs and debris sped past us. Fitz said we should not be concerned because the Pink Palace was much bigger than any of them.

Now safe from the Peruvian border guards, we decided to check our ransacked boxes. Our machete was missing.

"It would be worth a lot to someone out here," I said, reaching for canned sardines that were hiding behind a box.

"Let's hope we don't need it," Fitz said.

That night I slept poorly, worrying about the many loose logs in the river that might strike us in the dark. I also couldn't stop thinking about the frightening guards and what they might have done.

Chapter 11

Flying Free

FEBRUARY 18

For the next three days and two nights the river carried us through luxuriant rain forest. River songs ran through my head. Especially "Moon River, off to see the world—there's such a lot of world to see . . ." This was us. Here we were!

By the third day I was dancing on the logs and singing "Proud Mary." "Rollin', rollin', rollin' on the riverrrrr . . ."

Fitz looked up from his paperback. "This is what kids dream about." He shoved the book into the back pocket of his jeans, then reached for my hand to steady me.

The sweet scent of flowers floated past me, inviting me to daydream of Schcherazade, of princes and princesses in foreign lands.

"You're beautiful," Fitz whispered.

"You're handsome."

He threw back his head and laughed.

I leapt toward him, the heat of my skin touching his. He embraced me, his mouth making me quiver. We held hands, watching the distant jungle glide by. The silence was interrupted by one lone caw from far out in the lowlands. The wide span of water picked up the color of the purple sky. A shadow crossed the raft; I looked up to see a wispy cloud. Fitz pushed his hat back, his curls spilling out. The broad rim's shade moved off his face to show his sunlit smile, his white teeth, his mouth moving toward mine again. Closing my eyes at the touch of his lips, I surrendered to the strength of his arms around me.

In the afternoon, I tried to write in my journal, but the mesmerizing scenery made it too difficult to concentrate. I retrieved *Papillon* from the row of secondhand paperbacks in the tent. Even that book couldn't keep my attention. The canopy of trees along the banks of the Madre was embedded in what looked like the red-orange earth of Georgia. Some lone bare trees stood out, branches curled to the sky, green horizontal plumes at their tips. They looked like elegant umbrellas. Umbrella trees, I called them, promising myself to learn their real names someday.

Watching them go by, I broke into "Proud Mary" again, standing so that I could swing to the beat, careful to watch my step. "Rollin', rollin' . . . ," I burst out as I danced, my hair following my head's movements.

Fitz laughed. "You're crazy!"

"Dance with me."

"I'll fall on my ass."

"No you won't." I grabbed his hand.

"Well, I'll dance a slow dance with you. 'Michael, Row the Boat Ashore.'"

He gave a half smile but didn't budge. Maybe he wasn't at ease dancing, although he'd never said so, perhaps because he knew I enjoyed it so much. He slowly got to his feet.

"It'll be fun," I encouraged. His eyes laughed as he slipped his right arm around my waist, his left hand in mine. Our hats clunked against each other. We took them off and placed the paddle on them so they wouldn't blow away. Fitz began to hum and sway with me. I dropped my head on his chest, against the soft cotton of his T-shirt. Bliss, I thought. I wanted to tell Fitz, but I didn't dare spoil the moment with words.

When we stopped dancing Fitz gave me a short bow before we sat down. His bare feet were like mine, molded into the shape of the tops of the logs. I reached out to rub his, but being ticklish as hell he pulled them away.

Just then a breeze swirled a flight of butterflies toward the drifting raft. Pure white against the amethyst sky. One, two, three . . . seven of them, dancing, twirling up and down, flirting merrily in the sun. They hovered above us. Seven pairs of opal wings dropped soundlessly upon me, landing one at a time on my arms and hands and shoulders.

"Look, Fitz," I mouthed, eyeing my covering of butterflies, a necklace of pearls.

"Bejeweled by nature . . . ," my poet replied.

I sat still, beguiled by wings opening and closing, resting on my limbs. My arms began to ache.

"I have to move," I finally whispered, sorry for us as well as the butterflies.

Ever so slightly I adjusted my elbow. They took off. Our eyes followed them until they were specks.

Fitz pulled me close. He'd shaved, so his skin was smooth as a plum. I melted like chocolate, but when we lay down on the raft my back slipped and pinched between two gnarly balsas, the river spitting up between them. "I wish we had a cushion."

Fitz held me around my shoulders, his arms wedged between me and the raft, his knees likely aching on top of the uneven logs.

"I don't think romance on balsa logs is that great," I grumbled.

"They're ridiculous!" Fitz took my hand and led me to the tent.

The silky sleeping bag and the tent's platform were the Ritz-Carlton compared to outside.

Chapter 12

The Storm

We slept soundly during our fourth night on the river, trusting the Madre to carry us safely through the darkness, just as she had on previous nights. We'd become used to her soft movement.

I dreamt I was riding a merry-go-round, smoothly undulating up and down on the wooden horse, when abruptly the carousel's screws loosened. It spun high into the air then plummeted downward. I woke to the raft in a tailspin. Ernesto had warned us not to let the raft spin. It was too late. Thunder and lightning were right on top of us. "Fitz!" I yelled, yanking his shoulder as lightning flashed through the plastic tent, like giant floodlights.

He didn't wake up. "Fitz!"

"What?" he mumbled.

"A storm! It's HUGE!"

Cracking thunder muffled the sound of my voice. The raft rocked and continued to spin wildly, lifted then pounded hard on the waves again.

"Whoa!" Fitz yelled. "What the hell is happening?"

"Storm!" I shrieked over the thunder.

"Shit!"

Bolts of lightning illuminated the tent enough for me to see Fitz inching forward on his stomach to the door flap, a foot from our sleeping bag. He pushed himself up onto his knees then pulled back the flap to stare into the roiling night. His tall frame swayed as he hung on to the door.

"Jesus!" he yelled toward me. "I can't see anything!"

"Fitz, get inside! It's too dangerous!"

If he fell in, I'd never find him in the dark. Just then something slammed the bow, pulling the raft downward.

"Holly, watch out!"

I dropped my head, hearing *riiiiiiiiip* through the pink plastic wall.

"My God," Fitz screamed. "Holly, Holly!"

The ripping sound ceased as the motion of the raft stilled. My heart pounded in the darkness as I lay stomach down, silent, not daring to move. Rain pelted through an apparent hole in the tent. "Fitz?" I tried to raise my head but something jabbed me, held me down. The raft was tipped forward with the new weight.

"Jesus, Holly! Are you all right?" Fitz's voice hollered out of the night. "That goddamned tree trunk flew right in here. I thought, my God, your head . . ." His voice trembled as he moved toward me.

"Oh, Fitz," I said, still stunned. "I thought you'd gone over . . ." I let out a small sob.

"Baby, I got thrown forward, but I held on."

"Thank goodness . . . Fitz, I can't move."

He was next to me now, his hand feeling my scalp. He sounded like he was sniffing.

"Are you okay?" I asked through booms of thunder and howling wind.

"Of course!" Bravado now in his voice. "Does anything hurt? Your head? Can you move your feet?"

"My head seems okay." I wiggled my fingers then my toes. "Yes."

He patted my shoulder. "Thank God," he whispered.

"But what's holding me down, Fitz?"

Lightning blazed through the night.

"Roots. Sharp as spikes!" In the fast, certain voice of the *comandante* he said, "Holly, I've got to lift this goddamn tree off you. Hold on."

I lay flat, listening to him, trying not to panic at the tipping of the raft as the storm raged around us. I saw him through flashes of lightning, as if through a kaleidoscope. I told myself he's here and he's okay. I'll be fine, too.

He bent down close to my cheek. "We've got to hurry. This damn thing could sink the raft. Close your eyes so the roots don't scratch them. Cover your head!"

He groaned as he tried to lift the trunk. The roots scraped my naked back. They felt like they were going deep. I screamed.

"I'm sorry! I'm just one goddamn man here!"

The rain was piercing me like needles.

"It won't budge!"

I tried to be quiet so Fitz could concentrate. All of a sudden I felt a stinging, burning sensation. It began on my scalp then ran down my neck, onto my bare shoulders and then my back, like flames blistering my skin. "I'm on fire! Please, help me!"

Fitz jostled the tree trunk again.

"What is it? I can't stand it."

"I can't see anything," he yelled.

Lightning flashed.

"I'm burning!"

"Fire ants!"

I pleaded with Fitz to help me as the unseen ants rushed over my body, biting relentlessly. I tried to lift my head, but I was pinned down inside a chamber of tree limbs and roots.

"You've got to get out," Fitz commanded. "You're going to have to move backward, Holly. Can you?"

"Yes!"

As the raft thumped up and down on the wild river, Fitz crawled toward my feet to guide me out.

I started shifting backward on my stomach. Something yanked my scalp. My hair was caught! I could feel roots and branches surround me like stakes. Stay calm, I told myself. You can do this. Thunder bellowed as I reached up behind my neck to free my hair. I felt for the ends of the strands, trying to loosen them. It was taking too long. Streaming all over me were the biting fire ants.

"Keep coming!" Fitz shouted over the storm.

"My hair's caught!" I wanted to rip my long hair out. I wished I was bald. "I can't see what I'm doing," I cried. My hands kept working until I felt the strands loosen. I yanked until the ends came free. Then I wriggled backward, one hand over my head to cover my hair, the other hand pushing as the barbs scratched and the ants burned all over me.

"Come on. Come on. You're almost here!" Fitz lifted the last part of the roots and I was out.

He grabbed my shoulders. I collapsed into his arms, sobbing as we rocked violently back and forth with the waves. Fire ants still covered my skin. "I can't stand it, I can't stand it," I wept, pulling away from Fitz to slap at them.

The Pink Palace jerked up and down, tipping deeper into the river.

"The raft!" Fitz turned toward the bow. "We've got to get this tree off. Grab whatever you can and shove hard."

Despite the merciless stinging, I forced myself to help. My upper-body strength wasn't anywhere near Fitz's, but adrenaline helped me to push as hard as I could. Fitz shouldered the trunk, lifting and jostling it until it slid off the raft and disappeared into the river, we hoped moving beyond us, not to ram us again.

I held on to the tent frame and stumbled out into the darkness.

"Don't go out there!" Fitz yelled. "You'll go over!"

"I can't help it. The ants!"

The moment I got outside, most of the ants disappeared on the wind. I sniveled, hanging on to the side of the tent, swiping at the pinching creatures that remained under my arms and near my groin.

"Please come in," Fitz shouted. He leaned out and grabbed my wrist.

As I inched my feet along, my hands gripped the frame. Fitz held firmly to my upper arm. When I reached the tent door I fell inside. We both brushed off the rest of the ants, stomping our feet on the floor to destroy them.

Soon, the storm began to subside until it was nothing more than a few flashes of lightning in the distance. The Madre de Dios relaxed into her quiet, soothing flow as if the squall had never happened. Even the moon dared to show its face through the tent's sliced plastic.

The Pink Palace banged against something hard.. We peered out to see she was bumping up against trees at the river's edge. We hadn't touched trees since we'd left Puerto Heath.

"We can finally tie up!" Fitz leaned out to grab a branch

On top of the world in Peru on our second wedding anniversary. By this time we'd been traveling for two and a half months on our trip around the world, having already been down the East Coast of the United States, then on to Colombia, Ecuador, and Peru. (Photograph taken by our friend Yves Girault)

The plane crash-landed at a penal colony in the jungle far from Puerto Maldonado, where we needed to be to catch a boat to Riberalta. We were dazed and bewildered but without broken bones.

At the bank of Rio Tambopata near its confluence with Rio Madre de Dios. Six slender sticks held the shelter intact despite gunfire, storms, and tropical heat. To the left, tied near to us, was someone's dugout canoe, chiseled from a tree.

Our young friends climbed onto the raft to be closer to the action as I announced, "I christen thee Pink Palace!" The raft—named for the American ambassador's mansion in Lima—is made of just four logs with gaps of open water between them.

Onlookers gathered to wave good-bye to the two crazy gringos launching their uncooperative raft. Behind the onlookers is the roof of the open-air slaughterhouse.

Fitz living out his boyhood dream from his favorite novel, *Huckleberry Finn*: "Other places do seem so cramped up and smothery, but a raft don't. You feel mighty free and easy and comfortable on a raft." The river looked deceptively calm and manageable.

The Pink Palace near Puerto Heath, Bolivia. Without the inexpensive plastic sheeting, and *mosquitero* netting within, death by exposure would have come quickly in the wet, hot, tropical jungle.

This water-damaged photo of little Liza and our dog, Zelda, remained with us always: a reminder of what awaited us if we could only survive.

in the darkness. "Don't let go of this. I'll get the painter." He disappeared out the door.

I held on to the branch though my legs and arms were rubbery and my skin was still burning.

"I can't see a damn thing," Fitz yelled as he struggled to the stern to retrieve the vine. The raft was pulling away.

"Hurry, Fitz," I called out. "I can't hold on much longer!"

"I've got it!"

Through moonlight and flashes of distant lightning I saw him swing the vine over the bough. "Keep holding on, Holly. I haven't tied it yet." He wrestled with the vine around the branch. "Jesus, it keeps springing away from me!"

"You can do it, Fitz."

"Okay. I've knotted the damn thing!" He let the branch go and the vine locked around it.

"Let's get some sleep. We'll see where we are tomorrow." His voice was weighted with exhaustion.

My body sank into the sleeping bag. Through the huge hole in the plastic I saw stars emerging. I didn't care that the tent was in shreds, or that the sleeping bag was sopping wet. I was beyond feeling my body's mass of welts and stings. I warmed myself in Fitz's arms.

"It feels like a bad dream," I said. "I hope we wake up to find out this didn't really happen."

Fitz was already drifting off. I lay awake, listening to the departing thunder, unable to worry about wild animals that might approach us through the darkness now that we were tied to the riverbank.

Chapter 13

Where Are We?

Leafy branches hung above the torn tent. They were bathed in the soft light of dawn against a pale blue sky. A concerto of wildlife was erupting outside. My mind flashed to last night's storm and the spear-pointed petrified roots of the tree. Relief poured over me. We'd landed. We were safe. Ouch! My arms and legs were covered with scrapes, bruises—and, worse, itching dime-sized red welts. Before I realized it, I was digging my nails into them. I tried to scratch around the bites, but scarlet circles puffed up. Finally I forced myself to stop before they bled.

Parrots chattering high above us jiggled branches incessantly. I wondered if they noticed us. Fitz slept through the racket. We would have to repair the tent before setting off, but with luck we would be in Riberalta by sundown.

I couldn't believe our trip on the Madre de Dios was almost over. Pioneering down the river, just the two of us, had been delightful despite the storm, the border shooting, and the frightening abuse by the border guards. Still, I looked forward to seeing people again.

"Caw, caw, caw!" a bird called loudly.

Curious to see where we'd tied up last night, I crept outside the tent.

A red macaw cried shrilly before taking off over my head then disappearing into the foliage. Sunlight peeked over the horizon of trees to the east, melting raindrops, touching the mist that swirled above the placid water. Inhaling the moist air, I felt a promise of renewal, savored the tranquility of this other side of nature.

The raft looked intact, though thrust deeply into the bushes. Finding a clear spot to sit on her edge, I lifted my face to the light, half closing my eyes to relax in the sun's warmth. I felt so lucky after last night. I wanted always to remember how the air was baby's-breath soft, how the sun danced on the water then touched my skin.

All my senses were heightened, taking in the lily pads near our raft, big as platters; the chartreuse frog that sat languidly, like me, embracing the moment; a mystifying odor—faint but dank—that wafted on the sweet, clean scents. I couldn't quite place it.

Rustling came from inside. Seconds later, Fitz stuck out his head, knocking it on the low tent frame again. "Hi, Hol! How are you feeling?"

"Much better, thanks to you!" He came to sit next to me; we held each other, my head resting on his shoulder. I looked up at his unruly curls and tried to comb them with my fingers. My own hair was a tangled mess. "My hair got snarled by the tree attack!"

Fitz's eyes crinkled as he smiled, but then he grew thoughtful.

"I don't know how you got that tree off the raft before it sank us," I continued.

"It felt like a goddamn boulder. It shakes me how close that tree came to crushing your head."

"Fitz!" My back trembled. "I thought I almost lost you."

"It was awful."

We tightened our grip around each other for a few minutes. Then Fitz rose to check out the raft's condition. "Jesus, the tent's ripped to hell on both sides." He pushed his way into the web of branches that held the Pink Palace, thrusting his weight against one of the sturdier limbs. The raft didn't budge.

"I think she got twisted around after we went to sleep." I stood up to help.

"We'll get her out of here after breakfast. I'm starved," Fitz said, weaving his way out of the foliage and brushing a spider web from his cheek.

Following Fitz into the mangled tent to pull out the Spam and eggs, I noticed the wall flapping slightly behind the boxes at the foot of the sleeping bag. How had I not seen that earlier? It was no longer attached to the tent's frame. Two boxes were on their sides, facing the water.

Fitz reached them first, righting them. "I don't believe it! The food was knocked overboard by that damn tree!"

There were only six items left: a four-ounce can of tuna, a 1.4-ounce package of dehydrated pea soup, a small chunk of cheese, a jar of instant coffee, a half cup of sugar wrapped in plastic, and a can of evaporated milk. Two other boxes of food were missing completely. My heart plunged.

"Damn!" Fitz yelled. "This isn't enough food for a baby bird!"

"It's only for today, Fitz. We'll find a nice place to stay in Riberalta, and eat a big dinner at a cozy café. We'll celebrate over a beer." I glanced into the overturned toolbox in the corner. Our hammer was gone, but the nails and extra rolls of plastic were there. "Let's repair the tent and get going," I said.

Fitz didn't say anything. He stared into the almost-empty boxes, his hand rubbing the back of his neck.

"We can use my wooden sandal for a hammer," I suggested. "I knew it would come in handy sometime."

He reached for a cigarette.

I touched his shoulder. "Fitz?"

He shook his head. "There's nothing in here," he said, gripping his cigarette in his mouth as he shuffled through the same few items over and over. Then he picked up the small jar of instant coffee. "Let's start with this."

"Yes, let's." I let out a sigh.

In an undisturbed box, my pot-and-pan kit was nestled with the halazone tablets. So were the small bottle of iodine and two filled bottles of purified river water. Grabbing the pot and a water bottle, I ducked back outside.

Fitz brought the coffee and cups and removed the dry matches from the tin cigarette container. The kindling was wet from the rain, but he placed some into the oilcan anyway and was able to make a fire. We let the water boil for several minutes as an added precaution before we poured it into the instant coffee. Then sitting, feet resting on the log in front of us, we cradled our cups. The coffee tempered my hunger.

Fitz's cerulean eyes stared at me through metal-rimmed glasses, brilliant in the tropical morning light. He took a puff of his cigarette then gazed at the river. Just looking at his somber face made me worry.

"The river's a lot slower than it was before—and narrower," he said quietly. His eyes turned to the trees next to us. "I don't see any land."

"No land?" I followed his stare, bending my head to peer under the brush. Tightly knit bushes and trees were growing out of the water. As far as I could see into the thicket there was no earth. My stomach suddenly felt like twisted rope.

"Oh, Fitz." My voice rose. "Where are we?" I looked at the river. "Why's it so sluggish?" I felt like a little kid wanting to be reassured. "We can't be off course, Fitz. Juan swore that if we followed the river we'd be fine."

Fitz flicked his cigarette. "That's my point. This may not be the river. It's too damn slow for the river."

"It's got to be the river. What else could it be?" I jumped up. "Let's get out of here. It's getting late!" The sun was halfway toward the top of the sky already, so I estimated it must be about 9:00 a.m.

Fitz bent down to grab the pot and water bottle to take back into the tent.

The tepid morning wore off quickly. It was blisteringly hot. "Should we fix the tent or just push off to make sure we're still in the river?" I asked.

"Push off. If we find the current, we'll have plenty of time to fix the tent."

We rushed to free the raft and untie the painter. Fitz pressed the pole against the brush while I paddled in the bow. The minute I stopped for a breath we slid back into the trees.

Fitz gave up steering to use the rudder as a big paddle. Muscles straining, we tried to reach the center of the river to catch the current.

We kept paddling, but the raft was dead weight.

Fitz groaned. I glanced around the tent to see how he was doing in the stern. Sweat poured down his face and neck.

"Do you need water?" I asked.

"I've got a bottle. You?"

"Okay for now."

"She's a bloody ton to move. There's no current."

Finally, after at least two hours, we caught a current, but it was lackadaisical. Without continuous paddling we would have stalled listlessly.

"Something's very wrong," Fitz said, shifting his stance from one leg to the other. "I definitely think the storm blew us off course. We may be stuck in a dead-end channel or swamp."

"It's got to be a detour. Remember what Juan said? We came from that direction," I pointed. "You can see the current is coming this way." Then I stared toward the curve up ahead. "It'll take us back into the main river."

"We're going nowhere!" Fitz snapped. "Look at the difference in the water from yesterday."

"Please, Fitz, we have to try. It'll link back to the Madre. You'll see."

He flipped off his hat, dipped his hand into the river, and splashed water onto his head as he studied the water's slight swirls.

Exhausted, I dropped my paddle and walked toward him. "We've worked half the day to get into this silly current. Let's see where it goes. What else can we do?"

Fitz squinted at the wall of trees where I was sure the river turned. "That's a dead end, Hol," he said. "See, it's not moving down there?" He pointed almost wistfully.

"Please," I begged, desperate for him to stay strong even though we'd had little to drink and nothing to eat for hours. I honestly couldn't see if the river was moving or not. "We have to go down there and check it out." My voice felt like glass shattering.

Fitz could be right. What would we do if we were in a

dead end? I didn't even know there could be such a thing. Why would there be a dead end?

"All right, Hol, let's go," he said. There was resignation in his voice but perhaps a hint of hope.

He put the blade of his rudder-paddle back into the water.

Once again, we strained against our paddles. When I looked up we'd gone only a few feet. The Pink Palace was like an ox. I plunged the paddle back into the water, not wanting to complain for fear Fitz would give up. It ached to cock my head upward, to see what was in front of us while also peering down to be sure each stroke cleared the raft and struck the water. At last we gained momentum from the slight current. The Pink Palace began drifting quickly toward an island of huge bushes, which I realized were actually the tops of trees popping from the water. I couldn't steer her. "Watch out!" I sputtered, my tongue dry against the roof of my mouth.

"What?" Fitz yelled from behind the tent.

"Left. Your left! Port . . ." The Palace slid under the limbs and foliage. I extended my paddle to soften our crash. When we hit I fell backward against the tent. The familiar sound of *riiiiip* sliced the air as a tree tore through more of the tent's plastic siding.

"Jesus!" Fitz called out, running from the stern.

I ducked from under a branch to see Fitz's stunned face. Shrubbery bits were in my hair, hanging over my eyes. "False alarm," I called. "It's just another tear." The Pink Palace was tangled in vines, but her logs were unharmed.

Fitz smiled at the sight of me. "You look like a tree yourself." He gently picked twigs from my hair.

We hastily dislodged the raft and set out toward a pile

of driftwood across the water, just ten yards from the bend we sought. Finally we neared the spot. In a few seconds we should know if we were free.

Gaping toward the bend, I hoped to see the channel widen to open river. Then came the kick in the stomach—there was nothing ahead but a wall of green jungle flooded by lethargic brown water. The channel we had been following went no farther. Last night's storm had pushed us down a river to nowhere.

My blood seemed to siphon from me. There was no outlet. No riverbank. No land. Just impenetrable jungle submerged in water. My eyes quickly shifted over the landscape. There was no opening where the channel sliced through the trees to reach the Madre de Dios.

Juan's words echoed in my head: "Detours always return to the main river, but they take you longer."

Sergeant at the Bolivian border had scoffed at the thought of our getting into trouble on the raft. "You will be fine," he'd said, assuring us that we'd be the biggest thing on the river. He hadn't mentioned anything about flying tree trunks or violent storms or dead ends.

I looked at Fitz. There was no "I told you so" on his face. I could see he wished I'd been right. How could we possibly escape? A raft only goes one way, and we had run out of river.

It was 1:00 to 2:00 p.m. by the sun. We decided to paddle back toward the little cove where we'd tied up last night. If we could make it there, maybe we could get beyond it and find the river before sundown. The only way we could navigate the raft against the current was by pulling ourselves along branch by branch, not even stopping to purify water for the empty canteen or water bottles, afraid we'd slip backward. Panting, sweating, too tired to speak, we pressed on for several hours.

Fitz broke the silence between us, suddenly shouting, "*¡Socorro! ¡Socorro! ¡Socorro!*"

Birds ceased their chatter at this strange, loud wailing. The air itself seemed empty. Soon I began to shout, "*¡Socorro!*" too, more in solidarity than with any belief that anyone might hear us.

As our voices echoed across the water, unanswered, I shivered at just how lost we were.

Chapter 14

The Rains Poured Down

Fitz and I yelled until we were hoarse. Even droning insects seemed stilled by our voices, heavy in the dead air. We continued to grab on to flimsy boughs, reeds, vines, anything to pull the raft back up toward the true river. After another couple of hours, we'd made it a few yards beyond the cove.

Sheets of rain began to sweep across the sky. The petulant current shoved us backward as rain drenched the inside of the roofless tent.

"We've got to paddle her in!" Fitz yelled.

I barely nodded. My body felt like an elastic band ready to snap. Fitz threw the painter over a tree branch near the cove and drew the Pink Palace beneath it.

Light had been sucked from the sky by a thick, dark bank of clouds. We collapsed on top of the sopping sleeping bag, too weary to nail up new plastic. Hungry, thirsty, soaked, and shivering, I recorded a couple of lines in my journal before darkness descended: "Trapped. Will we ever get out? No one answers calls for help. Current pushes us back. Rain in tent from missing side. Scared."

We lay in each other's arms, whispering soothing words to each other beneath the steady splash of rain. The raft rocked in response to the waves.

It rained well into the night. When it finally stopped, we groped around for the flashlight then changed into drier clothes that had been protected in the backpacks under the one side of the tent that was still up. We then lay back down under the dripping mosquito netting. Even as I tightened my hold around Fitz, I felt my confidence slipping out of me. I couldn't speak my thoughts for fear I'd burst like a dam. Pulling out my journal again, I wrote by flashlight, "Please don't let us get sick, please give us the strength to get out of here. I'll kiss the river if I ever see her again."

A large animal growled in the dark. It seemed awfully close. There was a loud thumping overhead and off to the right. Of course—we were at the tree line. Animals live in these trees—they could drop down on us at any moment.

"Fitz! Did you hear that?" I quickly stuffed the journal back into the black bag. He lifted himself onto his elbow.

We held our breath.

"I don't hear anything." He patted my side.

His voice sounded so tired I wanted to crack. The thumping in the branches came again, right over our heads this time. "There!"

Fitz sighed. "Squirrels."

"In South America?"

"Then it's probably birds."

My back arched upward as I listened. "What about that growling? It was so close."

"I can hear weird sounds, Hol, but all this water could be magnifying them to seem closer than they really are. Come on, we have to sleep. Big day tomorrow, getting out."

"I don't know how you can sleep when we're so vulnerable."

"This isn't my first time sleeping in the jungle, remember?"

I thought about Fitz in Vietnam, where he'd been wounded twice. He'd told me he'd trained himself to fall asleep on his very first night in the jungle, surrendering to the prospect of death while sleeping, knowing that otherwise he would never make it home.

Fitz brushed his hand lightly down my hair. "I wonder how far off the river we are," he said. "Could be miles."

"I'm sorry I pushed to take the raft. I didn't know we could get lost." Tears swam in my eyes.

"Shhh, I didn't either. I wanted to take the raft. You know I'm too stubborn to do something I don't want to do." He rubbed my shoulder. "It was fun, wasn't it, before the storm?"

I could hear him smiling. I snuggled into him, sniffling.

"We obviously can't paddle the Pink Palace any farther," he continued, softly.

I nodded into Fitz's chin. I felt like we were in a giant labyrinth.

Fitz pulled me even closer. "The most important thing, right now, is to let yourself go to sleep."

He'd often called me "the princess and the pea" for being such a light sleeper. Noise, light, and even wrinkles in the sheets could wake me.

A long hissing sound joined the jungle chorus.

"What's that?" My body tightened again.

"Ignore it. Just get some sleep."

I tried to tune out a sudden staccato of belching croaks. They must be some big frogs, I thought. At least they sounded familiar. An alkaline odor enveloped the raft, broken occasionally by a fresher breeze from the forest. Berries, oranges. Do I smell oranges? Thirsty, I reached for one of the bottles of turbid Madre water. I slugged a little, pretending it was fresh water from my paternal grandmother's spring near our summer log house at Eagle Lake in the Adirondack Mountains. When we were kids, my sister and I would carry a chipped white enamel pitcher along a pungent path of pine needles to fill it with water from the spring. It was the purest water I'd ever tasted.

During the night we awoke once again to another downpour.

"This night is lasting forever," I whimpered. "Where the heck is the plastic? We need to put it up." I felt for the box and pulled out a roll of plastic and nails.

Fitz stumbled to his feet, grabbing the flashlight. "Let's make this quick." We nailed the plastic to the wooden tent frame, using my Dr. Scholl's as a hammer. Fitz whacked the last nail into the wood. "Okay. We're done," he said.

We pushed the wet sleeping bag and blankets aside then collapsed onto the bare boards. One board had warped beneath my spine. Could this get any worse?

Two years ago, my idea of being "trapped" had meant being stranded at home without a car. As newlyweds we'd rented an inexpensive cottage nestled in snow and pine on a small mountaintop far from the small town of New Fairfield. I'd used my savings to buy Fitz a secondhand Plymouth to cover his beat as a reporter, but the car soon broke down beyond repair. We didn't have money for another car, so Fitz had to drive my VW bug, leaving me in the country without transportation, knowing no one. Always open to new experiences, I found my life suddenly had become too small.

At first, I contented myself with painting the plywood living-room floor blue, sewing a synthetic leopard-skin bedspread, and decorating the headboard wall with reeds. I mailed out résumés, took Zelda for walks in snowdrifts where she sank up to her nose, cut out old *National Geographic* stories to fill scrapbooks of places I someday hoped to visit. There was no television, no radio. In an attempt to connect with my xenophobic neighbors, who spoke mostly German, I planned a party. I even walked to their houses to invite them personally, but when I knocked and got no response, I slipped their invitations under the doors. On the night of the party, Fitz; his brother, Chip; Chip's wife, Ellen; and I waited patiently. No invitees showed. Just before midnight, a frustrated, inebriated Fitz stepped into the blustery night, banging a pot with a wooden spoon, shouting: "Nazis! You're all Nazis!"

Fitz was working long hours and was rarely home, except on days off. When I tried to convey my isolation, he scared me by smashing his foot through a wicker chair. "Jesus Christ, Holly!" he said. "What can I do about it? I'm working, aren't I? Isn't that what a husband's supposed to do?" His sudden rage came out of nowhere. Stunned, I said nothing as he stormed into the kitchen and grabbed a beer from the fridge. I stared at the splintered wicker chair in the corner, feeling like Rapunzel in her tower. I knew I couldn't tell anyone about his outburst. We were newlyweds, so it was my job to try to understand him.

I comforted myself by anticipating the pleasure we would have together on his day off, but I didn't want that to be my life, waiting at the door like a puppy dog for its master's return.

Loneliness began to bite like ice. One day, I painted a Chagallesque portrait of a young woman with celestial blue hair, a small bride and groom in a gondola floating over exotic scenery beneath her face. It was only when I set down my brush that I realized I had also depicted a birdcage in the corner of the canvas. The cage door was sprung open and the bird had flown out. A curly-haired guy was trying to catch it.

Chapter 15

Hope

FEBRUARY 20

Second day trapped

I woke with difficulty breathing, as if a steel beam were crushing my chest. Fitz was staring at the peak of the tent. I folded my arms around him.

"Fitz, I'm scared."

"Me too," he whispered.

He made a fire. I stirred a tablespoon of powdered pea soup into boiling water, equal to very few calories. Already we'd needed to doctor more water with halazone tablets.

Although we'd never said grace together, we now thanked God out loud for the coffee and broth. With reverence we sipped every drop, using our teeth to filter the mud, leaf, and twig content.

Fitz peered into his empty cup then tipped it to lick the last bit. I scraped the sides of my cup with my spoon then licked it, too.

I suggested we hold off on the tuna, even though my

stomach screamed, "Eat it!" If Fitz wanted to eat it, I would agree in a second.

He studied the can. "Let's save it," he said.

I returned the tuna to the tent before we could change our minds. Then I sat down by Fitz again. This morning we had a choice to make: stay with the Pink Palace and wait to be rescued, or swim up the current and look for land so we could walk out of the swamp.

"If we swim," I said, "the closer we are to the Rio Madre, the stronger the current will get. I don't know if I'm a strong enough swimmer." The Madre could be a mile away or twenty. "Maybe we should follow the 'Don't leave the ship' idea."

Fitz acquiesced. "We should wait in case a plane is sent by the *aduana*. A pilot would see the raft better than us swimming."

"And we'd have shelter and could conserve our energy."

But the Madre de Dios twisted through hundreds of miles of jungle. Would anyone really be able to spot our tiny tent out here? What if no one ever comes to this godforsaken channel? Why would they?

We considered the danger of swimming in a channel that was most certainly teeming with piranha. Supposedly they wouldn't attack unless they sensed spilt blood, but we risked being cut by objects beneath the water. What about candiru? We remembered Juan's warning never to swim in the river. What would he suggest we do now? I heard a splash, then two more splashes a few feet away.

"What the hell is that?" Fitz turned toward the sounds.

We both scanned the wide swirls of expanding circles in the water beyond the stern.

"You don't think it's a caiman, do you?" I yelped, moving

closer to Fitz. Caimans could exceed fifteen feet and were far too big for us to defeat with our hands and two small knives.

"That machete could have helped us." Fitz sighed. "We could have cut a tree down and hacked it out for a canoe. Then we wouldn't have to swim in this swamp at all."

"There are big snakes around here." I had read of the boa constrictors and anacondas that swim here and crush their prey. Some snakes drop from trees, their venom so lethal that death comes in seconds after their bite. "And electric eels and stingrays." I twisted a strand of my hair.

It seemed safer to stay on the raft.

Fitz took out a cigarette. "I feel like the Christians in the Colosseum. Pick the wrong door and you're fucked."

We went back and forth for at least half an hour. I don't know who first thought of praying, but we fell into seeking divine insight.

"I think we should be proactive and try to escape," Fitz finally concluded, his tense brow softening. "'God helps those who help themselves,' right?"

For the first time in my life, that quote spoke personally to me. "It feels like the right answer." I took a deep breath. "Which way should we swim? Up the channel or into the trees?"

Fitz cleared his throat. "Look, Hol," he said in a firm voice, probably so I wouldn't disagree, "the best thing is for me to swim to land and bring back help. There's got to be a village . . ."

"Wait a minute!" I blurted out. Was he trying to change plans to protect me? "We're doing this together, like everything else." I was as firm as he was.

"It's just better if you stay on the raft. Anything could happen . . ."

"That's right. Anything could happen. What if a cai-man got you and you called for help? I wouldn't hear you. I couldn't get there."

"If a caiman gets me you couldn't save me anyway. There's no point in the two of us . . ."

"I'm going with you. Sitting here not knowing what's happening to you would be worse than hell. I just can't imagine that. I can't imagine being lost either, but that would be worse. I'm going." I spewed out my response like ammunition, so fast that it took us both aback.

"Okay," he shrugged. "We'll both swim out."

We looked at the channel in silence.

I envied the green parrots and the blue, elongated, deep-toned birds that darted across the water and up over the trees. If we only had their view we would know where we were and in which direction to go.

There would be less current to contend with if we swam through the flooded brush and trees. We could get disori-ented in the darkness and become fatally exhausted before we found land. And if we did find land, which way would we go then?

Fitz smoked a cigarette as we debated.

Our best chance might be to swim up the channel. Going against the current would eventually lead us to its source, where we at least had the hope of a settlement or a passing boat. Then again, fighting the increasingly strong current could debilitate us faster than if we swam through the trees. Either choice felt hopeless.

"Somewhere up the channel there has to be a riverbank."

"Yes . . ." Fitz's voice trailed off as he stared up the swamp. "It better be sooner than later."

I let out a sigh and reached for him. We both knew it was

going to be rough. We sat on the raft, cherishing this last moment of her solidity. I began to think of life preservers.

An inlet near the raft smelled of rot and detritus. The water was stagnant there. Just the sight of it depressed me. Then my mind opened.

"Fitz! Look at those logs. If they're not rotten, we could each swim with one. If they're light and buoyant they could work like floats."

Fitz's head tilted toward where I pointed. He took a last puff of his cigarette and stubbed it out. His mouth widened into a grin. "Great idea, kiddo. There's got to be a couple of good ones out there in the muck." He reached for another cigarette.

He was smoking more than usual. What would he do without them when he ran out? I leaned toward him and gave him a hug.

"Yes," I said, "for sure."

We stood up and scanned the lime-colored water plants, lily pads, floating leaves, dead branches. Many hues of yellow, green, brown—what were they camouflaging? Our eyes burned into the swamp, seeking the right logs.

"Look! Jesus! A small raft!" Fitz cried.

"Where?"

"Beside those dead branches, thirty-five, forty feet straight out!"

"Yes!" A small raft was mostly submerged, but the tops of three or four logs broke the surface. A thought flashed through my mind: Did its owner end up like us?

"How did you ever see it?" I asked, pulling Fitz into a bear hug. It was as if we'd hit gold. We could use it to go upriver instead of swimming. It would be safer. I laughed and squeezed him so hard he almost lost his footing on the logs.

We both laughed so loud that a startled bird flew from the foliage, which in turn startled us. It was iridescent blue, with a long, deep green tail that caught the sun so brightly that my eyes closed trying to follow it. I smiled at the hope we now had, and the beauty we'd just witnessed, if only for a moment.

"Now comes the tough part," Fitz announced. We couldn't reach the small raft without swimming. "We were planning to swim anyway. I might as well get started."

We spun it out as long as possible, studying the water, looking for signs of caimans and anacondas. A sense of dread made me shudder.

"What?" asked Fitz. "Do you see something?"

"No." Every dead frond, every slimy leaf looked ominous. Every swaying plant growing to the top of the water moved like a snake. Every stick and log glistening wet in the morning sun might have a head, a snout, teeth. "It's nothing," I said, not looking at him, but when I finally turned to face him my words tumbled out. "We don't know what's out there. Well, we know what's out there; that's the trouble . . ."

Fitz untied the long, thick vine that tethered the Pink Palace. The raft was so entrenched in bushes that it really didn't need tethering. He tied the vine around his waist. "I'll wear this. If something grabs me, pull this as hard as you can," he said, handing me the other end.

Nodding, I twisted the vine around my hands, hoping I had the strength—and, more, that it wouldn't be needed. It occurred to me that this vine was just an illusion to make us feel safer.

How could I possibly pull him from the jaws of a caiman?

"Maybe I'd be better at getting the little raft," I suggested, warily. "You'd be stronger at pulling me back."

I knew my husband. He would insist on getting the raft himself. And, of course, there was no way around it. He was stronger.

"That's ridiculous," he said, scowling. "You'd never get that raft out of there alone." Fitz put on his long jeans and a T-shirt for protection in the water, but no shoes. He squatted on the edge of the raft as if he was going in then thought better of it, grabbing another cigarette. "One for the road."

He smoked unfiltered cigarettes, so he tapped one end of the pack to settle the tobacco so it wouldn't flick into his mouth. He nestled the tip between his lips, struck a match, lit the end, and breathed in deeply. He exhaled, long and quietly, his eyes closed. Not a smoker, I imagined his habit must ease his nerves. I wished I smoked and could put myself in a meditative state, too.

"Okay," he said. "Wish me luck." He slid over the side of the raft into the water, keeping two hands on the edge of the outermost log. One hand still held the cigarette. The smoke drifted up and hung in the air. "It doesn't feel too bad." He made a face. He hung on to the side of the raft a little longer, thick mud, algae, and slime swirling around him. "It's warm . . . kind of refreshing." He took one more puff then flicked the cigarette far out into the swamp. "I'm ready."

"Be careful." I kissed him.

Fitz swam toward the tiny raft. Each moment I feared a caiman would pull him down or a snake would strike. Did something move, or was it Fitz disturbing the water? The tip of a log rose above the slime, reflecting light off its glossy, wet back. A knot in the limb looked like a yellow-and-black eye. The blazing sun jumped and flickered. Every branch with green, brown, black, or yellow leaves came alive. A splash a few feet to his left, a bubbling gurgle behind him, a low, seething growl. A quick snap.

I was perspiring profusely, but I didn't dare let go of the vine to wipe my eyes and face. My wet palms made the vine slippery. I played out more vine, at the same time bracing myself in case I had to pull it back in. Fitz kept swimming through the debris, shoving logs and branches aside, pulling himself over others if they wouldn't stir. He banged his legs and feet on logs and rocks below the waterline, uttering startled yelps and expletives. Dragging himself over a dead tree bough, he gave out a huge groan.

"Are you okay?" If he'd scratched himself the piranha could come like lightning.

"Yes," he answered, and kept swimming.

When he reached the small raft he turned toward me. "I made it!" he whooped, raising his arm in triumph, then leaned on the half-submerged raft to rest.

I marveled at his physical strength, with only a cup of thin soup in him, but I remained uneasy. He still had to bring the raft back.

He tried to jiggle it out of whatever held it down. "It's pretty well jammed in here."

"Please hurry."

"There's just one edge that's caught," he called.

He dove down into the muck. I watched his feet disappear. My eyes remained on the spot where he'd entered, where circular swirls rippled out on the surface. An eternity seemed to pass though surely it was only seconds.

When Fitz popped up, water flattening his mop of hair, he practically sang, "I got it out!" as the raft lifted to the surface. "Give me a pull."

I yanked the sweat-slick vine, back and legs rigid to maximize my strength. My arms burned as I tried to hurry.

Fitz held on to the little raft, kicking with his feet, pushing and pulling the raft over and under the obstacles he'd faced on his way out. "Pull harder," he directed, trying to drag it through the brush.

I pulled as if I were playing tug-of-war, bracing my bare feet one behind the other. I felt I might go overboard at any time, but I was stronger than I'd thought I was.

When he finally touched our raft, I pulled him up. He was shaking. He released the vine from his waist and tied it to the small balsa raft, then collapsed on the plank floor inside the tent. I gave him water.

The late-afternoon humidity lifted. Dusk drops like a brick in the tropics, so we had perhaps an hour of light to see if the raft was safe with both of us aboard. If it was, we could escape on it tomorrow.

After a few minutes' rest we extended our legs slowly out to the small raft. The raft was about two feet by four feet. It didn't sink with the two of us on it, although it was slightly submerged. There were two-inch spaces between the four crooked limbs held together by nailed boards.

We paddled it around the Pink Palace, discovering that it was clumsy to turn. Even the slow current here pushed us back, but we hoped we'd be stronger after a night's sleep. We both felt dog-tired, our stomachs hollow. We each chewed a small chunk of cheese before turning in.

"We'll get out of here in the morning," I said as we crawled under the mosquito netting for our last night on the Pink Palace.

Tomorrow night we wouldn't have the *mosquitero*'s protection, but we should be back on land somewhere along the river. I lay down and listened to the hum of the hungry mosquitoes outside, searching for holes in the netting. Relieved to have a plan, I ignored the nighttime jungle sounds exploding around us, choosing to focus only on hope.

Chapter 16

The Logjam

FEBRUARY 21

Third day trapped

We rose when it was still dark. The birds weren't even awake. Catching ourselves whispering as if not to disturb them, we dressed by flashlight in jeans and shirts then collected the few items we would take with us. I removed the camera from its bag along with the lenses and boxes of film. My camera had been with me longer than I'd been with Fitz. As much as it had been a part of me, I had to let it go. We didn't need it to survive.

Out in the blackness, on our side of the swamp, a sucking sound erupted—big as thunder, just beyond the trees. Louder and louder, like a tornado coming to squash us. It was a sound like none I'd ever heard. I reached for Fitz. "What's that?"

"Jesus, I don't know."

The noise grew even stronger, howling as it reverberated across the open water.

"It's too big to be alive. Maybe it's a whirlpool," Fitz whispered. "It just started up—like someone threw a switch." His arms trembled and so did mine.

I clamped my hands over my ears and leaned harder into him. We held our breath, waiting for the noise's source to reveal itself, waiting for the movement of a whirlpool that would suck us down.

As quickly as it came, the mysterious sound lowered to a rumble then vanished. We remained motionless, our arms still around each other, listening. I couldn't shake the thought that it was a bad omen, like the christening bottle that wouldn't break.

The sun finally peeked over the trees, bringing with it the distraction of jungle noises: parrots, birds, frogs, splashes in the swamp. A symphony of background music that was barely noticeable until it wasn't there, the way honks and sirens become white noise in the city.

Fitz opened the tent flap. "Let's get the hell out of here before it starts up again."

We skipped the coffee; a fire would take too long. Fitz opened the can of tuna fish we'd been too tired to eat last night and scooped two and a half ounces onto each plate.

I looked at my chunks, so small, my hunger so big. I looked at Fitz. "You're bigger than me. You should have more."

"It's not enough to even notice," he said with a shrug.

Not usually, but now it is, I thought. "Here." I handed him a small piece of mine. He shook his head firmly and put his hand over his plate.

I didn't argue. With one mouthful the tuna fish was gone. It didn't touch my hunger. Swirling my tongue between my teeth and around my gums, I ached for one more morsel.

On this third day I couldn't imagine being hungrier. Could it be worse for Fitz, who was nine and a half inches taller than me and seventy pounds heavier?

I rubbed his arm. "We better get going."

He nodded.

We packed the last of the food in the waterproof Naugahyde camera bag: the can of evaporated milk, and the remains of the sugar and dehydrated packet of pea soup. In went the can opener for the milk, then the cigarettes and matches wrapped in plastic, protected inside their small tin. Fitz pushed in slickers, towels, extra clothes, mosquito repellent, malaria pills, halazone tablets, and the tiny bottle of iodine. We didn't take the coffee.

"We've got to take these." I held up two cellophane-wrapped Kodak snapshots of our toddler niece, Liza, posing on my mother's lawn. Her cherry-cheeked face looked directly at me from one photo; baby doll rose lips spread to a big smile above her tiny shoulders. She was wearing her new red wool jacket, tied at the neck with yarn pom-poms; her red sneakers peeked out from under red-flowered overalls. I could have cried.

Beside her lay puffy-haired Zelda, pink tongue out. Her dark eyes looked alert, her front legs extended forward, haunches curled under, ready to jump. On the back of each photograph my mother had written "Oct. 13, '72," four days after Liza's second birthday. She'd mailed them to us in La Paz in time for Christmas. Now they were the only evidence we had of our lives back home.

Fitz slid the photos into the bag.

Beside them I shoved in a pen and my budget booklet, wrapped in plastic, to replace my journal. In it I'd write the date and weather and anything important. Without it we could lose track of the days. Knowing the dates somehow implied a future. My journal, thick with memories of our adventures over the past few months, was too big to take. There was no point to those memories if we didn't survive, although the journal, if found, might provide solace to our families.

The black bag bulged, zipper wide open. Fitz looked skeptical.

"Here, let me try." I squeezed the sides of the bag inward as Fitz pulled the zipper. The bag wouldn't close.

"The slickers are taking up a lot of room," he said.

"But we'll need them to keep dry or we could get sick. Remember what happened on the way to Puno?"

We'd traveled eight hours in the back of an open truck to Puno, an Andean town in Peru, with sheets of rain falling on us all day long. Fitz and I had gotten the chills because we didn't have slickers. Luckily, scotch, hot showers, and a warm bed had prevented us from becoming ill. We might not be so lucky today.

"Okay. What can we take out?" Fitz was impatient to go.

After we removed the clothes and towels, the zipper finally closed. We slid the Bolivian and Peruvian cash, our passports, and traveler's checks into our money belts so if the camera bag went overboard we'd still have our identification. We would need that if we ever saw civilization again—when, not if.

Fitz looped the canteen's strap around the belt of his jeans, which were rolled up to his knees. I'd pulled on my jeans and sleeveless white polyester shirt. The jeans would pad our knees as we squatted on the little raft, and would give us some protection against cuts from underlying boughs and rocks if we had to get into the water. They wouldn't protect us from the tiny candiru. We both wore Panama hats to shade us from the pounding sun. Like Huck and Jim, our feet were bare.

The little raft was slick with algae and misshapen; its four timbers were half waterlogged and cut at varied lengths, curved and bumpy. Yesterday we'd been so encouraged to retrieve it from the swamp that we hadn't noticed its flaws. Now we wondered how long it could hold us.

We climbed onto the small raft, trying not to rock it as we knelt to balance our knees between the logs. Fitz was in the stern, I in the bow, uncomfortable already. Still grasping the side of the Palace with our left hands, we juggled the black bag into position between us. Our weight submerged the raft a couple of inches, and within seconds our legs and buttocks and the bottom of the camera bag were wet. The water felt warm.

Fitz grabbed a board he'd found in the swamp to serve as a second paddle because our rudder-paddle was too big to handle on the little raft. We pushed off.

"Good-bye, Pink Palace!" I called out as we paddled away.

But there was no time for cheering. We had to fight the current immediately. As we moved forward a few yards I recalled how hard it had been to paddle even a canoe upriver or against the wind on Eagle Lake. Our family gathered there each summer to enjoy the clear, clean water where the sun sent its bands of gold down fathoms; to relish hot dogs cooked on an open fire, and board games at night; and to jump the twenty-five-foot cliff into the bottomless lake for fun and to prove our bravery. It's where I'd brought Fitz to get to know my family before we were engaged. He had jumped, too.

We struggled up the channel, sweeping our paddles deep, hard, and quick, over and over, encouraged by the late-morning sun and a slight breeze. My hat protected me from the glare, but perspiration dripped from my face. I wanted to rip the hat off, but I didn't dare take a second away from paddling. Already my arms screamed "Stop!" but I knew the raft would swirl backward and we would lose every inch we'd gained. With so little nourishment, I thought, we had but one chance to succeed.

Fitz and I fell into a rhythm, singing, "We can do it, yes, we can!" like an army running chant that kept our spirits up and our paddles in sync. I pushed through the current, singing until I couldn't anymore. Always the goal was to make it around one more bend. But with each bend we conquered, the current grew stronger and harder to fight. We were quiet for a long time, except for our heavy breathing and the stroking of the paddles.

"This must be like boot camp," I finally gasped.

"In boot camp you go home to a cot and a mess hall."

The jungle seemed almost benign as we concentrated on moving forward a few feet at a time. There were no more splashes or frightening sounds, just the gentle twittering of small, colorful birds.

As we approached another curve, water gushed over the front of the little raft. We quickly shifted from kneeling to sitting, and wrapped our legs around it so it wouldn't shoot out from under us. I felt like I was riding a slippery porpoise.

"Hold on!" Fitz called.

"I'm trying!"

We reached out and clutched tall, wheat-colored reeds sprouting out of the channel. Round and smooth, they didn't pinch our palms like other stalks had. Slowly, hand over hand, we pulled ourselves along. They looked like a regal mass of soldiers, towering fifteen feet above us, feathery plumes rippling in the breeze. We pulled ourselves to the next cluster of reeds, where we hoped the current would let up.

It didn't. When we were halfway to the next bend, Fitz nodded toward a passage among the stately reeds that appeared wide enough to paddle into. "Let's try inside there."

It was gentle paddling within the reeds. I breathed long, slow breaths, noticing how drops fell from the paddles into the serene water. A breeze, light as breath, twisted the solemn soldiers guarding this marsh, nodding their heads. My muscles relaxed as I inhaled the aroma of silty mud. A different scent, thick and dank, emanated from the jungle. This quiet water and the bright sun dancing in its reflections was almost cheerful, a surprise respite to rebuild our strength. My stroking was meditative now, synchronized with Fitz's.

We hadn't always been so synchronized. Memories of our day trip to Block Island washed over me. We'd caught a ferry from New London. A row of ornate nineteenth-century hotels and shops came into view as we entered Old Harbor. But what really caught my attention was the line of tandem bicycles flanked by waving colored plastic flags.

Smiling up at Fitz I softly sang: "We'll look sweet upon the seat of a bicycle built for two."

His eyes darted toward the bikes. "You're not thinking . . ."

"It's so romantic!" I implored. "You're the guy I was meant to ride tandem with. As a kid singing that song, I always imagined doing this."

The shaggy-haired man at the bike shop, jeans slipping

off his hips, seemed dubious when we asked for a tandem. "Are you sure? I have regular bikes, too."

"Oh, yes. It will be great," I said. It hadn't occurred to me that riding a tandem bike required a knack.

"Is it that difficult?" Fitz asked.

"It will take getting used to. Then you'll be fine." I had the feeling Fitz didn't believe him.

Fitz straddled the tandem up front, feet firmly on the ground. "I'll hold it steady while you hop on," he instructed me.

When we raised our feet to pedal the bike, we immediately keeled to the left. "Pedal!" Fitz hollered.

"I am!"

The bike skidded sideways, balking like a badly reined horse. We were nearly righted when we slid into the center of the road after Fitz inadvertently braked.

"What are you doing?" I protested. "I'm trying to pedal and you're braking!" We were about to crash.

"Watch out!" yelled a man in a rusty truck, honking his horn as he maneuvered around us. "If you can't ride, get off the road!" He then gunned his engine.

Fitz yelled back an expletive.

We moved to the side of the road and glanced up the steep pavement that would take us out of the village. How would we get momentum while coordinating our very different leg lengths?

Just then a child and his dad breezed by on a tandem. "We need to be synchronized," Fitz urged.

We both counted, "One, two, three," and pushed off. My feet and legs were aching it was so hard to pedal.

"What gear are you in?" I cried out as the bike wobbled slowly along.

"Gear? I've no idea. Never had one with gears."

So that's why I felt as if I were pushing a monolith up this hill.

"Watch out!" Fitz yelled as the front tire hit a large pothole. We collapsed to the pavement, bike crashing down on top of us, forcing cars to brake abruptly. Horns blared. People drove around us, glaring. One man clambered out of his car to see if we were okay.

Shamefaced, we walked the tandem the few yards back to the shop and talked the man there into a refund. We then found a café where we drank a cold beer and ate lobster at a table on a porch overlooking the harbor.

"We're coming out to the fast current again," Fitz said, eyeing me rubbing my lips together from the memory of lobster. The small raft floated toward the end of the soldier-like grass. "Want to tie up and have some of that soup?" he suggested. "I can't stop thinking of food."

"Me neither," I said.

We tied up to a cluster of reeds and each ate a teaspoon of cakey powdered soup washed down with water.

Ready to start again, I felt my jaw set, determined to succeed. I squeezed Fitz's hand.

His face was as tense as mine felt, but he looked at me straight on. "Okay, Hol?"

Leaving the relative safety of the marsh, we pushed out into the channel, resuming our hard strokes. We paddled half the afternoon, driven by instinct, like migrating animals, an inner force driving us forward as the sun crossed the sky.

Finally, when I thought I couldn't stroke even once more, we spotted a resting place up ahead. A mound of driftwood was caught in an elbow curve of the channel. Hundreds of dead trees had been thrown on top of each other against the flooded forest, washed down here, just like us.

Tears sprung to my eyes. "We'll be able to rest."

The thought of feeling something solid under my feet propelled me across the thirty yards of water. As we banged into the logjam, I reached out to massage the first log I touched, as if it were North American soil.

None of the logs budged as we tied up and climbed onto the woodpile. Our legs shook with cramps. We stood up to stretch before lying down. The huge logs were the closest thing to land we'd felt in days. I lay on my stomach, curved my arms around a weathered trunk, and hugged it.

Fitz sat, watching a bird fly overhead. He muttered that if the storm had pushed us into this curve with these other logs, we would have saved a day going back up this channel.

I felt the smooth driftwood with my hand, watched drops of my sweat fall onto it. "I know. We could say, 'If the storm hadn't happened . . . if the plane didn't crash . . . if we hadn't missed the boat.' It's like dominos that won't stop falling."

Fitz gave a short laugh and shook his head. "Luck like this has got to change!"

He slid the canteen off his belt and handed it to me. The water tasted good. When we'd both finished it off, I filled the canteen from the channel then dropped two halazone tablets down its neck to dissolve. It would take twenty minutes for the water to purify.

Fitz lit one of his few remaining cigarettes, still dry inside their plastic wrapping in the tin, along with the matches.

I looked around and wondered where we were in this green and muddy maze. How far had we come in comparison to how far we still had to go? Were we making any head-way at all, or were we fools even to try? We stared at the widening channel, then Fitz turned toward me and said, "I think we're doing great, Hol."

"Shoot, this is like running up mountains on your hands, Fitz."

His mouth started to curve up, wiggling his mustache. "You make me smile, despite everything," he said, rubbing his hand along his unshaven chin. "You've got to have the will to face this kind of thing." He pulled me to him. "You've got it."

"You do, too, Fitz. You're amazing. I always knew you were." I held his gaze. He leaned down and kissed me.

Looking across the swampy, vine-enmeshed bay, I wondered how deep the water was around the islands of trees growing out of it and even along the barrier of jungle. It could have been twenty or one hundred feet. Our pole never touched bottom. None of the trees bore fruit that I could see. I heard a large splash a few yards away, then another and another. Did I really have the will to get back into the channel? Who was I kidding? Whether I got back onto the little raft or stayed on these logs, I was trapped either way. My mind whirled to Fitz and Vietnam. Maybe he understood this jungle better than I did. "Does this look like Vietnam?" I asked.

"Some, but we never had this flooding." He wiped his forehead with the back of his hand. Then he sighed and sat quiet for a while. "The situation in 'Nam was totally different," he continued. "One thing, we had the radio to bring help when we needed it."

I scanned the jungle behind me, wondering if anyone was out there, for good or bad, then wondering how Fitz had coped with the incessant awareness that he might be shot at any second. It seemed no one was near here, either to help us or to shoot us. I caught myself. Fitz must be depressed enough without my probing. "Fitz, I didn't mean to bring up Vietnam . . ."

"It's okay." He put his arm around me. "You've got your own personal watchdog." His voice tightened. "We were never lost in 'Nam."

I looked up the channel to see another bend ahead, teasing me that the river might be around it. "The *aduana* will radio Riberalta," I said. "They could send out a plane anytime now."

"Maybe he went to lunch and forgot all about us," Fitz replied.

The *aduana* was our anchor to the outer world. It's his job to radio ahead, I wanted to say. He has new equipment that he wants to try out. But Fitz and I just sat in silence, occasionally scooping muddy river water over our hot heads with our hands. What a horror, I thought.

After a while I reached into the side pocket of the camera bag and slipped out the photos of Liza and Zelda. The power of the images surprised me. "We have to get home."

Fitz nodded, the raw, noontime sun burning his face. He pulled on his hat and stored the photos in the bag. "It feels good to sit on something solid, but we better get going."

"I just want to hug them again," I said urgently.

"You will."

As I locked my legs around the little raft, I clung to thoughts of our family.

Chapter 17

Dead Tree

The little raft kept us wet all day, a curse and a blessing. Water lapping over us made it difficult to paddle forward, but it kept us cool in the tropical heat. Our bucking bronco seemed as tired as we were, as if it wanted to slip into defeat and go back with the current. Sometimes we had to get in the water and swim in order to push it over logs. Swirling algae, fish, and other creatures bumped me. Had the candiru wormed up my jeans? Shuddering, I tightened my sphincter. After a while I resigned myself to the fact that there was nothing I could do about it if they were going to come. Afraid the next touch could be something deadly, I tried to concentrate on finding dry land.

By late afternoon we'd still found none. Not even a logjam. With the sun dropping, we had to find shelter. We couldn't sleep on the submerged little raft. Fitz and I decided our only choice was to sleep in a tree. It had to be a strong tree with branches low enough for us to reach. Such a tree would not be easy to find.

We spotted a ghostly one up ahead. It was tall, but not too tall, rising leafless among green trees, its gray shadow reflected in the water. It was majestic, with gnarled bare branches. A few entangled vines draped the limbs, which showed no obvious sign of rot. The tree wore root buttresses like a dress, tapering from waist to water.

"What do you think?" Fitz asked.

"Let's check it out."

We moored the raft against the trunk, swinging the rope around the first limb that was low enough for us to grasp. As I looked up, my heart thumped so loudly I could hear it.

When I was seven, my dad had built a tree house in a maple tree at the edge of the woods behind our home. I'd watched him winch up lumber for a large floor and sheets of plywood for the walls. It had a ceiling, two windows, and a trapdoor with a hook so we could let in people who knew the secret password. Everyone knew the secret password.

My sister, our friends, and I would hoist up food and messages in a basket by rope and pulley. We had peanut butter sandwiches and a thermos of milk. Some days, I'd lie on the tree house floor, reading books and imagining pirates below. Once we slept in there, protected by the glow of the light from the house's back door. Mom left it on so that we could follow it home if we got scared. We lasted an hour or two.

Reaching up to the first branch of the ghostly tree, I felt a spurt of energy thrust me back to all the trees I'd ever climbed.

Fitz was the opposite. He feared heights, probably because he had fallen down several flights of stairs when he was two or three. He'd tried to overcome this by becoming a paratrooper, making at least nine jumps. Although he'd forced himself to face his fear, he still fought panic when looking down from a ladder or a roof. He didn't complain and would climb if necessary, but I would go up first to find decent limbs for us to sleep on.

Fitz helped push me up to the first limb, four or five feet above the water, the little balsa rocking.

One hand leaning against the trunk for support, the other grasping the limb above me, I jiggled the branch with my legs, testing it. No cracking sounds. "It's strong. But a little low."

"Go up. In case of caiman," Fitz suggested.

Fitz pulled himself up to the first limb, shouldering the bag. "I'm okay," he said when I looked down.

We both paused to glance up the channel. Still no land in sight.

Then I stared back at the water we'd struggled against all day. My heart fell when I spotted the pink and blue of our tent. We'd paddled against the current for ten or twelve hours and we were still within sight of her. I couldn't take my eyes off the last of the light hitting the tent's peak.

"How's that limb?" Fitz asked, looking up at me.

"It's fine . . . but Fitz, I see the Pink Palace. I can't believe how little distance we've traveled . . ." I hoped he didn't hear the tremble in my voice.

Fitz turned his gaze down the swamp. "Shit," he muttered. "This is as far as we got?"

The darkening forest was coming alive with eerie night sounds. Birds began barking, hooting, and scuffling in the trees. Large bats swooped over the water. Fitz buckled the black bag's strap around a limb. Hanging on to the limb with one hand, he pushed his hat back on his head with the other and stared up the channel. Usually he would have added a few more expletives, or some thoughtful explanation. I didn't know what to think when he was silent.

Mustering himself, perhaps for my sake as well as his own, he finally said, "We never said we'd make it out in a day." His voice was strong. "Find us some limbs, Hol. We've got to rest for tomorrow."

I reached for the next branch. Climbing focused me so I couldn't dwell on the psychological punch in my chest—or the hunger in my stomach. "This is a good branch. Come up." Then I climbed onto the next branch, which had a nice curve for sitting.

"Watch your hands and feet," Fitz called. "There could be snakes or bats the color of the bark."

Or fire ants. The shadows of the last light played tricks and I couldn't be sure if the branch was safe. I banged the limb. It seemed fine. I put my whole weight on it, holding on to the branch above me for balance. Crack! The limb gave way under my left foot, crashing down into the water. "Aah!"

"Jesus!" Fitz yelled.

My left foot hung in midair, but my right foot was still on the unbroken nub of the branch.

I quickly wrapped my arms around the upper branch I'd been holding on to. If I couldn't hold on I would crash into the lower branches on my way down into the water. I would certainly break a leg or my neck.

"Inch your right foot closer to the trunk to make room for your other foot," Fitz urged. My left foot felt for the stub of the limb where my right foot was and found a place.

"Jesus," Fitz said again.

I positioned my two feet near the trunk then climbed down to the branch above him. My legs were melting like sticks of butter on a griddle. "I . . . can't move."

"You can," Fitz reassured me, his voice steady. "You've done the worst part already."

After a few moments my legs stopped shaking. "I'm afraid to pick another. What if they're all rotten inside?"

"This one's still holding me. Come back down here."

"But we don't know if it can hold both of us. I'll try this one to the side. I'll be careful." I felt braver again and started backing down to a side limb.

"Hol, that was close. Just get to another solid limb before it gets dark. I'm feeling a little queasy."

I landed on the side limb, a few feet down and to the right of the trunk. Its girth was at least three feet. I banged it then walked out on it, hands always grasping the limb above. "I don't see anything rotten," I finally announced.

"Okay."

Slowly inching my way to a sitting position, I straddled the limb.

Fitz took his time sitting down against the curve created by the joining of the trunk and the other branch.

"You're like a mountain goat," he sighed.

Lianas hung down from the branches. We used some to secure us to the trunk. We leaned against the fat tree, legs hanging over the broad boughs we'd chosen. As darkness turned into pitch-black night, we were grateful for the lack of rain. Our clothes, wet from rafting, were almost dry.

Roars of unknown origin echoed across the water. Other rustling, slithering sounds were too close. Creatures were hunting. Branches on nearby trees jounced, leaves fluttering. Something hit my face. Oh, my God, is it a vampire bat? I thought. They suck blood! I twitched my cheek, and the thing fell away. Something else bumped my branch.

I peered into the darkness toward the thump. This was our first time in the wild without the Pink Palace as refuge. Its mosquito netting had provided a gauzy separation from insects and, mentally, from hungry jungle animals. "We can't see anything, but everything can see us," I groaned.

"I have an idea," Fitz replied, his voice hopeful. "I'll pee a border around us to let the animals know this territory is ours."

Scared as I was, I nearly laughed out loud. "Sure." I was willing to try anything. He did.

It was a terrible night. The mosquitoes bit endlessly. Some pica ants crawled over us, though not many. They pierced and burned then moved on. Fitz had slept sitting up in Vietnam, but never in a tree. The vines could only do so much. Each time I started to drift off, despite fearing the bats, I leaned one way or the other and began to fall. The vines jerked me awake.

"This is miserable," I complained, slapping at mosquitoes. "Torturous little beasts."

Silence.

"Fitz?"

He could sleep even in a tree!

I clung to the vines, my legs knotted around the branch, trying to visualize a firm bed with smooth sheets and fluffy pillows. My body softened.

I was awakened by what sounded like a motorboat putt-putting in the distance. Someone's out there! "Fitz! Do you hear that? Wake up!" I tried to touch him with my foot.

"What?"

"I hear a motorboat! Listen."

The putting sound was still going.

"¡Socorro, socorro!" we yelled, but no one answered. The putting drifted away and was gone.

"They didn't hear us over the motor," I said.

"No."

Silence. Then hope burst through again. "A motorboat means civilization is out there," I said. "We've got to be close to the river. Maybe there'll be another boat tomorrow."

"Let's get some sleep so we'll be ready."

"I love you, Fitz."

"I love you, too."

Would this night ever end? I needed sleep but was afraid it would send me crashing to my death despite the lianas. How did birds and animals sleep without keeling over? Each time I succumbed to exhaustion I was immediately yanked awake by the lianas stopping me from falling. Oh, my God, this is unbearable. I remembered the prayer I'd learned as a child, and recited it to myself while thinking of my mother: "If I die before I wake . . ."

Chapter 18

Wrestling Match

FEBRUARY 22

Fourth day trapped

In the morning I awoke with a crick in my neck. A patch of pale yellow sky hung overhead, crisscrossed by skinny gray boughs, like a quilt. I unwrapped myself from the vine that had kept me from falling, and peered through sandman eyes at Fitz on the thick branch below. Rustling leaves in trees next to ours suggested other creatures were also awake.

"Good morning," I said. I was relieved that the night was finally over. "Fitz! We heard a motorboat last night. The river has to be close."

Fitz nodded. "Gotta be."

This cheered me. Instead of grumbling about the masses of mosquito bites I'd gotten last night, the horrendous lack of sleep, and the hunger pangs in my stomach, I asked, "What would you like for breakfast?"

"A stack of flapjacks with a fried egg on top, and sides of ham and sausage."

"You don't even like eggs."

"I do now."

"I've got a bit of sugar, powdered pea soup, and a can of milk."

"I'll take it."

I thought of all the wonderful Saturday morning pancake breakfasts we'd enjoyed in Connecticut on the one morning a week when we weren't working. Sauntering into the kitchen from bed and love, tousled hair, sun streaming from the window onto the old Formica table. Fitz making the pancakes, light as air, the bacon crisp. I loved that smell. Zelda, lying in the doorway, her puffy tail wagging, hoping for a dropped morsel.

As the sun showed itself, we climbed down from the tree and slipped onto the waterlogged raft, carefully positioning ourselves and the camera bag, one at a time.

"Damn!" Fitz said.

"What?"

"My hat! It must have fallen off in the night. Where the hell is it? I'm going to need it."

We searched the immediate area but saw no sign of it. We decided it must have fallen into the channel.

"What the hell am I going to use now for the glare and that goddamn heat?"

"Use mine."

Half the time it was too hot to wear hats, but they did protect our necks. Fitz's neck had burned red even with his Panama. I had been braiding my hair to keep it off my skin while wearing my hat, but I could let it hang down to cover my neck. We were usually soaked from the splashing paddles anyway.

"I'm not taking your hat."

"Your neck already looks like a boiled lobster," I pointed out. I scooped up water with my hands, soaking my hair. "See? My hair will protect my neck—it feels cooler anyway."

Fitz agreed to share the hat. We would each get some protection on our faces and scalps.

We sat on the little balsa, still tied to the tree's lower branch, our legs dangling in warm brown water, to share a teaspoon of sugar and a smidgeon of dried soup. I glanced at the ingredients on the packet to learn its nutritional value: dehydrated peas, carrots, and dozens of chemicals with unpronounceable names. "Look what's keeping us going!" I handed it to Fitz.

He read the ingredients and shook his head. "We'll die from other things long before we have to worry about these chemicals."

We each took our sugar first. I let the sweetness sit in my mouth to dissolve. The powdered soup was salty, with a bitter aftertaste, and it stuck to the inside of my cheeks.

"Hand me that canteen, will you?" I asked, swirling my dry, gritty tongue around my teeth. Before pushing off, we held hands for a moment, just as we had on the Pink Palace, and gave thanks for our food.

God rapidly was becoming more real. Neither of us presumed he would focus on us. Still, it was comforting to feel there might be a greater being in charge. Perhaps he would take pity on us and get us out of here.

We started up the channel. My muscles, which yesterday had endured more than I had ever thought possible, were now locked in knots. The current lay waiting for us, like an enemy. It was slower at the tree line, but we kept snagging on submerged growth, hardly making headway.

I glanced at the fifteen-foot rope we used as a painter for the small balsa. "Fitz, let's weight the painter with a stick then throw it over the low limbs so we can pull ourselves along." Fitz agreed. "It's got to be better than just paddling."

He clung to a bush, holding the raft still, while I reached for a loose piece of wood floating by. Then he knotted the rope around the wood and tossed it toward the closest branch. The raft floated backward, making it difficult to throw the rope effectively.

I clutched brush to help keep the raft stable. Fitz took several attempts to catch the branch. The painter had to loop around the branch twice or it wouldn't hold. Once it caught, Fitz slowly pulled as I paddled forward.

When we reached the branch, Fitz jiggled the piece of wood free and we started the process again. As we became more adept we slipped backward less. The rope served as a fifth arm, and while throwing it was hard work, pulling and paddling became easier.

Logjams became goals to reach and to pass. We clung to each as we reached it, reining the raft in, in order to catch our breath. A few minutes later we were ready to start off again.

"Ready?" I asked after we'd paused for longer than usual. I lowered my paddle to push off for the next logjam.

Fitz didn't respond. I turned toward him.

"It's those damned butts," he blurted. His breath was coming hard.

I'd never heard this admission before. I laid my paddle across my lap and didn't mention the cigarettes. They'd be gone soon enough. "You're in great shape," I protested. "Look at those pecs. Anyone would be out of breath doing this job."

"You're not out of breath."

"I was breathing hard a minute ago."

"Let's go. I'm fine."

We inched our way slowly upriver until we came to a place where dozens of logs were jumbled together. A few feet of water and debris were caught between many of the logs where the current gathered power, forming a low waterfall. The little raft jolted in the rapid current. We tried to cling to the logs with our fingertips, but the wood was too slippery to grasp.

"Hol, we can't paddle the balsa through this. We'll have to drag it over the pilings," Fitz yelled to me over the sound of the waterfall.

"What if it gets caught on stuff under the water?"

"Then we'll get in to free it."

The falls swept hard over the raft's port side, knocking our hands from their tentative grip; the raft lurched backward.

"Grab the logs!" Fitz cried.

I was thrown upside down into the muddy water. No chance to take a breath. Through the ghostly darkness I twisted around, trying to see which way was up. There was light below me. I scissors kicked toward it. Something hard stopped my head from breaking the surface. My lungs wanted to crack open. Knowing I had only seconds, I swam sideways seeking a place to raise my head. I spluttered to the surface, water up my nose, struggling to catch my breath. The raft was stuck on something near me, so I grabbed it.

Fitz had pulled himself up onto the log pile and was clinging to the raft's rope and the black bag. He reached for my hand. "I've got you, Hol." His arm around me now pulled me up.

I coughed hard. Water spurted out of my mouth and nose. Fitz slapped my back. I took in a deep breath then began to breathe more evenly. "Thanks," I wheezed.

The slippery logjam was piled every which way. I tripped, my left leg flying up. Fitz gripped my shoulder. I thought we would both go over, but we clung to each other until we'd righted ourselves.

"Jeez, it's really frightening under the water." I wiped my eyes. My legs were shaking. "I didn't know if I'd make it."

"Jesus, Hol, I was scared, too." He kissed my forehead. "It's good you have nine lives."

"Don't jinx me." I began to tremble all over despite the scorching heat.

Fitz tightened his arms around me and rubbed my back. I looked at him. "Let's go home, George."

"I wish," he said, then smiled. "Say good night, Gracie."

I was so glad Fitz was with me. I reached up and kissed him, long, to take us somewhere else. A loud crash in the water yanked us back.

"That was big," Fitz said. We spun around, listening intently, looking in every direction for loglike reptiles, eyes searching for snakes and caimans. We knew they napped on logs. We'd been lucky so far, but how long could our luck hold?

"The rainy season isn't officially over for another month, so we should be safe from caimans right now," Fitz said. He sounded reassuring, but he really didn't know any more than I did.

It had been sunny a great deal lately, signaling the rainy season's end. But there were no guarantees out here. We were going on hearsay, and we'd learned firsthand just how unreliable that could be.

"I don't see anything. Do you?"

"No." Fitz sighed. "Shall we bite the bullet and drag the raft over the log pile?"

"It's safer than paddling up the waterfall. We'd pitch over for sure," I said, apprehensive about falling into the water again.

We hoisted the little raft onto the wide logjam at the edge of the falls and dragged it up, stumbling over and around logs that were half underwater. Near the top of the logjam the raft tipped and caught on something under the channel. We wrenched and pulled but couldn't dislodge it.

"We'll have to go in to see," Fitz said. Resigned, we forced ourselves into the raging cascade, no time to worry about going under.

Blinded by water rushing against my face, I felt for the little raft. Finding it, I yanked it with one hand while holding part of the logjam with my other. Fitz and I banged and tugged. The little raft broke free. We clambered onto the logjam again along with the little raft, and continued hauling it to the top, repeatedly falling on slimy logs. It would have been easy to twist an ankle, or cut ourselves, but we were fortunate.

Past the waterfall and at the end of the logjam, Fitz and I pushed the raft back into the open water, climbed onto it, and started out for the next bend. The channel narrowed to just a hundred feet wide in places. We paddled forward, passing marshes, the endless jungle stretching out behind them. In other places, we tried to stick close under the submerged trees for security. The current was stronger with every stroke.

Overhead, dark clouds swallowed the sun, blackening the sky. The channel became furious now, kicking up small waves. Birds cawed and fled into the canopy. The clouds' bellies burst, releasing a pelting downpour that slashed against our skin. I threw my arm over my head.

"Ow! I guess it is still the rainy season."

Relentless, flat sheets of vertical and diagonal rain fell for hours. Black raindrops peppered us like BBs without mercy. I felt so angry I wanted to cry. Our meager fuel from powdered soup and sugar was long gone, but still we bent to the paddles and fought like hell. We were half sinking on the little raft, our legs and hips in the water, waves whipping us as pails of pellets fell and fell. I can't, I can't, I can, I can.

Hope dropped like a barometer. Help us! a small voice inside me cried. I was sobbing silently but had to keep paddling. God help us! I pleaded for strength.

I bent my head to my chest, jabbed the paddle into the water, pushed it back wearily, lifted it up again. Over and over I thrust my paddle into the channel on either side of the raft, trying to push away the pain, to make my motions robotic.

We hunkered into porcupine balls, backs to the sky, seeking protection from the furious rain. It was impossible to measure progress. "Try grabbing the slickers while I paddle," Fitz yelled.

Twisting around to unzip the bag, I glimpsed Fitz's face, red from the strain of paddling by himself. We were slipping back. I forgot the slickers and grabbed my paddle. We paddled as hard as we could just to stay where we were. Up to now we'd held our own with the river and the jungle. But the storm was too much. The fist of the storm surged sideways. The small raft began twirling like a baton.

"Stop us, stop us!" I pleaded to Fitz as I reached out for anything to grab.

"I can't!" he yelled as he reached out, too.

We seized a tree submerged in the water and clung by numb fingers to its branches. The storm raged around us as tears flooded my eyes. In seconds, Fitz and I had lost half the distance we'd gained in a day.

"We can't do this," Fitz cried. "It's insanity."

"I don't want to give up. What was the point if we go back now?" I yelled through the wind. "We'll be right back where we started."

I heard no answer. The wind and rain slapped my face. My fingernails dug into the branch but were slipping, the little raft pulling out from under us like a wild pony. I wouldn't believe we were beaten. I'd thought that as long as we tried our utmost, we would make it. "What was the point? What was the point?" I choked.

"I don't know," Fitz yelled back, his face contorted. "We can't do this."

But neither of us let go.

Chapter 19

Little Balsa

Waves smashed over the little balsa, slapping our thighs and stomachs.

"God Almighty!" Fitz yelled.

"We can't go back! Not after all this!" My hands locked onto the branch like gnarled, swollen fungi. Letting go meant being swept back to the Pink Palace, where slow death awaited us. My arms throbbed; my fingers began to give way. Anticipating the sweet relief of surrender bade me let go.

My parents would never know what had happened to us. I imagined my mother's beautiful brown eyes, watering and red with grief, my dad's cheerful blue eyes, puffy behind his glasses. I strained to grab the ends of the bough. I had to hold on, for them.

Scenes of ordinary life flashed through my mind: my dad calling from the ladder for nails to complete the octagonal playhouse (that was never used as a playhouse because my sister and I had grown up); my mom singing cowboy songs on family car trips when the radio stations didn't come in; that last intimate weekend with our friends and family at the lake before we left on this trip—all of us laughing, playing hearts, talking of who was doing what and going where.

"We can't give up!" I screamed over the wind. But desire counted for nothing. We didn't have the power to save ourselves. Clutching the branch, I pressed my eyes against my upper arm, trying to wipe away the tears.

My fingers slipped, my hands releasing against my will. I was thrust into a free fall.

Fitz also let go.

We clenched the little raft with our arms and legs as it took off downriver, unsteady as a new colt. Hurtling into the relentless current, it wouldn't stop spinning. Rain and wind howled, as if everything in the universe was ganging up on us. I heard a deep moaning inside me as we whirled down the channel: You'll never get out. You should never have come. We flew by all the landmarks we'd fought so hard to pass: the small waterfall, the logjams, the dead tree, the regal reeds.

I couldn't swallow or catch my breath. My lungs seemed filled with stones. Succumbing to the force of the water, I couldn't believe that just a few days ago I'd embraced the joy of the ride, thrilled by the fun of the adventure. Now the river was whisking us back to hell. My mind groped wildly for something solid to cling to. Fitz. He was my stability. "I'm sorry, Fitz," I yelled, desperate for him to understand that I had never wanted this.

"What?"

"I'm sorry I was so insistent that we take the raft." I'd wanted to get out of Puerto Maldonado so much that I couldn't see the danger. My face felt contorted by the rain and my furious tears.

"For God's sake, Holly, we had to get out of there."

"I talked you into it," I choked.

"You didn't."

I felt reassured to hear Fitz's gruff voice, letting me know I shouldn't condemn myself. We were in this together.

The stench of stale mud and swamp water greeted us as we neared the end of the channel. The Pink Palace came into view, looking ethereal through the sheets of rain, her robin's egg blue and hot pink plastic walls in clear contrast to the jungle. She was a reminder of our failed escape, yet my heart leapt upon seeing she was still here. We'd abandoned her, but she'd held strong. She was the only solid surface we had to stand on in this endless, flooded swamp.

The rain turned to drizzle, and the sun peeked coyly from behind the heavy clouds. A rainbow appeared as we closed in on the Pink Palace. My thoughts raced from fear to hope. I had to contain myself from leaping at the large raft, throwing us off balance. All I cared about now was collapsing on her uneven floorboards, wrapping the dry sleeping bag around us, and letting the raft rock us into the deepest sleep.

We paddled hard for a few more feet until I could grab her and tie up. Hoisting the black bag onto the logs, we pulled ourselves, like soggy rats, out of the water. I was desperate to lie down. We were still alive. That was good enough for now. I leaned on a tent pole to get my bearings just as a distant humming came from the sky. It was moving toward us, getting louder. I searched the cloud bank over the water.

"Sounds like a plane!" Fitz gasped, struggling to catch his breath. "My God. Look!" He pointed to the western sky where the sun was bursting forth. A small two-propeller plane emerged from the clouds, bathed in a halo of sun. It flew low over the swamp toward us.

"Fitz! Oh, my God." I wanted to believe that God had guided us back here just so that we could be found.

We frantically waved and shouted together, "Here we are! Here we are!"

The plane flew alongside the swamp but not directly overhead. It occurred to me that the *aduana* might have radioed Riberalta after all. Why else would a plane be flying so low? We grabbed each other's hands and raised them high, yelling as loud as we could, "WE'RE OVER HERE! WE'RE OVER HERE!"

As quickly as it had appeared, the plane departed. We watched in silent disbelief as it vanished into the clouds. Then we listened to the drone of the distant engine until we heard no sound at all.

We stood for a long time, waiting, hoping the plane would circle back. The last drops of rain tapped lightly on the tent beside us, accompanied only by the sound of our breathing.

Chapter 20

SOS

I wanted to scream, to crumple and not get up, but I knew that wouldn't help. Fitz looked numb, his curly hair flattened into corkscrews from the rain. If I lost control he might fall apart, too. We'd been so sure the plane was looking for us. I'd even believed that God had sent us back here because he was sending the plane. So much belief, so much hope, bottomed out. I stood bracing myself against the tent frame, waiting for the plane to return. Fitz looked over the trees, watching also. He didn't swear once. Not even under his breath.

I needed to keep up my spirits for Fitz, for both of us. If we gave in to despair it wouldn't be the jungle that killed us; it would be our own despondency. My thoughts began to rally. We can last longer than this. It's only been four days. "We can't give up hope," I told Fitz. "People have survived all kinds of things."

Fitz's stunned look gave way to a nod. "True." He rubbed his neck. "What about that psychoanalyst you always talk about?"

"Viktor Frankl?"

"Yeah, him."

As a student I'd read that Frankl observed how others had endured the concentration camps during World War II by clinging to hope. He'd held on to it himself by longing to see his family again. So did we. Hope could make the difference between life and death. If we held on to it, we at least had a chance. As a therapist I'd helped clients find hope in the smallest places and build on it. Now I needed to do that. Splashes in the water meant fish. We had hooks. We could catch our food! A plane had come today. So why wouldn't another come tomorrow?

"They'll find us," I finally said.

"Tomorrow I'll make a big SOS sign from that extra pink plastic. When they come back they'll see it and know that we need help." Fitz looked at me and smiled.

I reached for his arm. "Huge letters so they can't miss them." I could have kissed his feet for the idea, but I hugged him instead.

We entered the tent, pulled off our soggy clothes then dumped them in a pile in a corner. I found a towel in a backpack. As I dried my skin I was grateful for the flat balsa platform, the soft sleeping bag, the dry tent still holding firm. No drips, no leaks, no rips. We stretched our legs straight out for the first time in two days.

"What luxury! A couple of days ago we thought this was roughing it," I said. "Little did we know that the Pink Palace is a palace."

Fitz's eyes were closing, his glasses resting on his nose, but a flicker of a smile crossed his lips. I pointed my toes then pressed my heels forward, stretching out my tense calf and thigh muscles, like a cat. It felt so good to lie down. My stomach yearned for something to eat, but we were down to almost nothing. Sleep first. Tomorrow we would catch a fish. "Are you awake?" I whispered.

"Barely," he murmured, reaching for my hand.

Turning onto my side I put my arm around his waist. I watched his breathing, his strong nose, the stubble growing longer on his cheeks, his jaw even more prominent than it had been this morning. I marveled at his tenacity. "I love you," I whispered as I lifted off his glasses and put them carefully to the side of the sleeping bag.

Chapter 21

High Noon

FEBRUARY 23

Fifth day trapped

A bright light expanded out to pale angel wings, reaching for me, like hands from heaven. "No!" I heard myself howl, coming out of sleep. I whimpered, changing positions on the sleeping bag. Every muscle burned from yesterday's exertion, my empty stomach most of all. We'd better catch a fish today.

Fitz was already making coffee. I raised my head then lay right back down. "Uuugh."

"What is it?"

"Everything. My head, my stomach."

"It's from not eating," he said. "Coffee will help. I'll bring you some."

I told him I would come out; I had to relieve myself anyway. I didn't want him exerting more energy than he had to.

We didn't urinate as much as I thought we should despite drinking the treated channel water. We didn't move our bowels at all; our bodies had nothing to waste. As I raised myself onto one elbow, my stomach cramped. I felt feverish, as if spiders were crawling up and down my back. Before this, the closest I'd ever come to feeling hunger was when dieting in college. The moment I felt hunger pangs I would give in to a burger and fries. Until now, I had no idea of real hunger: the aching, nausea, shaking chills, like a bad flu.

Yesterday, ignoring starvation, I'd used up my adrenaline because we'd had a plan to escape that propelled me forward. Now I couldn't leave Fitz to fish and make the SOS sign alone. I moved slowly, gradually rising to my feet.

Balancing against the tent frame, I stood shaking. Fitz was standing up to bring me coffee, his pants falling in folds, like draperies around his legs. He'd looped a rope tightly around his waist to hold them up.

"I didn't hear you get up."

"You were out cold," he said. "I didn't have the heart to wake you." He walked toward me, watching his feet on the logs and the cup of coffee jiggling in his hand. "My stomach was raging. I had to scrounge up what food we've got left. I used the last halazone tablets, but we've got the iodine to purify the water." He'd found the evaporated milk and the end of the powdered soup and sugar in the bag from yesterday.

Reluctantly letting go of the tent frame, I staggered to him. "Let's have it all." I leaned in for a kiss.

Fitz embraced me and kissed me softly on the mouth. "Hi." He looked intently into my eyes then handed me the half-spilled coffee in the tin cup. The coffee stung my hollow stomach.

"Hot, thin soup coming up. I'm going to toss the line out. We'll catch a fish for lunch."

Fitz was anticipating a fruitful day. I wished I felt more interested. "What'll we use for bait?" I asked.

"Algae? What else do we have?"

"Nothing." I leaned on him to steady myself. "I'm like a drunken sailor."

"What a pair!" He took my hand and led me to sit by the stove. "The coffee will give you a little zip."

"Thanks." I felt like a squeezed lemon, no juice left. "That awful sound came again last night. It really frightened me, Fitz. I thought it would suck us right up." I drew my head back and downed the last of my coffee. "It only seems to come at dusk and dawn. I wonder, did we pick a bad place to tie up?"

Fitz shook his head. "We didn't exactly choose this place. I don't get what the hell that sound is." He blew on the fire, stirring a tablespoon of pea soup powder into the water. "If it comes again we can move the Pink Palace—if we have the strength." He glanced at me warily.

"I think we should open the can of milk. I was only saving it because we're trying to be so cautious," Fitz said.

"Soup's fine. I don't think we should use up our last supply. It's a security blanket."

"As I see it, the plane that came yesterday should be back today," Fitz assured me. "I think they're looking for us. It's only a matter of time before we get out of here."

"You think so?" I didn't dare hope, afraid to be disappointed again. What was the matter with me? What was happening to my will to live, my belief in Frankl?

"You saw how they circled around? It wasn't just a plane on a direct flight path," Fitz said, and swirled his hand in the air. "They were looking for us."

There's so much river, with probably hundreds of offshoots, just like this one. We're a needle in a haystack. I squashed my thoughts before they reached my lips. I couldn't slap down his optimism. I wanted to feel it, too, but right now I was too weak to feel anything but fear. "I love your outlook," I told him. "That's part of what I loved about you from the start."

"Well, it's not a pipe dream." Fitz sounded a little defensive. "I think it makes a lot of sense."

"Okay. I just need to get my energy back."

"You'll feel better when I cook up that fish." Fitz rose and headed for the tent to find the huge hook and fish line.

I realized that if we were dehydrated, as well as famished, coffee was the wrong thing to drink, although it was a stimulant that might help to motivate us. We had to replenish the fluids that had been sucked from us by yesterday's tropical sun. But first I needed to lie down before I keeled over.

Fitz buzzed with ambition as I crawled back to the sleeping bag and collapsed, cradling a bottle of water. Please let me feel better so that I can help Fitz, I prayed.

The plastic tent was a sweatbox. I yearned to dip into the swamp but couldn't move. I heard the fire spit as Fitz put it out, then the coffee cups clinking as he dipped them into the channel. The satiny sleeping bag felt hot against my cheek. My breath was shallow. Closing my eyes, I tried to imagine something cold . . . our wedding day.

DECEMBER 12, 1970

The tent my dad had rented for the reception was close to collapsing under the weight of the falling snow. It was the biggest snowstorm in ten years. At 3:00 a.m., long after we'd returned from the rehearsal dinner, my mom, dad, and some friends and I found ourselves banging snow off the tent roof with brooms. It was coming down so hard we couldn't work fast enough.

Fitz's friend Nick had hitchhiked in from California and called at midnight from a telephone booth to say, "I'm here! Can you come get me?" I'd never met him. Bejou, my bridesmaid, and I skidded down the long plowed hill in my blue VW bug to fetch him, grateful to have his help.

The flakes swept across the sky and landed, heavy, on everything. The tent's canvas roof sagged, and the sides leaned in. Nick and Dad waded through knee-deep drifts, lugging two ladders through the howling storm.

They managed to lean the ladders against the tent poles. Then we took turns unsteadily climbing the rungs, brooms in hand, to drag the snow off the roof. Bejou held the ladder for me as I went up. A burst of wind rocked the ladder, pulling it away from the edge of the tent. It slipped sideways and crashed, taking me with it. I fell on my back into the softest mattress of snow I could imagine. After the shock of dropping through the air, I lay cushioned on the deep drift, staring up at the falling crystals, just like I had as a child. Snowflakes on my face were a cooling mist. I tasted them. So cold! Then I moved my arms to make a snow angel, laughing as I pushed them back and forth.

After a chorus of concern, Bejou pulled me up. "You'll go to any lengths to make this the wedding of the year!" she chided me good humoredly.

We used only one ladder after that, with three people holding it for the brave soul climbing up, and two more holding flashlights. Even so, the swirling storm made it difficult to see anything. The snow was so deep and so heavy it was difficult to remove, but we kept at it.

Fitz was oblivious to our situation because he was spending the night at the new rental cottage in the woods, an hour away. I was glad he was catching up with Chip and

Ellen and some of his buddies, whom he hadn't seen in months.

"Come on, everyone! This part of the tent is still laden," my dad warned. The strain showed on his face, but his voice, normally quiet, was strong. As father of the bride, he bore the responsibility of the wedding and the reception on his shoulders. He'd organized the tent reception at my parents' home after persuading the rental agent into breaking his "no tents after Thanksgiving" rule and putting one up on what had once served as a small macadam basketball court.

The tent vendor had voiced his doubts. "I've never put one up this late in the season, Mr. Conklin. Snow and all."

"We'll be fine. It's rare for it to snow more than an inch or two before Christmas," my father insisted.

But it was snowing a blizzard.

My dad was sixty but had always seemed ageless. We looked to him to fix things. I inherited his optimism and never doubted that everything would be all right.

When it finally stopped snowing, we paused to examine the mystically silent world around us. Pure and perfectly white, the snow had buried everything. Huge drifts had settled against our modern house, designed by my dad to resemble the glass prow of a ship extending from a Roman courtyard. The snow was piled two feet high along the walls in the courtyard and had also climbed the sides of the tent and hung from the cryptomeria and pine. It was exquisite.

I wished my curly-headed Fitz were here to see this sight. He'd write a poem about it, like his award-winning "One Icicle Tree," which was published in his college literary magazine. He'd tell the story of our fight to save the tent in the middle of the night.

Fitz was my poet and storyteller. I was so happy knowing I was going to marry him. We'd have stories for a lifetime.

In the morning we woke to a world of sun-glittered wonder scattered across all the fields and trees around us. The upright golden tent gleamed in the new day. Fresh, virgin snow signaling a new beginning.

"Why the smile?" Fitz asked, leaning over me.

"I was thinking about the night before we got married," I replied, reluctant to let go of the memories of frigid air.

"Ha! When your dad planned on a tent in December, I knew I was marrying into an adventurous family." He chuckled into my collarbone, carefully lying down beside me. "I was a little intimidated by your parents."

"You were?"

"They're so nice, even though I didn't have much of a job back then, not much college even . . . to court you. What was I thinking?"

"You had confidence! How could they not like you?"

I touched his cheek. We were quiet as I drained the water bottle he handed me. "I feel a little better," I said. "Maybe I was just dehydrated."

"That, and not eating. Are you up to seeing how the sign is coming along?"

"Sure."

Fitz gently pulled me up. "Bring your sewing kit."

Clutching my box of needles and thread, I made it across the raft to where Fitz had cut out three giant plastic pink letters, SOS, and a six-by-six-foot piece of bright blue plastic for the background. The sight of them renewed my desire to be helpful, giving me the strength I needed to try to sew on the letters.

My fingers shook as I threaded my biggest needle then stabbed it into the plastic. I was too weak to push the needle through it. After cutting small holes with the scissors, I sewed large basting stitches around the edges of the letters, securing them. The logs scraped my shins as I kneeled over the sign. I continually glanced toward the sky, wanting to get the sign finished before the plane came back.

When it was done, I stood up for a better view. The hot pink letters looked cheerful against their blue backdrop. "This has to be visible from the air. Who could miss bright pink in all this green?" I said proudly.

While we waited for the plane to reappear, Fitz fished with the hook he'd baited with algae. I paddled the small raft along the tree line in our little bay, hoping to find something for us to eat besides the fish that were not biting, perhaps some berries, or a frog for better bait. I watched intently for any sign of life, taking slugs from the canteen and sometimes throwing swamp water over my head in an effort to stay cool. Each time a splash erupted nearby or a branch swayed I paddled to it. But by the time I arrived, all signs of life had vanished. I yearned for lemonade and ice cream. Again I thought of the snow.

The afternoon settled into evening without Fitz catching a fish. I'd paddled around for hours but hadn't found a single berry. We broke down and opened the can of evaporated milk. It was sweet and rich and delicious, the most food we'd had in days, though in no way satiating. We agreed to save the two teaspoons of sugar now that all the milk and soup were gone. For hours our eyes shifted between the sky and the SOS sign. A plane never came.

Chapter 22

Swimming with Becky

FEBRUARY 24

Sixth day trapped

After yesterday's bad luck we decided to try to escape again. This time we would avoid the current entirely by attempting to go perpendicular to the channel, heading straight through the flooded jungle. We figured this was where the earth would be in the dry season. If we paddled the little balsa far away from the channel, we might finally reach dry land.

Fitz thought he saw a small break in the tree line. Maybe we were close to the Madre but just couldn't see it. The channel twisted so much that there was no sure way to know how to find the Madre other than by following the dead-end channel all the way back to its source. During the night we had spent tied to the tree, we'd thought we heard the sound of a motorboat coming from the south, so we packed the camera bag with necessities and set off that way. Our load included the very last of our food: two teaspoons of sugar.

We paddled the small raft to the end of the swamp, gliding with the light current. The water grew muddier; each stroke felt like stirring pudding. Mud sucked at the boards each time we raised them. Lifting boughs that hung into the water, we peered through gaps in a wall of gigantic vines, thick as hawsers. The vegetation looked like gnarled, interlocked knuckles. After less than an hour we discovered a face-scratching waterway into the jungle.

The small balsa was no canoe. She continually snagged on underwater brush, her bow bumping against every barrier, seen and unseen. We made little progress into the dizzying forest where darkness enveloped us. Bugs swarmed around our faces and limbs; we grew confused about which direction we were headed. It would be easy to push ourselves in circles. Bitten and bewildered, after hours of trying, we could barely see one another. Once again we surrendered.

Fortunately, we eventually found an opening through the trees to the channel and struggled on in the late afternoon toward the Pink Palace. At last, by glint of starlight, and with a lot of guesswork and tremendous luck, we made it to the raft. We each savored a half teaspoon of sugar, leaving the last teaspoon to split tomorrow.

When we turned in, I lay awake, listening to the jungle howl, trying to recall difficult circumstances in my life through which I had prevailed. Nothing had ever been like this. Not even close. Once I'd hitchhiked from college to the airport, to save a few dollars. I'd done it often with friends, but this time I was alone. An older man, with a huge stomach squashed into his three-piece suit, picked me up at the entrance to the highway. Soon he veered onto a remote country road surrounded by trees, then settled his hand on my knee. I looked for any way out. As we neared a gas station, I managed to reach to the brake with my foot, hitting it hard. The car slowed enough for me to open the passenger door and roll out. The driver took off.

Another time, my friend Jeff and I were walking along-side a bog in a Connecticut field when I stumbled and fell into what looked like grass. The ground gave way slowly, swallowing me. Each attempt to climb out sank me down farther. The more I reached out my arms, or kicked my legs, the deeper I sank into the curdling mud. Within seconds, I was covered to my shoulders, then to my neck.

"Don't move," Jeff yelled. "Stay still and you won't go down farther."

It was the opposite of what my body was screaming for me to do. My arms were above my head. He was too far away to reach me. "Get something to pull me out!"

We were out in the open, with no bushes, no branches. He looked wildly for a stick.

"Your belt," I called, so grateful Jeff had worn one and that my head was clear enough to notice.

He tossed the buckle end toward me twice before it was close enough for me to grab. As he pulled me to safety I shuddered, wondering if there were other bodies in the bog. Shaking off my thoughts, I curled closer to Fitz and wrote in my budget book journal. "These days have been hard. Perhaps they have made us better people. Hope we'll have another chance to put our lives to use."

FEBRUARY 25

Seventh day trapped

I woke with a start and shook Fitz awake, announcing that we had to try again, this time to swim out. We would each take a log for support when we tired or cramped. When the current became too strong, we would go under the brush and pull ourselves along. It was too cumbersome to paddle the little raft, but if we swam maybe we would have a chance to reach the river.

"What else can we do—just sit here and wait to die?"

Fitz didn't hesitate. "Okay."

We agreed to leave right after coffee. Since we'd be swimming, we couldn't take anything but our money belts. In them we crammed our passports, notebook and pen, traveler's checks, cash, photos, the remaining teaspoon of sugar, malaria pills, and iodine. Fitz would carry the canteen on his belt. We nixed the Panama hat, the rim so wide that we wouldn't be able to see while swimming.

I put instant coffee in our cups then handed them over to Fitz so he could add the boiling water. Fitz leaned over the port side and drew in the rope that held our little balsa. We pulled nails from the crosspieces and took off a four-foot log for each of us to use as a float.

Swimming made me think of my childhood dog, Becky, an Irish Water Spaniel, bred to swim. "I hope we'll be as strong as Becky was," I said.

Slugging the last of his coffee, Fitz nodded. He knew about Becky. You could throw a ball into the water all day and she would always jump in. She never tired. When she submerged herself, her long, curly brown ears floated way out to the sides of her head; her pink open mouth seemed to grin, her long tail wagging high above the water. Becky's brown corkscrew bangs flopped over her gold-brown eyes as she swam to shore with the retrieved ball and shook water all over us and the picnic blanket. I also wished for her determination so I could conquer my fear of what lay beneath this water.

Fitz doused the fire while I filled the canteen with swamp water and two drops of iodine. Although the tiny iodine bottle was full and should last awhile, we were drinking water continually.

I looked out beyond the Pink Palace to where dew glistened on lush leaves. It was maybe 6:00 a.m.

"Ready." Fitz closed the tent flap even though we weren't coming back.

Tightening my money belt around my waist, I stared into the opaque water. *We've got to swim out of this mess.* This was for real, an extended swim against the channel in a final, desperate effort to reach the river. *Don't think about what's in or under there. Just do it.*

I slid into water that was the consistency of liquid velvet, shuddering at what might be around me, and then I swam a few feet away from the Pink Palace. My arm around my log, I turned to face Fitz. "It feels okay. It's cooler than on the raft."

Fitz edged into the water. "Not bad."

The sun was shining, the warm day urging us forward. We held our logs outstretched in front of us and kicked hard. The current increased as we headed upriver, but we were able to move ahead, staying close to each other.

Excited, I was feeling strong, ignoring any frightening thoughts. I mentioned Becky again.

"Holly, don't talk. You're going to need every breath you have."

"I just wanted to tell you something positive."

"I know. But you'll just have to think it. We can't talk and make it."

Ahead I could see logs thrust into a curve of the swamp amongst the reeds. It was the logjam where we'd rested three days earlier. We stopped there again then pushed on, resting at other spots that we had reached while paddling the little balsa. Passing these landmarks instilled confidence.

Although we were now weaker, we made better headway swimming than we'd done paddling. The current was mild and the breeze was light. I became accustomed to the slimy, swirling things around my legs. I didn't see or hear anything dangerous. Nature appeared to be on our side, though that could change in an instant. I had to stay alert, but my mind wandered.

"You okay?" Fitz could hardly talk.

"No cramping." I glanced sideways to see him. "You?"

"Yeah. Thirsty?"

"Always."

"Let's find something to hang on to."

We plowed forward.

"There." I jutted my chin toward a small logjam up ahead. Clambering onto the logs, we gulped at the canteen.

"Look at the brush along the tree line," Fitz said when he'd caught his breath. "As long as it's there let's stay close to it; the water's quieter and we can grab on to the branches."

The sun was with us still, joined by a gentle breeze. Fitz's blue eyes sparkled behind his glasses that were tied around his head. He looked bronzed and muscular even though he was thin. We'd finished off the canteen so I refilled it then added the iodine. We set out again, keeping close to the brush. The jungle was silent in the hot sun.

Chapter 23

Log Bed

After we'd swum for many hours, the channel was ever stronger. Exhausted, we agreed to stop at the next logjam. After a couple more bends, I sputtered, "Fitz," pleading for a rest.

"Reeds," I moaned, adjusting my direction. Fitz swam toward them.

We hung on to the willowy stalks. Clutching them was our respite, the only time we weren't moving forward or falling back. Even so, my arms ached. This posture was about as restful as hanging on a cross. Fitz raised the canteen to my mouth while he clutched the reeds with his free hand. I did the same for him.

Advancing slowly, we shifted between swimming and pulling ourselves, hand over hand, along the grasses. Whenever I heard a splash I barely turned now. I kept my eyes ahead, my arms reaching in front of me, stroke after stroke, my log beneath my chest.

"There must be an inlet where we can rest," Fitz said.

The sky turned pink and yellow. We saw nothing but water, reeds, and trees with branches too high to reach.

"Fitz!" I pointed.

A few logs were perhaps twenty yards away. Each rose vertically two to five feet out of the water, like elderly crooked fishermen bowing to the channel. Hot afternoon light bounced off the water between them. Two or three of the vertical logs were long-dead trees with crooks and stubby limbs.

Reaching the logs, Fitz squinted into the muck, hoping to pull out a couple to make our bed.

Treading water, I held on to our safety logs while he dove to determine if any of the vertical logs could be loosened below. He surfaced, raising his thumbs, then rested his arms around one upright log before going under again. It took several attempts for him to yank three logs to the surface. Each was about seven feet long, and one had spiked, hardened roots at its end. We created a kind of logjam between two upright logs, wide enough to support both of us.

"This should be better than sleeping in a tree," Fitz said.

Although the slimy logs had sharp points protruding at all angles from broken branches, it felt good to stretch out.

It wasn't long before the sky released torrential rain. We lay curled in fetal positions, shivering on the logs, just inches above the water, fully exposed. Rain poured under the small piece of plastic Fitz had pulled from his pocket and placed over our heads.

"It's trickling down my neck," I whimpered.

"Mine, too."

I turned my face upward to catch the rain in my mouth. It tasted so clean after the muddy canteen water we'd been drinking. My cold, wet jeans and shirt clung to me. Broken stubs of branches poked at me no matter which way I lay.

"Damn, this is beyond awful," Fitz moaned.

Unable even to groan, I squeezed his arm in response.

Our knees and shins hung like bait over the channel, so we had to change positions carefully. Moving an inch either way could topple us into the water.

As I peeked into the darkness from the plastic headdress, all I could think of was caimans.

How could I know for sure that they would stay dormant until the rainy season ended?

The rain lessened just enough for mosquitoes to swarm. They hovered over us with their high-pitched, taunting whine, looking for our most tender spots. I slapped at them, but it did no good. They stabbed us, even through our jeans, desperate, like us, for food.

Once they'd found us, the mosquitoes remained even when the rain kicked up again. They were bigger than the mosquitoes back home, and I decided that they would be the last to survive global annihilation. The pests would inherit the earth.

"Are you crying?" Fitz asked.

"Yes. Are you?"

"Yes."

Lightning struck the water so near us that we felt the roaring smack of thunder immediately after the flash. It struck again and again, turning the sky white. It seemed nothing alive could be more vulnerable than we were—two creatures huddling without shelter, Nature's force and utter indifference inflicting arbitrary cruelty. I felt like meat on a platter. How could we survive?

What the hell did we know about this jungle? People like us shouldn't be allowed on the river without a guide. Neither Juan nor the officials had thought we would need one. I wanted to blame them, but the fault was our own ignorance. Had I thought that we could treat the river like a ride at Disneyland?

I clung to the edge of a log with my fingernails, praying for the lightning and thunder to stop, praying that nothing would devour us. Brilliant white light struck water perhaps ten yards away, leaving an acrid odor. In that moment, the night was brighter than day. The thunder left me trembling. I curled up as tightly as I could and closed my eyes, hands over my ears. Lightning flashed outside my eyelids for what seemed like hours.

This was our most defenseless night yet. At least when we'd slept in the tree we were above the channel. Now we were at water level, there to be taken by any curious or hungry creature. If I could catch them I would eat them. Why shouldn't they eat me?

Eventually, the lightning and thunder moved off, leaving only a drizzle. I peeked out from the plastic. Two glints of light, like cat's eyes, stared at me from a few yards away. Were they moving closer? I stifled a scream.

I clutched Fitz's arm around me. He hadn't said anything in a while. Again, I peered into the darkness at the mysterious glints. Would rain keep animals from hunting? Probably not. They were the survivors. We were their prey.

"Fitz, are you sleeping?" I blurted out, unable to hold back any longer.

"Hell no."

I was relieved not to be alone with my thoughts.

"These damn mosquitoes!" Fitz groaned. "And all this balancing on logs—shit—I'm not a ballerina."

I smiled inwardly at his image. I tried to give him a gift in return. "If it's any consolation to you, I took ballet, and I don't think it's helping all that much."

"Humph."

"These mosquitoes are unbearable, but it's the caimans and the lightning that I'm most scared of," I said.

"I know. If it happens at least it'll be fast."

"I can't believe you're saying that."

"What can we do about it? We have to stop thinking about what we can't change."

He was right. We had to try to sleep with half an eye open. Just like the wild animals around us.

I don't think I slept at all.

FEBRUARY 26

Eighth day trapped

I was grateful when morning broke. It had been a worthless night. The channel was much wider here. Surely this meant we were closing in on the Madre? Between the width and the stronger current, I wondered if we had the strength to get out at all.

For breakfast, we drank a few ounces of filthy water after waiting for the iodine to temper the bacteria.

Fitz pulled out the last of our food, a half teaspoon each of sugar. "This is it," he said, shaking the final grains into my palm before his.

The pit of my stomach lurched. We'd been so disciplined over the past week to ration our meager food. The remaining grains of sugar offered only a few calories. They wouldn't save us. Momentary sweetness left us with nothing at all. It felt like a dark tunnel had opened beneath us and we were falling fast.

Fitz studied the empty plastic for stray grains. How could I not love a guy who would hand me the last of something when he wanted it so much himself? We both looked longingly at what wasn't there.

We had more than a hundred yards to swim to reach the next visible cluster of logs. The closest log in the group was a tall post, with another leaning against it at a forty-five-degree angle.

"Oh brother, this is going to be hard," I murmured while gazing at the small whitecaps flowing toward us.

"We can do it," Fitz replied.

"We're way beyond the tree we slept in," I added.

Fitz nodded. "It's going to be tough because we're closer to the Madre, but if we get lucky with the weather I think we'll reach it today."

I'd never feared the power of the weather before, but now I knew it could either help us to survive, or kill us. "We better get going." I pointed to the gray cumulous clouds rolling above our heads. "It could turn nasty."

We swam out together, each straddling a safety log. One hundred yards was a long way off. I sidestroked, then laid my stomach on the wood when I got tired, clinging clumsily to it with one arm while doing the breaststroke with my other. The log bucked out from under me. I grabbed it. I couldn't propel forward very quickly, though the frog kick did help.

Fitz followed behind, shortness of breath slowing him down. I turned often to track him. His head bobbed in and out of shadows on the channel. On land I was used to trying to keep up with his long, loping gait. Now I was the one ahead. Each stroke was a struggle for both of us.

We'd swum practically nonstop all day yesterday.

Fitz caught up as we neared an upside-down tree trunk with a branch forking off, like a children's slide, flattening out as it reached horizontally across the water. We could use it to take a break!

The current ran stronger around the trunk. We swam our hardest for the last ten yards, making no progress, gasping for breath. I thought of Becky's determination. It had worked yesterday.

I reached for the horizontal branch at the same time as Fitz. We heaved ourselves onto it, but the branch snapped and broke from the post. The crack was loud as I fell backward under the dark water. Clinging to my log, I flailed my free arm and clawed toward the light. I kicked hard against something, caught my foot for a second, then yanked it away and rose to the top. Shaking water from my eyes, I tried to get my bearings. The post was thirty yards away, now thirty-five. As I searched for Fitz I saw I'd lost perhaps one third of the distance we'd swum this morning.

I started to swim hard but couldn't move. I'd expended every ounce of physical and psychological fuel in me. The current beckoned like a siren: "Don't resist. Follow me."

Fitz saw that I needed help and started toward me. "Come on, come on, Hol. Don't give up!"

"No, don't," I screamed. "Keep going!"

He looked as if he wasn't sure.

"I'm coming." I did the sidestroke until my lungs burned, my mind fixed on a vision of Becky swimming ahead of me.

When I finally reached Fitz, we swam toward the reeds. Our fingers clutched at the tall stalks, but they tore off in our hands.

Quickmud

Our logs were like sails dragging us back downriver. I searched frantically for something to grab and hold. Please don't let us lose all we've gained, I prayed, not daring to think of the Pink Palace. I never wanted to see her again.

Flailing the water with one arm and kicking my legs, I reached for another clump of grasses.

This time the blades of grass didn't break. I hung on, panting, as Fitz swam up behind me, his contorted face reflecting how I felt inside.

Waves splashed into my mouth. "We've got to find somewhere . . ." I coughed, spitting out water. "I don't know how much longer I can hold on."

Fitz took one hand off the grasses to wrap around my shoulder, but he was immediately yanked by the current.

"Please, both hands!" I cried. Craning my neck, I pointed to thick brush along the tree line. "There must be a branch we can rest on over there."

Fitz was breathing hard. He could barely nod.

"If we could just find a gap in that brush," I gasped, "there might be calmer water on the other side." We scanned for an opening.

"Is that a space?" Fitz stared toward a dark area in the midst of the trees.

"Yes! Come on."

As we swam through the gap, dense brush gave way to open space with ropes of lianas hanging over our heads from the high canopy. Shafts of light illuminated patches of the water's surface, where shifting shadows moved between the tree trunks spaced a few feet apart. Silence reigned but for a bird cry once in a while. A strange, awesome beauty countered my rising trepidation.

Branches shook above me, sending fronds spinning into the water. I swam cautiously as thick muck swirled around my legs. Something was bumping me, brushing against my skin. Fear fluttered in my chest. Probably just weeds, I thought. Don't panic. Fitz was right next to me.

"It's creepy in here," I whispered. "The water's so black I can't see a thing. At least it's a rest from that current."

We lay on our half-submerged logs, barely having to push ourselves forward. The swimming became easier the deeper in we went. My breath steadied. Fitz was breathing more easily, too.

Our safety logs buoyed us past tall trees, their trunks resembling smooth columns. None of them offered low limbs for us to rest on, but we could float here for a while. All we wanted was to pull ourselves out of the water. I finally spotted a tree ahead with a fat, low branch.

"Fitz, look!" My voice practically danced as I swam toward it, anticipating the relief of its support.

I was within a few feet of the tree when mud, the consistency of clay, enveloped my left calf. I was unable to see below the black surface, but I felt the slime reaching higher up my leg. I kicked hard, frantic to free it, but my leg sank deeper, taking my thigh and hip with it. The mud was like molasses. I stopped kicking, recalling how every move I'd made in the Connecticut bog had taken me farther under until only my head was visible. I felt like a fly stuck to flypaper. How could I get out this time? If Fitz got close enough to throw me his rope belt, he'd be trapped, too. I had to keep my arms and right leg from touching the dense sediment. If I could just ride high on the water, I might stop sinking.

Fitz was twenty feet behind me.

"Don't come any closer," I warned. "It's sucking me down."

"What is?" he yelled, speeding up his pace.

"Mud . . . like quicksand. I can't get out!"

"I'm coming!" Fitz started toward me.

"No, don't! We'll both be sucked under."

Fitz's legs were so long he'd be caught in the bog before he even got near me. He knew about my experience in the Connecticut bog. Shock flooded his eyes.

"Stay back," I said firmly. "I can do it."

My throat was so dry I could hardly swallow. The mud was like an underwater creature, its mouth clamped to my leg. I squirmed a little and it devoured my hip, then my waist. It was hard to lie still, even with the safety log, but now I worried that it, too, would sink. I glanced up at the lianas. Too high to grasp. Realizing that only one leg and part of my left side was trapped, I wondered if I could slowly frog kick my right leg and breaststroke my right arm while carrying my log with my left arm. I'd have to keep them close to the surface so they wouldn't get engulfed in the mud, too. If I then turned slowly around toward Fitz, I might be able to maneuver my left leg and hip free.

Concentrating on twisting my torso toward him, I fought

the instinct to kick my trapped leg. Hugging my log, I made wide strokes with my right arm, frog kicking near the surface with my right leg. At first I seemed to be splashing in place, but my left leg loosened a little. I powered ahead then felt my hip and thigh burst away from the mud. I threw myself forward, and my stomach skidded above the mud as my leg came free.

"I'm out!" I heaved a sigh.

Fitz's face relaxed a little. "Thank God."

We both swam toward the patches of light that pointed our way back to the channel.

It took us a while to find a hole in the tangle of trees where the sun was peeking into the darkness. Through it we stared at the sweeping channel before us. Wind kicked up small whitecaps. I'd been desperate to get out of the quickmud, but did I have the stamina to swim against the current again? The water inside the tree line was calm, like a cradle.

"Can we rest until the wind dies down?" I panted.

"We can't just stay here, clinging to these logs. We're vulnerable. We need to keep going."

"The current looks worse than before we came in here."

"But we're rested now. We couldn't even talk before," Fitz urged.

"I'm not that rested. I can hardly move!" I could feel my face flushing.

I looked at Fitz and he looked at me. "You're right. That mud was terrifying." He looked away. His fingers were shriveled from being so long in the water. "Listen," he said, looking squarely at me again, "we can rest in here as much as you need."

I swallowed hard. "It's just I know it's going to be worse out there. I wish we were salmon!"

The twitch of a smile crossed Fitz's lean face. He reached out and pushed a strand of wet hair off my cheek. "You always say the river could be right around the bend. The stronger current means we must be getting close."

Our legs splayed out behind us, but I could still feel muck just below my stomach. I wanted to tell him that we were going to have a whole life ahead of us. Instead, I touched his shoulder and whispered: "I'll try."

Fitz started out first. I took a deep breath then followed. My left arm around the log, I stroked with my right. Low waves slapped my face, as if displeased by my audacity. The merciless current pushed against me. No food, no sleep, no energy, nothing but wishing kept me afloat.

I needed my dad's tenacity now. As a boy he'd fought polio, then in his thirties contracted tuberculosis in North Africa during World War II. He'd spent his first eight years of marriage, and seven years of my childhood, in and out of hospitals. Knocked down but never out, he'd kept going. So had my mother, always by his side. I kept swimming. Survival, I realized, isn't a choice; it's instinct.

Chapter 25

Rant

The churning channel was at least a quarter-mile wide, so we tried to keep to the side of the current to avoid spinning backward. As it was, we could barely advance. Where trees and bushes disappeared behind large reeds, we had no choice but to swim along the grasses, some of which were so sharp we couldn't cling to them.

The wind kicked small waves against my face; an undercurrent yanked me backward. Fear of quickmud kept us from venturing into the reeds or trees to rest. I thought of Becky. She would have continued swimming until her heart gave out.

Fitz was slightly behind me now, breathing so hard I thought he might pass out. There was still no land, nor logs. I noticed the veins of leaves, every limb shaking in the wind, and heard every sound from some unknown bird, but I couldn't make headway, no matter how hard I stroked. The distance between my nose and the choppy water at my lips was the distance between life and death. I glanced back at Fitz. He was fifteen feet behind, unable to keep up.

A veil of weeping leaves hung low into the waves up

ahead with something pale gray beyond. "Logjam!" I blurted to Fitz.

Reaching the logs, I pulled myself up as Fitz panted forward.

He grabbed my hand. "This is murder," he coughed as he climbed the logs, his ribs protruding through his wet shirt.

I leaned over, trying to catch my breath.

"It's . . . crazy." He was wheezing now as he sat down. Algae and mud coated his arms, shirt, jeans, and feet. He stared at the channel for a few minutes but didn't seem to see it.

Then, amazingly, as his breath became steady he thrust his head back, body taut. "How dare you!" he yelled up to the sky, shaking his fist at the clouds. "We haven't done anything to you! What the hell are you doing?"

My mouth fell open. I imagined a bolt of lightning slashing through the sky. God would pulverize us.

"We can't do this anymore," Fitz raged. "The river isn't around the bend, is it? Damn you! Damn you!" he cried, eyes flashing.

He was losing all control. I put my hand on his arm. "Fitz, honey . . ."

But he didn't hear me. He was like a train without brakes. "What are you out to prove? You've made your point. You could help us if you wanted to!" His face became flame red. "Why won't you help us? What have we ever done to you? We're good people. What is it you want? Jesus Christ!"

"Baby . . . darling." I shook his arm.

Fitz turned to me, his eyes brimming tears. "We can't stay in this current. It's too strong. We can't go under the brush because of the quickmud. What are we supposed to do, Hol?"

Before I could say anything, he glared up at the sky again.

"You tell us what you want!" he yelled. "Why did I make it through 'Nam, wounded twice? Why didn't that shell explode in my foxhole on Thanksgiving? Why did I survive the coma with spinal meningitis? I was out for three days. They gave me the last rites! What was the point of it all?"

"Fitz, Fitz . . . please." I rubbed his arm, trying to get his attention. The wind flattened my hair across my cheek and tore at his curls.

Defeat settled in Fitz's eyes. "Everyone told us it was safe to go down this damn river. They knew we had no experience. What is the *meaning* of going through everything if we're just going to die now? Why didn't God let me die before?" Tears spilled onto his face.

It frightened me to see him so distraught.

Fitz dropped his head into his hands and began to sob. "What's the matter with him? He could get us out of here. Why is he punishing us?"

I moved closer and put my arms around Fitz. His body gave in to me as his rage subsided.

"We'll be okay, Fitz. Really, we'll be okay."

I wasn't sure that we would be, but I was afraid, aware that one of us needed to stay strong.

Fitz was shivering all over. "We can't do this anymore. We have to go back." He was silent for a few moments then he raised his head. "We'll find food near the raft. We know there are fish because we've seen them jumping."

I was relieved to hear his confidence, but I didn't want to turn back. Is this really God's plan after all our struggles? The current was so angry now that the waves were breaking over each other. I felt sure we had to be close to the river, that if we kept trying we'd make it out.

My husband was at his breaking point. So this was it. We were giving up. I couldn't believe we'd swum so far just to go back now. Hot tears cascaded down my cheeks as I wept for all the hours we'd spent trying, only to see our hopes shattered once again.

"You're right," I said. "We need to focus on finding food." I nudged Fitz to look at me. "Let's go. Floating back will be easy."

Slipping off the logjam into the current, I let my body float with one arm over my log, my eyes fixed on Fitz close beside me. I didn't cry anymore. I just wanted him to be all right.

Within fifteen minutes we could see the pink-and-blue plastic tent awaiting our return.

Back on the Pink Palace we fell onto the tent floor.

"We tried everything," I said, trying to console myself as much as Fitz. "We had no choice but to turn back."

Fitz smoothed my tangled hair. "I've always admired you more than anyone I've ever known. Now I admire you even more."

Those were the most precious words I'd ever heard. I realized that we finally had to let go of the dream to reach the river.

Fitz and I talked quietly into the evening, setting our sights on new goals of catching fish, looking for planes, and making a kite with a message on it. Darkness wrapped herself around us as the jungle resumed its incessant nighttime noise. We would wait until tomorrow to get started on our new plans. We curled into balls beneath the mosquito netting. Despite the haunting fear that this was it for us, my heart clung to the possibility that we might still get out alive.

Chapter 26

Desire

FEBRUARY 27

Nine days trapped in the swamp, yet I awoke happy to be alive, inspired by our plans for finding food. I wrote a line in my budget notebook, now serving as a personal journal, "We have found in each other and perhaps in ourselves more strength, courage, and faith than we realized was there—and a great desire to live."

Fitz and I watched the sun glide up the plastic siding as we talked of our new focus. We would take the little raft along the small area of trees and logs in our bay of the swamp and find something to use for bait. Algae didn't work. There must be something big enough to stay on the hook, a snail or grub perhaps, anything that a fish would bite. Despite conversing, we lay listless. I had to force myself even to sip water.

The tent soon turned into a sauna. Pulling myself up, I suggested coffee to get us going.

"Make it iced coffee."

Fitz rubbed my shoulder tenderly, which made my skin tingle. His fingers attempted to smooth the snarled hair that fell down my naked back. I couldn't resist. I lay down with my head in the crook of Fitz's thinning neck, his collarbone digging into my cheek. We were both sticky, but I didn't care. The smell of Fitz's sweat was an aphrodisiac that made me want to linger for just a little longer. This languid mind-set was seducing us into not moving at all.

"Come on, Fitz, we've got to get up. I'd much rather lie here with you, but a fish isn't going to jump into our laps." I pushed myself onto my haunches. "We have to get out there." Kissing him I reached for my shirt and jeans.

Fitz boiled the water. After we'd drunk the bitter, twiggy brew, we climbed onto the small raft and set out to search for anything edible. Paddling through the swamp, we studied the two-foot-high, half-inch-wide yellow and chartreuse grasses for bugs, ants, snails, or anything that might be nestled along their spines.

"I wonder if we can eat any of these leaves?" I asked, my stomach driving hammers into my core. "Do you think they have any nutrition?"

"Hol, let's focus on the bait. If we get a fish, we'll be all set. We don't know anything about these plants. They could be poisonous." Fitz waved his hand over his head to brush away mosquitoes. They were especially bad today since there was no breeze. "Damn these things and damn this jungle!"

My mouth opened and shut, chewing nothing as we searched the hundreds of lily pads surrounding the raft. "You're right about not eating the plants. But there must be frogs or something we can use for bait around here," I said.

We stared at bark on the trees that reached up through the water, hoping to find a lizard or a sleeping bat lolling in the dappled shade of the feathery, fernlike leaves.

"A fish might eat a bat," I whispered, trying to say it

quietly so as not to disturb anything catchable. "It would be chunky on the line."

"Ugh," Fitz grimaced. "If we're lucky enough to get one, we'll try it."

Everything was deathly still. I squinted into the shadows at the trunk of a tree, looking for the slightest movement.

"What about a bird?" Fitz peered into a hole in a long log in the water then shoved his paddle handle into it.

"What if something aggressive jumps out?" I held my paddle defensively although it would be useless against anything big.

"Nothing there." Fitz shook his head, sweat rolling down his cheeks.

"How would we catch a bird?" I asked, hoisting up my jeans, which were loose around my hips. When we're back at the Pink Palace I'll tie my purple sash through the jean loops, I thought. "Maybe there's a nest of eggs," I continued, lifting a low branch. "I'd feel bad, but we need to eat."

I'd always been excited to find a nest of eggs, or baby birds, but hunger was twisting my thoughts beyond the beauty of nature. The thought of food was haunting me.

"I'd feel bad, too," Fitz sighed, shaking his head. The neck hole of his shirt fell over his right shoulder, and shadows now filled the inlets in his cheeks.

We kept watch in silence, but my mind raced with possibilities. What if we saw a snake swimming by us? How would we know if it was edible? In my hunger, my mind jumped from thinking about a snake as bait to eating it. What if we found berries, or frogs, or grasshoppers, or dragonflies? We had no idea which ones were poisonous. I remembered from *National Geographic* that dangerous things often had bright colors.

I was startled by a green frog. "Look, Fitz!"

It stared at us from a log. He was just like the frog I'd seen the first morning here, when I wasn't thinking of food but enjoying the virgin jungle kingdom. I reached for it, but it was gone in an instant, leaving swirling circles on the swamp's surface. "Oh, gosh! He could have been lunch."

"We're not going to catch a frog that easily. At least you spotted something big enough to eat." Fitz smiled at me. "If there's one frog out there, then there's got to be more."

We hardly made a sound as we paddled among the skillet-sized lily pads, broken branches, and downed dead trees. Soft gulps and glugs came from the swamp every now and then, while mosquitoes and other bugs hummed through the air. I heard scampering over lily pads, but when I turned to look all I could see were quivering lily pads.

Fitz finally spotted a gelatinous-looking glistening thing attached to a log. It looked slimy, like a slug. He pulled it off the log and plopped it into a tin can. "It'll make good bait." He was almost jubilant.

We called it a slug although it squirmed like a worm.

"We'll catch a fish!" I grinned.

The sun was casting shadows across the water. "We better hurry back and try it on the hook," Fitz said, his face pinched as he saw the day was ending with only one small slug in the can and no dinner yet.

While we paddled back to the Pink Palace, louder sounds erupted from the jungle creatures that were preparing for night. Rustling, chirping, and cackling ascended into the trees as animals and birds sought their places. A croaking chorus emerged from the grasses. Soon the demonic howl began. With our legs and hips submerged in the water, we were even more vulnerable on the little raft than on the Pink Palace.

"It's so menacing," I stuttered.

"Let's hurry. It started early today," Fitz said, urgency in his voice.

There was nowhere to hide from the ghostly sound. We paddled fast, bumping into logs, catching on underwater plants. My heart thumped against my chest so hard I thought it would jump out of my body. When we clambered onto the Pink Palace, Fitz was still determined to catch a fish. Despite the heinous roar that ended in a growl, he picked up the fish line and tried to steady it in his trembling hand. He struggled to push the squirming grub onto the end of the large hook that was hanging off the fish line, which he'd attached to a stick. When the point went through its soft flesh, the grub curled into a ball. Fitz flicked the line out a few feet. A fish splashed but didn't nibble.

After a few minutes, he pulled in the line to discover the bait had fallen off. The hook was just too big. With only a half hour before nightfall, our stomachs hollow, we became desperate to find more bait. We made ourselves get back on the little raft. Fitz undid the rope and we paddled out, hearts hammering. The source of the roar hadn't revealed itself in all the time we'd been here.

On this search we found a few minuscule, wriggling, wormlike things lying on a log. The frightening sound petered out, as if it were creeping back into the earth. We quietly returned to the Pink Palace.

Fitz pushed the tiny worms onto the hook, but they disappeared without a fish even tugging at the line. I sat gazing at the empty hook. After a whole afternoon of work, we had not even a morsel to eat.

A honking noise reverberated above me as a fat, goose-like bird flew into the trees. Dusk teased us with so many birds. Longing was in my belly as I watched them skimming across the swamp, playful, oblivious to us.

"Damn. I wish the hell I'd bought a gun," Fitz yelled. "I could have shot that bird with my eyes closed."

Marksmanship and jump school were the only army classes Fitz hadn't slept through. He'd shot "expert" with each type of rifle. In Vietnam he would sleep with his boots on, rifle strap wrapped around one arm, ready to respond to any sudden noise. He'd fought in a unit whose soldiers were dropped by helicopter into enemy zones. On Thanksgiving Day, 1968, an artillery round had ripped open Fitz's shoulder before landing at his feet in a foxhole. The shell, which would have vaporized him, failed to explode. Three months later he was hit by shrapnel while on patrol, just seriously enough to be evacuated for stitches and a couple days of rest. After that, Fitz had a reputation among his buddies for being lucky. His best friend, a Cuban named Sugar Suarez, would stay as close to Fitz as possible, sometimes rubbing his curls for luck.

Fitz had been in enough firefights, lost enough friends, to drain all the glory from war.

Even as he was about to board "the freedom bird" to return home, the enemy had begun shelling the airstrip. He'd spent his last moments in Vietnam huddled inside a sandbag bunker with mortars exploding around him. When he'd scrambled onto the plane he'd prayed it wouldn't be blown from the sky.

Fitz made it home, but Vietnam never really left him.

"Once you've spent time in the field, you never get out," he would explain. "You're in the field forever."

I watched another large bird fly overhead. I could almost taste it. My mother had roasted a goose for Easter when I was twelve. It was so plump it had taken two of us to plop it into the pan. Over the next few hours, Mom had siphoned off a quart of fat, and still it kept rising up the sides of the pan. "Never again," she'd said about cooking a goose. But in the end, when Dad brought it to the table on a gleaming silver platter, the goose was a masterpiece: perfectly golden brown, moist and tender, its cavity stuffed with apples and onions.

Wistfully, I watched the swamp birds. If we could only catch one, I'd sear off its feathers then rip and gnaw every last piece of meat and gristle off its bones. This jungle must be full of food. We just had to find a way to get it.

Chapter 27

Butterflies

MARCH 1

Eleventh day trapped

Fitz was sitting on the stern of the Pink Palace when a butterfly landed on his shin. How pretty, I thought, mesmerized by its violet wings that opened and closed as it rested. Fitz instantly pressed his hand over it, hard.

"Oh!" I gasped.

When he opened his hand, the butterfly lay still, its wings crumpled. Fitz picked up the hook and poked it through the small green body. "Let's hope this works."

Two more butterflies flew in. One settled on my arm. I waited a few seconds before I brought my hand down, cupping it over the butterfly. I felt the wings flutter against my palm before I squashed it.

A dozen butterflies landed on the raft. Beautiful, iridescent in the sun. We killed them all.

Fitz fished all morning off the little raft using butterflies for bait. He was hunched over, sagging beneath the burning sun.

"Please come in, Fitz. It's too hot."

But he stayed out there, my hat on his head, his eyes boring into the murky water, as if he were willing a fish to bite. When no bait remained, he slowly paddled in and tied up to the Pink Palace. "The butterflies just disintegrate or get nibbled away," he complained. "I can't see what's happening in the water. I wish we had something bigger for the hook."

I reached for his arm to help steady him as he climbed onto the raft. "If it were bigger we'd eat it!" I tried to be light but I meant it. I thought of the green frog I'd seen yesterday. "Look, I found a slug on one of the logs."

It was only the size of a finger knuckle, curved like a fat quarter moon. Sticky to the touch. A grub, a slug? It could be poison or protein. The thought of putting it in my mouth was sickening, but I hoped a fish would want it.

Fitz dropped it into my small aluminum pot. "It's something, and we've got the afternoon to find more."

It was midday. The sun seemed to focus all its rays on us. Black dots swirled in front of me. "I feel woozy." I took a swig of water then grabbed Fitz's arm for balance. "We're crazy to be out here at this time of day. We can search for bait when it cools down a little."

We shuffled along the logs, reaching for anything to hold on to. The humidity was extremely high, so it felt like we were walking in water. My feet stuck to the logs, my hair to my head, and my clothes to my skin. I tried to inhale but I could barely breathe. I wondered if my eighty-nine-year-old grandmother had felt so weak before she died.

As we took off our clothes inside the tent, I discovered that I didn't need to unzip my bell-bottom jeans. They dropped right off me. Fitz's jeans fell off his hips, too. We uncurled our stiff bodies onto the reddish-purple sleeping bag, grateful for the trees swaying in the heavy heat and casting shadows over the plastic tent.

"When we get home we'll have a separate room for a delicatessen off the kitchen," Fitz announced, wrapping his arm around me. "We'll have fresh turkey, beef, and ham behind a glass counter, and I'll slice it on one of those machines they have at the store. We'll stock every kind of bread you can think of: rye; pumpernickel; the croissants you love, fresh baked, so we'll have that wonderful smell all through the house every morning. If we don't have time to bake ourselves, we'll have someone come in and do it."

Fitz had dreamt up his deli in Vietnam, where he'd subsisted on C-rations. He'd told me how cases of canned goods, some in storage for years, had been dropped by helicopter to clearings cut in the jungle by soldiers using machetes.

"Cold scrambled eggs and ham in a can," Fitz said. "Oh, how I'd welcome you now."

I turned toward him. "Tell me again how you traded those cans of eggs with the other soldiers to get the canned peaches in heavy syrup, or the canned pound cake."

"If I had to, to close the deal, I'd even throw in the cigarettes the government sent with the food." He grinned, going on to explain that he would hoard Chuckles or chocolate Tropical Bars to give to the village children, but also to feed his own sweet tooth.

A smile of ecstasy crossed his face as one hand squeezed my shoulder, his other arm now resting under his head on a lumpy mound of clothes we used for a pillow.

"I can taste the bread, all soft and squishy." I smiled. "So hot it melts the butter. The croissants will be light and flaky, with almond slivers all over them." I rubbed my stomach, trying to override its queasy, gnawing ache as my mouth began to water. "While you're in the deli, can you grab me half a pound of cheddar? I'd like to make a fat grilled-cheese-and-onion sandwich."

Our food fantasies soothed us, offering us a lifeline to hope as we lay in the blistering heat of the plastic tent. Fitz talked of the mustards and relishes he'd serve, hot with garlic and onion or sweet with honey and dill. "Don't forget pepper for the New York hard rolls, soft in the center, with real butter, not margarine, of course."

I closed my eyes and imagined them.

"You won't have to go out, Hol. We'll have it all right there in the house."

"Mmm." I shifted position on the hard boards. It was such an effort to move our bodies at all now. "I like that idea of the food coming to us."

Hours passed as we languished in the tent, detailing meals we loved, ones we'd be sure to serve once we got home.

"How 'bout that chateaubriand we had for our anniversary in Cuzco, Peru? It was so rich it made us sick, but boy was it good!" I could feel the smile growing on my face. "I'll broil a big one just like it."

We discussed a litany of our favorite foods: asparagus, rare roast beef and Yorkshire pudding at Christmas, roast leg of lamb with mint jelly at Easter, ice cream with chocolate sauce, blue cheese on a crisp salad, avocado, charcoal-broiled burgers with tomato and onions. We relished our memories of food.

Fitz touched my hand. "Remember the onion soup at the elegant French restaurant in Montreal?"

I licked my sunburned lips. "With that crouton baked across the bubbly cheese on top. There were so many onions the spoon stood straight up!"

It had tasted so good that we couldn't wait to replicate

it when we drove back to Eagle Lake. Without a recipe or herbs, we had exuberantly thrown a dozen braised onions into a big pot of water and boiled them. The soup had turned out so watery we threw it out.

Fitz looked regretful. "If I had that onion dishwater now I'd drink every drop."

I touched his cheek. "Oh, Fitz, we're going to get home, and when we do, let's go to Montreal and find that restaurant. I know they'll give us the recipe. It'll be the best soup we ever had."

The tree shadows playing on the tent wall fell across Fitz's face.

"Onions are good luck for us." I massaged his neck and shoulders, trying to bring him back. "Don't forget . . . your bag of onions brought us together."

He smiled.

"For better or for worse," I added.

Fitz's smile broadened as he struggled up on one elbow to kiss me. He moved his other arm across my bare breasts. Our ribs were so pronounced that it hurt when we touched. I tried to hide a flinch, reaching my hand up to his whiskers, his sunken cheek. His eyes were still sky blue, hidden under bushy eyebrows, but they didn't sparkle anymore.

Drifting in and out of sleep all afternoon, we always woke hungry.

"It's still brutally hot out there." Fitz peered through the tent door. "We'll have to wait a little longer before we can look for more slugs."

He ducked his head back into the tent and shifted his weight toward me. Patting my head, he asked, "Do you want to hear the story of Skeeter and the mashed potatoes?"

"Sure." I nodded. I knew all about Skeeter Johnston, Fitz's buddy from Vietnam, but I could hear the story again. I laid my head on a cushion of clothes in the crook of Fitz's bony arm.

"Okay, so when we were on patrol, we'd get a hot meal flown out by helicopter from Tay Ninh, once every ten days or so."

"How did the food stay hot?" I asked, already knowing the answer.

It came in large thermos containers, Fitz explained, two feet high and three feet long, with lids that snapped down tightly enough to keep the meals steaming hot. It was rare to find a spot clear enough for the helicopter actually to land, so they'd use Charlie-4 to blow down trees to make room for the helicopter to hover, stump high. The bird would get as low as it could, and then the guys on board would pass down the heavy containers to Fitz and the others below. The men would line up the canisters, and then one soldier at each canister would sit on his helmet to ladle out portions to the passing chow line.

Fitz described in detail how the soldiers' thin olive fatigues tore easily, and no one carried a change of clothes, other than extra socks. Guys wore the same ones for weeks.

"You wore the one pair of dark green underwear until it grew stiff." He grinned. "Then you went without."

Similar to us, I thought, noticing the humming mosquitoes gathering outside our *mosquitero*, trying to get in.

"Donald 'Skeeter' Johnston was a bucktoothed Georgia country boy who had ladle duty in the middle of the chow line one afternoon. When the soldiers reached him they began laughing hysterically."

I was laughing, too, because I knew the punch line.

"So Skeeter looks down and realizes his pants are torn so badly at the crotch that his privates are dangling over the mashed potatoes!"

This was the first time I'd laughed in days.

"He saved my life," Fitz continued, his voice shaking a little. "I was supposed to take five days' leave to Sydney, Australia, but a new guy with more seniority came in the night before and bumped me off the list."

Fitz told his top sergeant that he would wait another month in the field for the next Sydney slot. But that night, Fitz and Skeeter shared a foxhole. Skeeter was just back from R & R in Singapore, and he kept whispering to Fitz about how great it was. Kneeling in the bottom of the foxhole, by the glow of a cupped cigarette, Skeeter showed Fitz a Polaroid shot of him and the girl he'd met there.

"You gotta take R & R in the morning, man, you're all pumped up for it. Forget Sydney, go to Singapore. I'll give you her phone number."

Skeeter had talked him into changing his mind. Fitz left for Singapore the next morning. A day or so later, Company D had headed into LZ White, a forward base, to take a short break from patrol. On March 21, 1969, LZ White was overrun. Skeeter and others were fighting from within a sandbag bunker when an NVA soldier tossed a satchel charge inside.

Fitz's eyes watered. "Skeeter threw himself onto the explosive, pulling it under his belly. He gave his life for his buddies."

That night more than twenty soldiers in Company D were wounded, along with others from a second company, and at least six Americans were killed. Fitz was not among them because Skeeter had talked him into forgoing Sydney for Singapore.

Donald "Skeeter" Johnston received the Medal of Honor posthumously for saving six American lives.

"That bucktoothed country kid was a real hero," Fitz concluded.

"It brings tears to my eyes every time you tell it, Fitz. He was so young and brave." Fitz's face was brooding. I kissed his cheek and told him he kept Skeeter's memory alive by talking about him. "How 'bout something funny? It's still too hot to go out."

He smiled, ready. "Once I was on KP duty, stateside. I had to do whatever the mess sergeant demanded.

"So he tells me that Supply is coming to determine how many fresh eggs the mess hall would get. Every box of powdered eggs had to be used up before more fresh eggs would be delivered. So the sergeant told me to dump all the powdered eggs and hose them down the drain before the supply man arrived. Of course, I tried to suggest that there might be a better way. He told me to do what I was told and to do it fast."

I grinned, encouraging him to continue over the noise of the ravenous mosquitoes outside the netting.

"The drain area behind the mess hall was a square of cement about six feet by six feet," he continued. "It slanted down to a round metal drain cap with slits. I'd opened each of several large boxes of powdered eggs and poured all of them into the drain, making a mound of yellow powder more than a foot high." Fitz's hands sculpted the air to show the size of the mound.

"I began to hose the powder, just as the sergeant had ordered, but the more water I used, the bigger the mound got. You should've seen it morph into a shimmering, slimy yellow mass, like something out of a horror movie . . . just as the supply sergeant came around the corner."

Fitz chuckled as he slowly sat up in the tent, recalling the mess sergeant's screams and the supply guy's anger at the waste of food. He wondered if I'd ever tried to shovel a mountain of slippery scrambled eggs into garbage cans.

"Can't say I have," I replied.

We heard a large splash outside the tent. Excited, Fitz looked out. "I don't see anything."

My stomach lurched at the possibility of food. "I suppose it is time to go out. It feels less muggy."

Fitz said that it must be about three o'clock, that we had a couple of hours to find dinner.

Once again we had to face the swamp. "I'd give anything for a shovelful of those cold eggs," Fitz stammered as we struggled over the raft logs, tipping sideways then catching each other. Moving at all was increasingly difficult. Talking, unless we lay still, was labored, slow and breathy.

I reached for his hand so he could help me onto the little balsa. As I settled in the bow I twisted around to smile at him. Even with his tan and the golden hue of the late afternoon sun, his face looked much thinner than it had just a few days ago.

We were quiet and focused. Every movement took effort and concentration. We heard a few splashes and saw ripples in the swamp. By dusk we still had no food.

Chapter 28

Little Moments

MARCH 2

Twelfth day trapped

Fitz fished off the raft while I paddled through the swamp searching for a grasshopper or a slug for bait. I couldn't stop thinking about the open-faced sandwiches I'd enjoyed in Copenhagen, and of small shrimp prettily placed on salad greens. During my college term in Denmark, my host family had served a breakfast of thin wafers of chocolate on crusty bread. At night, we students ate *fricadillars*, pork-and-herb meatballs served on forks, washed down with Corona beer. Right now any food at all would be paradise.

I thought of Machu Picchu. Fitz and I had hiked all morning to reach its summit. When we arrived at the top, we found many other tourists and their drivers had flooded the ancient stone buildings and courtyards that clung to a ridge far above the Urubamba River. After everyone else left, we lingered to absorb the silent majesty of the peak and its ruins, admired the misty, forested ravines and mountain range that ebbed and flowed in waves to the horizon. Birds flew below us while llamas grazed, unimpressed by the view. We ate cheese and bread and watched the sunset then walked hand in hand by moonlight down the twisting road, just starting to notice our hunger. When we reached the base, we learned the last train had left. An Indian woman invited us into her small house with its dirt floor and kerosene lamps. Chickens, ducks, and guinea pigs scuttled amongst the furniture. She sat us down to a meal of spaghetti topped with canned sardines. The aroma of oil and herbs still swirled in my nostrils. The next course she served was a guinea pig, halved and proudly displayed on plates adorned with greens. Fitz got the worst of it, though it was probably an honor: the head, front legs, and torso. Its face was looking right at him, as if pleading. I received the rump.

Something moved in the swamp: green on green, a small frog on a lily pad ten feet away.

Oh, please, let me get you, I thought, staring at him. Neither of us moved. How could I catch him without a net? I quietly steered the little lopsided raft a few feet toward him then sat like stone as I drifted in his direction. I was within four feet when the gentle current turned the raft. I would have to be right over the frog to grab him. My paddle was in the water already, so I cautiously moved my arms back to steer a little closer. Two feet is all I need. Please!

The frog jumped away before I could reach him.

After my morning hunt I returned empty-handed. Fitz had done no better. At high noon we lay in the tent, the heat burning into the plastic, our mouths drooling as food memories flooded us again.

"Fitz, I can't think of food anymore," I finally said. "It's too painful." I didn't care about fancy meals now. "Why can't we just catch a fish?" I touched his cheek, alarmed to see his skin collapsing at his neck and around his collarbone. "We've got to get up and try again. Come on, let's get on the little balsa and find some bait."

He grunted, getting up slowly.

I wobbled out of the tent onto the deck, aiming for our small raft. Before we'd become trapped, I'd felt lithe as an acrobat, curving my feet around the Pink Palace's logs. Now I stumbled across them, almost too weak to walk. I got down on all fours and crawled toward the little balsa like a baby learning to move. Fitz did the same.

When we reached the small raft we sat cross-legged, paddling slowly along the tree line, within a short radius of the Pink Palace. I scanned the two-foot-wide lily pads, the bark of trees, and the leaves of bushes. Unseen life, like lost keys, must be right in front of us. We focused on one small area at a time, scrutinizing browns, greens, and yellows for nuances that might hide a bat, an insect, a grasshopper, a lizard.

Fitz found a one-inch squishy grub tucked into a log. On top of another log he found a clump of minuscule worms— maybe an eighth of an inch long—too small for the bait hook. I watched them wiggle. With no soil, they seemed to exist on air.

"Where do they come from?"

Fitz shook his head. "No idea. It's kind of eerie."

We picked them up and plopped them in the can.

"Fitz! Berries!" My heart leapt at the sight of a few smooth, purple-green berries in the undergrowth. I plucked all six from a branch and held them out in my cupped hand. It was barely a mouthful, but I could imagine their sweetness rolling around my tongue. But would they be sweet? Were they poisonous? They felt hard and looked like unripe blueberries, but their bush had wider leaves than blueberry bushes back home, and their skin had a sheen to it. "Almost like blueberries" wasn't blueberries for certain. Although ravenous, we were still cautious. Was it worth taking a chance for just a few berries?

I dropped the berries into a second can to leave on the Pink Palace deck. "A bird might see them and land on the raft," I said, smiling.

"Then we can grab it!" Fitz's eyes welled up. "I don't even care if we cook it. I'll just eat it raw."

"Me too."

We fell silent again as we paddled.

It hadn't occurred to either of us to eat weird grubs or squirmy worms. They were so unappealing to the touch and we assumed they'd be poisonous. We thought of them only as bait to catch something bigger to eat. I'd been drilled to be cautious of berries as a child, but nothing was ever said about not eating worms.

I looked around at this strange and beautiful swamp, not knowing where to turn except to Fitz, and I thought of God. I felt his presence in the breeze, in the silence, in short, shrill bird calls, a fish splashing, and the crack of a rotten branch. I felt he held all things in his arms, connecting us and our world into one large circle.

We'd started to pray out loud together, so now we asked God's advice about eating the berries. Deciding whether to eat them was a dangerous crapshoot. I heard God's voice in our words as we talked out our decision, and I felt his love giving me strength. As I struggled for life, turning to a power bigger than me was as natural as breathing. I treated God as my therapist. What would he do with these berries?

A client often carries the therapist in his mind away from a session into daily life, using the therapist as a model, an aid to decision making. That was me with God.

My parents didn't attend church. They would drop us at Sunday school then go home to work in the garden. Nature is where I felt most connected to God. This jungle was raw, unyielding nature. Feeling God all around us did nothing to alleviate my hunger. Fitz attended a parochial school, so he breathed religious ritual more than I did. He knew more prayers, too.

He would pull them out when we were desperate, and I, for the first time, saw how comforting that could be.

We had gone to church for Christmas Eve service in La Paz, where animals were brought down the aisle to be blessed. That was the closest I'd ever felt to God inside a building. It wasn't because of the icons and gold figures of saints, the crucifix and the stained-glass windows. Beautiful, yes, but they were art. It was the barefoot Indians in handwoven shawls carrying babies on their backs; it was the chickens, the goats, the dogs and hens that made me feel God's presence.

We returned to the Palace after several hours of searching beneath the draining sun, with only the six berries, one grub, and a half-inch ball of tiny worms. One thought pressed against me like a concrete slab: if we can't catch a fish, God must want us to die. Even though I'd felt so sure he would help us. He must have some other plan, I decided. There are fish here. I just saw one jump. So why can't we catch one?

I knew our families would eventually wonder why they hadn't heard from us. They would call someone, but what if that wasn't for a month, or two, or three? If we had fish to eat, perhaps we could make it until help came.

We set the six berries on a log of the raft in the hope of attracting a bird. We pushed the tiny worms and the grub onto the huge hook then watched them disintegrate.

Fitz pulled out the toothpaste and began eating it for dinner.

Chapter 29

Bees

MARCH 3

Thirteenth day trapped

I opened the mosquito net and tent flap seeking the cooler air of morning. "Watch out!" I yelled, trying to close them again as hundreds of bees flew inside. Within seconds they were in my hair, on my face and neck, descending on every part of my naked body. Flapping my hands, I tried to brush them away, but they stung me every time I moved. "Fitz!" I screamed as I reached to tighten the flap where others were pouring in.

He was flailing, too. "Damn these things!"

"Stop moving!" I said.

With nowhere to run, I carefully lay down beside Fitz. My chest was heaving as the blanket of insects moved in different directions over me. As long as I remained dead still the bees seemed to calm down. "Oh, God, where did they come from?"

Fitz was staring at me, his eyes wide open in shock. The

bees covered him like clothing, emitting a continuous purring. "Are they eating us?" he asked.

"I don't think they're biting," I said. "I think they're slurping our sweat. Maybe they're after the salt?" I whispered. "Oh, God, what can we do?" Bees crawled in the creases behind my knees, under my arms, stinging repeatedly.

"I'm going to roll out of the tent into the water," Fitz said. "Perhaps they'll drown."

He yelped in pain as he opened the flaps and pushed himself off the raft into the channel.

I followed him, the bee stings as unrelenting as a tommy gun. The warm water felt soothing, but the bees did not drown. They swarmed above our heads. Fitz submerged again then surfaced. We both hung on to the raft while treading water. The swarm grew bigger and louder, hovering over us. The bees were not leaving.

"The *mosquitero!*" I yelled. "We've got to get under the netting. That'll keep them off us." To go back inside to where the netting was hanging down from the tent peak meant passing through the bees again.

"You first," Fitz said. "I'll try swatting your back."

I thrust myself onto the raft as Fitz, treading water, tried to push up my legs. The bees were not fooled. The swarm moved instantly as one, but they hesitated to attack, perhaps because my sweat had been washed away. Fitz followed right behind me, screaming loudly. Most of the swarm turned and flew toward him, but they didn't land.

We crawled under the *mosquitero*, slamming our hands down on the few bees that made it inside behind us. They looked like yellow jackets but were slightly smaller. I picked up a paperback, using it like a hammer, squashing the bees as quickly as possible. Some stung me before dying. Between us we killed all the bees inside the netting, including a couple stuck in the folds, which we pinched with our fingers. We pushed the drape of the netting as wide as possible within the tent, using paperbacks to hold down the folded edges on the board deck. We lay down, stroking each other's backs in a desperate search for comfort.

The bees imprisoned us, flying against the netting all morning. "Let's hope this is just a stopover for them," Fitz said, and rubbed his thin beard. "They weren't here before. Maybe they're heading north."

Just then I heard a plane. Without a word, we struggled onto our knees and out of the tent. The bees immediately swarmed us again, but Fitz grabbed the SOS sign. Standing, we held it as high as we could, bees stinging us at every movement.

The small plane was flying low over the trees at the horizon, coming our way. It bounced toward us and looked like it would be here in a minute. "They've got to see us!" Fitz cried.

The plane flew near us, to the right. "Help! Help!" we screamed.

Surely it would spot us. Perhaps it was looking for us. By this time, the *aduana* must have figured out that we were missing. Maybe our parents had called my mother's childhood friend, the American ambassador to Peru, and he'd sent the plane to find us.

I jiggled the sign. "They'll see us!"

"It's got to be!" Fitz held his end high, as excited as I was. Bees clung to us, bands around our necks and arms, covering every inch of exposed skin.

The plane flew over the channel so close to us, perhaps fifty yards away. It flew off above the trees, almost touching them, before vanishing into the cloud bank. We stood motionless, watching, continuing to hold up the sign as the bees traveled up and down our bodies.

"It'll turn back," Fitz said quietly, an echo of ten days ago. I saw that he was having trouble standing, so I leaned into him like a prop.

The jungle closed in on itself as if the plane had never come.

Slowly we dropped the SOS sign, trying not to agitate the bees. Planes were our only visible connection to the outside world, our best chance of being found. This one had come so close. How could the pilot not have seen us? My emotions yo-yoed between hope and despondency. We were a flicker away from salvation and then it was gone. I noticed the birds hadn't eaten the berries we'd left out on the raft. The berries no longer looked like berries but were shriveled to nothing.

Slipping into the water, we momentarily banished the bees. I had some optimism every day, but it was always snatched from me. It was ever harder to believe that we would survive. That yo-yo of hope and despair was squeezing us like a vise. Don't think this way! I scolded myself.

Don't let your mouth quiver. Don't look at Fitz until you're okay. He's depending on you. If you fall apart, he might, too. I wondered if he fought off thoughts like mine, trying to protect me.

My arms were trembling from raising the sign for those few minutes—they'd been so strong from swimming only four days ago. It doesn't take long for the body to deteriorate, I thought grimly.

Fitz and I struggled to pull ourselves out of the water and then panted as we sat down on the raft. I watched water trickling down Fitz's face as the bees hovered nearby.

"How come they're not landing on us?"

Fitz looked at his wet arms and legs. "Maybe it *is* the sweat they like," he replied.

"We should dump water over our heads while we're out here then make sure we get under the *mosquitero* before we start sweating again."

We sat listening for planes while searching for minnows, using the tin cup to pour water over us every few minutes. The sun burned into my scalp so I leaned over the side of the raft and dunked my head.

When I sat up, Fitz was smiling. He could make a fish net out of his white nylon shirt. We could catch a minnow, or maybe more, he said, his new idea energizing him.

He started walking toward the tent, but his leg flew out from under him so fast that he slammed hard onto the raft. He was all right, but we decided from now on it was safer always to crawl across the slippery logs where there wasn't a post to lean on. We'd both begun to fall often.

Fitz's body looked skeletal as he crawled slowly inside the tent to find his white shirt. I could hear him rummaging through his bag.

"Here it is!" he called out as he returned, trying to hold the shirt and scissors and crawl at the same time.

Sunlight shone on his intent face. He wobbled, tipping to one side, then sat beside me to cut the polyester into a two-foot triangle.

I realized I could help by sewing the sides to form a cone, and said I'd get my sewing kit.

It took me much longer to crawl in and out of the tent than it had yesterday, and yesterday I'd been slower than the day before. Black spots began to whirl in front of my eyes again. I couldn't feel the skin on my palms and knees, only my bones knocking against the hard, curved logs. I was twenty-seven, yet I moved with the slow deliberateness of my great-aunt Nancy Hale. At eighty-six she was still walking around Back Bay without a cane.

When I returned to the deck, I carried a needle and a spool of thread, afraid to drop them through the cracks between the logs. Settling next to Fitz, time and again I attempted to poke the wobbly thread through the eye of the glinting needle. Each time the thread collapsed. Like us, it had no muscle. I licked the thread and tried again. Finally, my eyes and shaky fingers coordinated enough to push the thread through.

I began to sew the shirt around a thin, supple branch Fitz had bent into a hoop. He'd panted from the effort of holding the branch in a circle while I'd tied the ends with a vine. The project fostered a soft exuberance between us. We were doing something positive.

It was slow-motion sewing. My breath felt constricted. I couldn't push the needle through the polyester. How can I be this feeble? I poked the needle between the threads of the cloth, eventually jabbing it through to the other side, then back again. For over two hours, with the sun burning slowly across the sky, and with bees crawling on every part of my skin, I attached the two edges of the cloth all the way down to form a net.

Fitz and I carefully slid into the water to ditch the bees. They swarmed as a cloud above us. Ignoring them, we climbed back onto the balsa and leaned over the side. Holding the rim of the net, we pushed the cloth below the surface, certain that a wriggling minnow would soon come by.

Taking turns to pour swamp water over each other, Fitz and I held the net for hours. Small fish were close but didn't swim into the net. Did they see the shadows of our hands? We were thirsty and gulped water, but even with the steady irritation of the bees we didn't dare dunk into the swamp to cool off for fear of scaring fish away.

My vision had begun to blur. As I leaned over the channel, holding the net, I lost my balance. When I hit the water it felt sublime. Getting out was becoming more difficult.

Fitz held me under my armpits as I pulled myself up. "If we add a pole to the net we won't have to hang over the water to hold it," he said, his chest heaving. He wiped his brow with his forearm. "I wish I could do it now, but I've got to lie down."

Despite yearning for nourishment, we couldn't do any more. I knew that getting me out of the water was the last physical exertion for both of us today. We wanted to attach the net to a pole to fish. We could visualize it. We were so close, but we were too weary to try.

Somehow we managed to get back under the *mosquitero* without the bees. The air inside the tent was stifling, so we left the plastic flap open. Within minutes the bees were buzzing around the netting, but we were too tired to care, protected in our cocoon, secured by a perimeter of paperbacks.

Chapter 30

What I Want

A couple of weeks trapped in a jungle swamp, alone, without food, skews perspective. Suddenly we became the impoverished urban children staring at the gringos through the restaurant windows, not able to get anyone to give us a bite to eat. We just wanted one diner to wave us inside for a bowl of spaghetti. Hunger pangs begin like puppy-teeth bites then morph into starvation until you see everything through only a thin vertical space, like slats in a fence, big enough only for thoughts of food. Then comes a feeling of hollow transcendence filled with "if only" and "how different the future will be." You continually think you're dreaming until you realize that your present is horribly real and your future is the dream. Soon come thoughts of all the ways to cook a hamburger, followed by the vow never to be anywhere without a Snickers handy, followed by "What's wrong with God?"—just before the list of things we did not do to deserve this. I tried to imagine if I'd ever done anything that might have changed another life for the better. If you didn't count Fitz, some friends and family, and perhaps the clients I counseled as a therapist, all I could come up with were the black Baptist kids in New Haven.

Walking past the church one day, I'd noticed a sign offering summer camp. On impulse I ran up to the door and knocked. Did they need a volunteer teacher? Yes, they could use all the help I could give them. It didn't matter, apparently, that I was white and not a Baptist. It was 1968, an extremely hot summer in the city, with fears fanned by New Haven's very assertive Black Panthers.

Living at home two summers after graduation, each morning I drove to New Haven to greet ten lively boys and girls, six to ten years old. No one provided a curriculum, and that was fine with me. I designed a program that gently steered away from the Bible, leaving that to others. I wanted the kids to discover their own city through field trips to places they'd never imagined visiting. At the Peabody Museum of Archaeology, they stared in awe at dinosaur skeletons and at gems and artifacts from the Lost City of the Incas. In class we discussed art along with how we would act on a field trip to the Yale art museum to explore realistic and impressionist paintings. They painted their own pictures in class, and once we trekked to the studio of a bookbinder/artist friend. She set up paper and glue, needle and thread, and taught us all how to make books we could take home. Another day we returned to design batik book covers from cloth, dyes, and wax. The children worked with great concentration; not a single boy or girl was disruptive. We walked to the Yale Co-op, where I worked in the afternoon in the children's book department. The kids had eagerly chosen books I could buy for them with my 40 percent employee discount. Together we discovered the public library.

Sometimes I'd borrow a car and corral a friend with

another car for excursions to places we couldn't reach by foot or bus. We drove to my friend's parents' summer home at the shore. The kids made sand castles and bounded into the water, some for the first time in their lives. We visited my family home. The kids played dress-up from a trunk of silk costumes and straw hats, then had ice cream and cake in the courtyard. Beneath the weeping cherry trees, I read aloud limericks my dad had composed for me when I was a baby. Then, clothes on, we all jumped into the garden's reflecting pool. "What will we do tomorrow?" they asked as we left. Not one child ever missed a day.

That had to count for something, I hoped, in totting up my score toward getting out of here or into eternal life.

By contrast, Fitz had missed as many school days as possible. He'd cut class the first day of first grade, and he'd never forgotten the girl who ratted him out. Youngest in his class, he quickly became the clown. By third grade, he'd done time stuffed into the kneehole of the teacher's desk. Sister Frances would then scoot her chair in as far as she could, the smell of wool and her black polished boots vivid in his memory along with the clack of her oversize crucifix and rosary beads. In his Brooklyn high school, he devised a way to beat the attendance system, spending whole days at the public library, the Metropolitan Museum of Art, the Cloisters, or anywhere interesting and open for free. Fitz was fifteen when he was caught. Knowing there would be hell to pay, he and a buddy began to hitchhike to California. They ran out of money in Tennessee. So they hitched back home after ten days to face their parents.

Besides his family and me, the love of Fitz's life was children. He couldn't see one on a bus without trying to play peekaboo. I had relished the joy of being with my Baptist kids. At our last class they surprised me with handmade thank-yous that I proudly tacked to a beam in my bedroom. Now, aching with hunger, I barely noticed the hard boards against my spine. I knew, at last, what I wanted.

If it wasn't too late.

Chapter 31

Epiphany

MARCH 4

Fourteenth day trapped

I want to have a baby! This was my first thought as I woke.
I listened to small bird sounds outside the tent and inhaled
dank, tropical air, so uplifted I forgot to worry about dying.
I didn't feel nauseated anymore. My stomach didn't churn,
and my head wasn't dizzy. I felt attuned to myself as I imagined my belly swelling with pregnancy sometime in the
future, because we were going to have a future. I touched
Fitz's cheek. In a moment he stirred and opened his eyes.

"Morning. It's a beautiful day."

He rubbed his eyes, and his brows moved together as if
he thought I was nuts. "Really?"

"I want to have a child with you." I looked deeply into
his eyes.

His brows relaxed as he pushed his arm under my shoulders then moved his face toward mine. "Oh, Hol, that would
be wonderful."

I wanted to do something purposeful with my life, and I wanted to share it in the most loving way: by creating new life.

I was filled with contentment visualizing three or four children underfoot. Little babies, curly haired, like Fitz, or not. It didn't matter. We'd love them all. I couldn't see them clearly, but I envisioned them toddling after Zelda down a sandy lane by a beach, so intrigued with a pebble, a leaf picked up and studied.

I wondered if it made sense that I was so happy at a time when we were starving. Were our bodies entering a euphoric phase of starvation? I'd read that Buddha had sought enlightenment through fasting, but he'd had to moderate his approach when he realized fasting was killing him. He chose to fast; then he chose to stop fasting. We couldn't choose. Fitz and I weren't seeking a spiritual high or aiming for Nirvana. We just wanted to be two regular honeymooners on a grand Amazonian adventure.

Despite my physical debilitation, my mind had achieved a heightened clarity. My vision of life was now stripped to the bone. As starvation consumed my body, its effects also trimmed the fat and gristle from my thoughts. Things were no longer complicated. I could see my place in the grand scheme—I would be a mother. Fitz and I would have a family and help each other and our children and our community and maybe in that way help the world. What more important job could there be? I saw holiness in the body, creating flesh and blood, nurturing children to become the best they could be. Motherhood itself was holy, beautiful, fulfilling. I craved it all: creating life, carrying life, bringing little ones into the family of man. I wasn't ready for death.

I'd come all this way to this hole in the wild to discover myself. No matter what happened, I knew who I was.

Hunger had brought me like a fasting monk into an almost blissful realm I'd never before experienced. Pressed against unblinking fate, I looked death in the eyes. Cold, merciless, the end was no longer a "someday" hypothetical. Yet I could taste survival again.

If we were to have our baby, I had to ignore my spinning head and crawl outside in search of food, bees or no bees. We would endure their stings. We had to catch a fish.

"Come on, Fitz, we have to do this. We can do it."

"Gotcha, I gotcha." He began to rise.

Recharged by fantasy, we struggled to our knees and slowly made our way out. We were dripping in sweat. The bees covered us within seconds. Without a word we both slid into the water. We watched the bees hover over us for a few minutes before we climbed back onto the raft. As before, the bees stayed away until we began to sweat again.

Fitz attached a long stick to the net. "Maybe we'll catch some piranha or even a *bocochita*." He plunged the net below the water's surface.

My heart leapt with his enthusiasm. My mouth watered. I told him I could smell the fish cooking; even a raw fish would be delicious.

We sat all afternoon under the hot sun, periodically dipping into the water to escape the bees. Fitz's arms were drooping, but he wouldn't let me take the net. Instead, I took the small balsa twenty feet up the cove and fished with the line and the small bait of butterflies and tiny worms that kept falling off the hook.

Eventually, the net and Fitz's patience worked and he caught three minnows. They weren't big enough to attach to our fishhook to use as bait, so we decided to eat them: two for Fitz, one for me. We dropped them down our throats in one gulp, not touching them with our teeth. They were the first food we'd caught in two weeks. It gave us hope that we would do even better tomorrow.

I tried to ignore my intense nausea and light-headedness, but the awesome power of starvation was all too clear. Inside me was a pack of famished, frothing dogs, sharp teeth tearing at the lining of my stomach. Gulping dirty river water didn't calm them. The teensy fish didn't either. Fitz cutting open the tube of toothpaste to lick its insides clean did not deceive those wild, howling hounds.

My hunger made me think of a strange couple who'd rented my parents' lake cottage. They took off for a week, leaving four dogs in the house without food. Neighbors finally broke in after hearing their high-pitched, desperate whines. They found one dog dead, one dying, and the other two so ravenous they'd begun to feed on the carcass.

I understood, now, how organs turn on themselves near the end. Starvation had consumed our body fat then started on our muscle, eating our strength. Lethargic, we looked at our watery world through rapacious eyes. The sight of fish swimming in the swamp was relentlessly teasing.

We had to stay positive, to set goals, and to keep talking about family. Dreaming of our future was a new weapon to help keep us alive. The slightest task required enormous effort. Death was knocking loudly at our door. We were determined not to answer.

Chapter 32

Snails

MARCH 5

Fifteenth day trapped

It had rained all night and into the afternoon. We ventured out to collect water and relieve ourselves, but hunting food was impossible. The rain finally let up, but minutes after it stopped, the tent became a sauna. It was getting harder and harder to breathe the heavy, stale air. My abdomen felt like an empty bowl. A desire to chomp my teeth into something consumed me. I thought about chewing Fitz's leather boots or my Dr. Scholl's straps.

"Fitz, I really want to bite into something. Do you?"

"Yes, I can't stand it." He was grasping his stomach. "Why the hell do we want to chew so much?" He pushed at his jaw.

"Our primeval urges are taking over."

I heard tapping on the plastic. "Oh, no! Are the bees back?"

Fitz darted a look at the tent wall. The tapping was

much heavier than the bees could make. It started slowly, but within a few seconds we were bombarded by giant raindrops again.

"Good." I sighed. "This will keep the bees at bay and cool us down a little." I was already sweating and felt utterly weary, despite my full night's sleep.

An hour or so later, the rain stopped and the air had cooled. We were anxious to go outside.

Fitz opened the flap. "Don't see the bees. I'll make a fire for coffee. I really need to taste something."

We slowly struggled out of the tent with some kindling that we'd brought inside to keep dry. The swamp smelled fresh; large leaves dripped like newly washed green robes. Small birds swooped overhead, and macaws greeted us from the canopy as Fitz and I found our places on the raft. Every day we hoped this might be the day. I opened my journal and read the previous entry's date, March 4. My heart quickened as I realized the implications of our having made it to the fifth. We had grabbed at any goal—one of them being dates.

"It's March fifth."

Fitz was crouched over the stove nurturing a tiny flame. "So it is."

Setting down my journal I inhaled the swampy air. "Juan should be back in Maldonado today. When he asks the *aduana* about us, he'll find out we didn't get to Riberalta. Unless he found gold. Then he would stay longer in the jungle," I said nervously.

"If he did find gold, he would probably still have to go back to Maldonado for supplies. I bet he's already organiz-ing a search party." Fitz sounded reassuring, but the indentations in his cheeks were deep, warning that we didn't have much time. We needed Juan to find us soon. We waited in silence for the water to boil as the heavy rain clouds lifted.

I mixed the powdered coffee into our cups. "This is the last of it," I said. I felt saddened to be losing this small but cheering ritual.

Fitz looked down at the murky water as he sipped his final cup of coffee.

"I'm going to miss it," I added, wondering if I would get a headache from lack of caffeine.

"Holly, look!" Fitz fell to his knees, reaching his hand down the outer log.

The anticipation in his voice had me on my knees, too. "What is it?" I asked, peering over the side of the raft at a cluster of wormy-looking creatures that had attached to the logs near the water's edge. Some of them were even up on the top of the logs, underfoot.

"What the hell are these?" Fitz asked excitedly. "They're moving! Hol, they might be something we could eat!"

My stomach lurched into a spasm at the thought of food.

We studied them closely. The worms were each about an inch long and three-quarters of an inch round, were perfectly camouflaged, a mix of greens and browns, almost the exact color of the balsa wood. They were covered in a glossy film that caught the sun the same way the wet logs did. They were different from anything we'd ever seen.

As we stared at them, Fitz noticed something. "They have two tiny antennae popping up from their heads, like snails without a shell."

"Have they always been here?" I asked, amazed that we hadn't seen them, or stepped on their squishy bodies.

"How could we miss them? We know this raft backward and forward."

"This is incredible!" I was salivating.

As we squatted down, we saw more and more of them. First there were half a dozen, then a dozen, almost invisible, moving soundlessly in their microcosmic world.

"It's fantastic!" Fitz yelped, throwing his arms into the air in a wide "yes!" sign.

I laughed with delight. The worms definitely appeared to be some kind of snail, or at least it seemed more palatable to call them that. Although we were famished, we still discussed whether or not they were safe to eat.

"What if they're poisonous?" I cautioned.

"We could die if we don't eat them," Fitz replied, his eyes fixed on them.

We turned to God for the last word. The snails had appeared overnight either to save us or to kill us.

"This is crazy!" Fitz finally announced. "Here's food, right in front of us! It has to be a sign that God wants us to eat. What are we waiting for?"

"Okay," I agreed.

Fitz nodded.

As we took the leap of faith, the weight of uncertainty fell from our shoulders, leaving us euphoric. We carefully plucked every "snail" we could find, plopping them into our frying pan of simmering water, killing, we hoped, any bacteria.

As I pulled the last snail off the log I saw something move a foot away. It was a tiny frog, no bigger than my thumbnail, like a spring peeper from back home. I was stunned when I was able to snatch it. "Fitz! Oh, my gosh!" I held it between both palms, afraid it would jump, then quickly dropped it into the pan.

"There might be others." Fitz put the lid on the pan so he could look, too.

We found three more baby frogs. They appeared from nowhere, as if by magic. Was this some kind of spring spawn? I felt sure God was providing us with the food we so urgently needed. I couldn't wait!

When the snails and frogs were cooked, Fitz and I prayed that they'd be safe to eat. They looked meager and repulsive, but we were going to have our first meal in fifteen days, nine snails and two frogs each.

I picked up a snail and stared at its little snout and antennae. Wincing, I popped it into my mouth then swigged some water. When my tongue pushed up to swallow, I felt a large, gelatinous lump against the roof of my mouth. Fighting my gag reflex, I got it down. I managed three more snails this way, ignoring a strong desire to spit them out. Then I tried to think of how lucky we were to have food at all, and I got two more down. "They're like escargots," I joked, my shrunken stomach starting to feel almost as full as my spirit. "We're supposed to chew them." My snails looked nothing like the escargots I'd enjoyed in France.

"Go ahead, Hol, but I'm just dropping mine down my throat. I can't bear to bite into them."

My urge to chew was overwhelming. "It's the garlic sauce we're missing," I reasoned.

"Yeah, but the garlic sauce is all I'd like about escargots. That's why I've never had them." He always got to the heart of things.

"That's really all I like about them, too," I said, laughing. "But I'm still going to try chewing the last of these."

I squeezed my eyes shut and crunched on a curled snail, imagining the garlic. The snail's exterior was rubbery against my teeth and tongue. An icky texture, yet it felt magnificent to clamp down on it. Cringing, I bit deeper into the snail's flesh. It felt spongy; then came the ooze. Grabbing the canteen, I chugged water, washing the snail over the back of my tongue in a waterfall to my stomach. "That's it for chewing," I said, gulping down my last two snails like massive pills, followed by great swigs of water.

Fitz wiped his mouth with the back of his hand. "Yum!"

I chuckled. "You're really going to gross your readers out over their breakfast with this story." Now for the two baby frogs. I held up the first frog to my mouth by its tiny foot, trying not to think about its little head, three small toes on each limb, and its luminescent white belly. I closed my eyes as I placed it on my tongue. A wisp of what must have been legs brushed against the bridge of my mouth, light as flower petals, as the baby frog slid down my throat. The second little frog dropped down the same way.

The Pink Palace was becoming part of the environment, a tiny floating island in this jungle world, watching out for us by welcoming life to form on her logs.

Fitz put his arm around me as the sun dropped, decorating the sky in hues of lilac and deep purple, slashed with magenta-rose. "Don't worry, Hol, Juan will send someone for us tomorrow."

Chapter 33

Like Sticks

MARCH 6

Sixteenth day trapped

We both woke up! Our hot meal of snails and tiny frogs was not poisonous. It bought us two more days during which time it rained sheets constantly with lightning, thunder, and high winds. We couldn't risk crawling out onto the slippery logs. We had to be patient, sure we'd find more snails once the storm was over.

The swamp current was faster and the water was rising higher up the trees. The discolored plastic of our tent was weakening. A gust of wind had jumped up one side and ripped the plastic right off. We'd scrambled to rescue it from the water then managed to nail an extra piece of plastic on top to secure it. We were so light that we almost blew overboard ourselves. Heaving hard, we lay back down inside, waiting for the storm to end.

Rain still fell in buckets, but the wind began to let up. The incessant downpour had cooled the air and kept the bees away. Their effects on us were still visible on our arms, hands, and legs, reminding us that they might return.

As the day wore on, we hunkered down and read books to distract ourselves. I was still reading *Papillon*. Reading was helpful, but my mind drifted. I missed my family and friends. I promised to be a better person if we survived.

I thought of how my sister-in-law had given me a tombstone rubbing she'd made in England of a young woman with my name. I'd framed and hung the rubbing in our hall. The woman had died at twenty-seven. Now I lay dying beside Fitz on the raft. I was twenty-seven. Coincidence or fate? If it was fate, I had to master it to the best of my ability or die trying.

We began telling each other stories again about people who had survived drastic situations, looking for hope from their success.

"Tell me again about Rickenbacker."

Fitz was happy to oblige, weaving a dramatic tale of the pilot crashing his B-17 into the sea in 1942. Surrounded by sharks, he and several others had drifted in inflatable rafts with a few oranges and little water for twenty-one days. Fitz had read about the World War I ace when he was a boy. It helped to know that Eddie Rickenbacker had survived. Surely we might make it, too.

Torrential rain and wind continued to batter our spirits as we lay in our tent through the afternoon. I listened to leaves being turned inside out and the cracking and breaking of boughs as they were ripped from their trunks. The tent shuddered as heavy tree stumps hurtled past our violently flapping plastic. Had Juan forgotten us?

Two thoughts consoled me. First, I now believed that we were being held in the hands of God. Second, I imagined my grandmother waiting to greet us, standing tall and dignified, younger again and without her cane, netted dark brown bun atop her head, her patrician face watching for us, eager to hug us tight.

My personal pendulum swung between hope and doubt. Hope was like cupping water in my hands. No matter how I held my palms, it could trickle out. Doubt, however, lay like granite on the heart. I looked at Fitz lying by my side. "Love is what's really important," I said, looking into his eyes. "We have plenty of that."

He looked away. "I could have been much better. My temper . . . I'm sorry." He paused. "I love you so much."

I took his hand as he tried to hold me closer.

"We need to find more food," he whispered, his eyes glazing over. "We're like sticks."

The wind pulled and yanked at the tent as Fitz placed both his hands around mine and softly massaged my fingers. "If I do die, I don't think you'll be alone for long. You'll have your old guys to choose from."

"How do you know you will be the first to die?" I wailed. "Look, we can't give up." I squeezed his arm, imploring. "As soon as this blasted wind stops I'm going to look for more snails."

I knew that if Fitz had any strength left in him he would rise and join me on the deck. I hoped he would.

But he didn't. He couldn't.

Chapter 34

My Hero

MARCH 9

Nineteenth day trapped

Over the past two days, the plastic had torn off the tent frame three times. Exhausted, we'd hammered it back onto its wooden frame. The downpours eventually became intermittent. When it seemed safe to go out, we searched for food.

Snails and little frogs again appeared on the raft, this time a few more than we'd found four days ago. They popped up in groups. We assumed this resulted from the onset of spring, bursting forth new life. Whatever the origin, we took anything we could find. It was cooler to work between the rains. The sun soon brought the bees back. They hovered above us, awaiting our sweat.

As we pulled the suction-cupped little snails off the Pink Palace's logs, Fitz looked out at the current, strengthened by the storm. It carried debris, including a log raft, about six feet by four feet, which floated by us thirty feet away. He stared like a hawk at its prey. "We could use that!"

"How are we going to catch it?" I asked.

He didn't take his eyes off his bouncing quarry.

I saw what he was thinking. "Fitz, that's too far to swim. You'll never get back. We're fine with the little balsa."

"We need it. We sink to our waists on the little balsa. That one's bigger and sturdier," he insisted. "We'll go faster on it and find snails more easily."

"But you're not up to this. We'll make do."

He'd already slipped into the water and was stroking toward his target. Desperate to find food, he would see hope in anything. I couldn't be upset with him for that. When he was just feet away from the new raft he disappeared underwater. Seconds later he emerged, gasping but determined. Please make it back, I thought, gripping the edge of the balsa.

Fitz dragged the new raft to the Pink Palace. Kneeling, I put my hands out and helped him climb aboard. "Take the line . . . off the little balsa . . . and put it on this one," he panted, his chest rising and falling as he rested at the stern. "This raft's a lot better."

Still stunned at his feat, I swapped the painter then turned to him, laying my hand on his shoulder. "My amazing husband." I said the words reverently, proud of our inseparable bond. "What willpower you have." I felt humbled at the apparent return of his resilience.

I helped him into the tent, where he collapsed onto the sleeping bag and fell asleep immediately. I crept out to try the new raft. It wasn't waterlogged like the little balsa, and was much less rocky to sit on. I paddled the area, finding a few more snails, a couple of grubs, a dozen berries. I found three tiny frogs and dropped them into the bottom of the can. They were so light they barely made a sound. But they were protein.

Up ahead, growing on long vines that clung to logs and bushes not far from the Pink Palace, I spotted purple grape-like berries. They smelled so sweet, so ready to eat. The sight of them triggered the pinching tweezers in my empty stomach. Starvation is a kind of madness. My tongue wanted to flick like a lizard's, to curl around the berries, to sweep them into my mouth. It was a great struggle not to eat them. The birds had eaten most of them already. Didn't that suggest they were safe? I plucked the few berries that were left. Their red juice dyed my palm, dripping toward my fingers. Just one lick. Oh, what the heck, I thought. We have to take a chance before they're all gone. How could they smell so sweet and be poisonous? Just the same, I made myself hold back. Fitz and I would decide together.

"I've got frogs, snails, and berries," I called to Fitz, pulling myself aboard the Pink Palace. I peeked into the tent to display my bounty.

He was groggy but awake, lying on the maroon sleeping bag with clothes bundled beneath his head. "Supper," he said, peering into the can.

"Why don't we each try a berry. Then if we're okay we can eat more tomorrow?" I suggested, taking a berry out of the can to show him. "The birds are eating them all. Pretty soon there won't be any."

Fitz sniffed at it. "All right, I'll try one." He took the berry and popped it into his mouth.

"I'm eating one, too," I said. "If you go, then so will I." I reached for a berry.

"Holly, don't. If I get sick, I'll need you to take care of me, get me water."

I put the berry to my mouth to take a bite. "I'll compromise and have half."

"No!" Fitz pushed my hand and the berry flew out of it,

rolling onto the sleeping bag. "For your size it could still be too much."

"Fitz, stop! I'm not sitting back and having nothing while you take a chance." I was dumbfounded that he had the physical strength to push the berry away. I picked up another berry and took a bite. "It's delicious."

It didn't appease my stomach, but I held on to the flavor in my mouth, swirling my tongue around and around. I thought of my mother's small Concord grape arbor and the jelly she made.

Fitz pulled me close to him. His beard scratched my cheek but I didn't mind. I felt blessed just to be with him.

Chapter 35

Marsh Birds

MARCH 10

Twentieth day trapped

This morning the air was dewy cool with a soft sun and no bees. We'd made it through the night. The pink plastic glowed on Fitz's sleeping face. He looked like he didn't have a care.

I had no cramps, so I decided to take the new raft to search for more berries before the birds ate them all. Pulling my baggy jeans up my toothpick legs, I tightened them with my sash before dragging a shirt over my head. I moistened my mouth with water from the canteen then gulped it down and started out the door.

Fitz yawned.

I turned back. "How are you?"

He rubbed his middle. "No repercussions! Let's have the others."

We each ate five berries, sweet, with an aftertaste of dirt.

"I'm going for more," I said.

"I'm going with you. I feel lucky today."

I smiled at that, but I was worried about him. "Please rest. You did too much yesterday."

"I'm all right," he said, trying to get up onto his knees. He rocked and staggered.

"Please. You'll be worse if you come."

His blue eyes looked glassy, but he was persistent, dragging on his jeans and shirt then crawling after me.

We saw no bees as we set out on the new raft.

"I like her," Fitz said.

"Easier to maneuver." I glanced back at him, cocking my head. "You gave me a lot of gray hairs, though."

Fitz smiled. "I don't see any."

The smell from the jungle and the marsh was dank, but the sun sparkled on the channel, making me feel hopeful as we moved slowly across the swamp. Small sparrow-sized yellow birds chirped and flitted nearby. Not near enough to capture.

Fitz's eyes began to flicker: he wanted to cut branches to widen one of our unused tightly woven fiber hammocks. "It'll make a big fish net. We'll get that damn fish yet."

As we paddled along the bushes of the tree line, he cut small branches with the Swiss army knife I'd given him in La Paz for Christmas. "At least we have this," he said, and smiled as he laid the branches between us in the middle of the new raft. "Not quite a machete. Not that I could lift one anyway."

We picked off snails from the logs and headed to where a mild breeze blew the hay-colored marsh grasses. Colorful birds flew in and out of bushes as we skimmed right by them. Other water plants had short blades of brilliant chartreuse, which, I hoped, hid snails and frogs and lizards.

Intermittent bushes and small trees grew from the mud and water. Dead branches were strewn throughout, all places for marsh birds to land.

A flash passed me. It was a four-inch grasshopper, bigger than any I'd seen at home, and it landed right on a reed beside me. I swept my hand down fast and caught her. When I took a peek I saw she had a little one on her back. I placed them carefully in the tin.

"It's amazing we're so close to the birds and they're not upset. They don't even seem to notice us," I said. I watched one with a twig in its mouth dart out of sight into the trees.

"It must be making a nest," Fitz said.

Another bird went into a bush. We didn't say a word, just paddled the raft in that direction and followed the trees.

"There's a nest!" Fitz whispered as we came to a forked branch overhead.

"Are there eggs in it?" I asked, wetting my lips.

Fitz reached up and touched the nest. No birds squawked a warning. Using both hands, he pulled at the nest and carefully lowered it down to the raft. Three baby birds were huddled together, their eyes open and their mouths gaping, pleading for food. They were tiny but already had brown and yellow feathers. They looked almost ready to fly. Fitz handed me the nest to hold as he paddled.

"Oh, Fitz." I choked up. At home we would have fed them with an eyedropper. Here we would eat them. I tried not to look at the little birds.

Fitz cut their heads off and drained their blood into the frying pan. He skewered their minuscule bodies on a stick and held it over hot coals. The feathers singed, burned, then disappeared. The birds had hardly any meat on them, but we chewed every morsel and sucked every bone, cracking each one to try to reach marrow. When the blood was heated, Fitz carefully poured some of it into my cupped hands then put the pan to his lips. I slurped the blood, licking my palms and fingers.

The grasshoppers steaming on top of the grill turned bright red. Their sliver of meat tasted like bad lobster. The snails, a few berries, the three baby birds, and grasshoppers together constituted our biggest meal in almost three weeks.

Fitz gave me a half smile. "Things are starting to look up," he said as he ate the last fleck of grasshopper leg.

We both felt lighter in spirit. Our meal wasn't enough to live on, but hope had brightened us like coals in a breeze. We held hands and gave thanks both to God and to the creatures who'd forfeited their lives.

"Want to help me make the big fish net?" Fitz looked eager.

We trimmed the leaves off the branches we'd collected and wove them through the sides of the hammock to stretch the netting. We tied lines to either side of it and attached them to the raft. We thought that we needed only to wait for a fish to swim over the net; then we would easily lift the net and grab the fish. We shoved our net over the side and watched it gurgle as it slowly sank into the swamp, its sides barely visible. I wondered how we would know if a fish swam in. We would have to watch it constantly for any ripples and then quickly pull it up before the fish swam out again.

Wordless, Fitz and I sat waiting at the edge of the Pink Palace as dusk and the mosquitoes came. An occasional fish did break the surface but was always outside the net. We tried pulling up the net to see if we'd caught anything by chance. It was heavier than we'd expected. Pulling it against the weight of the water drained us. Soon we were gasping for breath.

"Let's leave the hammock in the water. It's too heavy to pull out," Fitz said, and twisted his growing mustache. "It seemed a good idea at the time."

"It is a good idea. If we hear a fish in there our adrenaline will make us get it."

Fitz continued to stare at the submerged net. Then he turned to me, his eyes brightening.

"I've got a wonderful dinner I'm going to make for you when we get home." He slapped at the mosquitoes around his face. "Let's get inside and I'll tell you about it. I've gone over it a hundred times."

Appreciating the distraction, I listened as Fitz described his seven-course meal, starting with appetizers, ending with strawberry shortcake.

We grew silent as the sounds of dusk began to wind down. The buzzing, the chirping, and the sawing of grasshoppers' legs all gave way to night. The sounds came every day, in the same order, so I was getting used to many of them: the mosquitoes' hum, the monster whirlpool roar, the trees rustling with animals we could never see. Nothing had tried to kill us yet. It was the sounds I didn't hear very often that unnerved me.

"When we have children, I think they should take a survival course and learn what's okay to eat in the jungle," I suggested.

"Yes. We should take it, too."

"We'll all take it together. Maybe they'll be the kind of

kids who want to stay home." Fitz chuckled. "Wouldn't that be nice?"

Shrieking shimmied across the swamp during the night, waking us up with a start. The sharp screams were so loud they seemed to rock the rain forest and reverberate around the tent. Lying under the mosquito netting, we sought solace in each other's arms. We guessed it could be a jaguar roaming the hardened earth somewhere beyond the quickmud. Its cry suggested that there was land out there, and if we ever got to the land it would be waiting for us. Each time the jaguar screeched I felt my back quiver. I drew closer to Fitz until there was no space between us.

"I don't like this," I murmured.

Fitz kissed my mouth. He rubbed my shoulder and my arm and then touched my wilted breast. For a few seconds my mind was diverted to a suite in the Plaza Hotel, in New York City. Then the jaguar howled again, an angry street cat hiss.

"What if he climbs from tree to tree and jumps in here?" I whispered.

"These trees are flimsy," Fitz countered.

"The tree we slept in was strong."

We waited in silence for the next scream.

"Cats can swim when they have to," I added, apprehensively.

"Not in quickmud. That'll trap him."

I prayed that the jaguar would not smell us and come any closer. I also prayed that the caimans would not swim up onto our low-riding raft, snapping jaws ready for what was left of our flesh. As always, I prayed desperately that we would be saved.

MARCH 11

Twenty-first day trapped

Today was rough for Fitz.

Each time we paddled in search of food, we also looked for sticks and rotting branches to use for fires in the stove. We had been snapping branches off of a dead tree that was conveniently lodged horizontally into the marsh, not far from the Pink Palace, but today I realized it was becoming increasingly hard to snap off the brittle twigs. Fitz had pulled the red Swiss army knife from his jeans to cut off the deadwood. His hand trembled as he tried to open it. He couldn't grasp the blade with his fingers. The knife slipped from his palm and slid into the water. We each gasped as it disappeared.

Fitz's head fell forward onto his chest. "I couldn't catch it." His voice shook as if he were in mourning.

"Oh, Fitz, please don't worry. We've still got the Girl Scout knife."

"But you gave me that knife," he sniffed, lifting his hand to wipe his eye.

"It's okay."

We foraged for food in silence, picking twenty berries, pulling a few snails off logs, and just missing two frogs. Fitz was totally dejected. It was as if, with each day, we were losing pieces of ourselves in a protracted struggle with the jungle. I wasn't sure what I could say to console him. This was a new Fitz—a peeled-away, weaker Fitz.

Chapter 36

Rising Fear

MARCH 12

Twenty-second day trapped

Tap, tap, tap. The round shadows bounced against the plastic as we were pulling on our clothes.

"They're here again." I fumbled to button my blouse.

"Damn."

The air was stagnant and excruciatingly hot. Already we were sweating copiously.

"We need to get some air in here! We'll just have to endure them," Fitz muttered.

I opened the *mosquitero* and the tent flap, hoping for any possible breeze. The swarm of bees burst in. Half of them landed on me, the rest on Fitz. They moved over my lips and along my hairline, where perspiration dripped down my face. Closing my eyes, I tried to keep control of my mind. Freaking out would waste precious energy. The bees crept over every inch of our exposed skin, into Fitz's beard and the creases of our eyes. Their continuous hum was a warning not to stir, but it was impossible to lie perfectly still. My bare foot landed on a bee. It stung me before dying. I yearned to wipe the sweat off my brow.

"I can't stand this," Fitz cried, rising stiffly to his knees to go outside. Bees were crawling up his jeans and into his sleeves to his armpits. Every time he moved they stung him.

"Ow, ow, ow!" he groaned as he banged through the door.

"I'm coming in a minute," I called after him.

I lay back on the sleeping bag, gathering strength to rise again. Abruptly, through the buzzing, I heard sobs. My head rose fast. "What's wrong?" I asked. I struggled to my knees.

Perturbed bees stung me as I pushed out to the deck through air so humid I felt I was submerged in water.

Head in his hands, Fitz sat at the stern, weeping.

"Fitz, what is it?" I looked for blood, but he appeared to be unharmed. I couldn't see his face. "Fitz, please, tell me what's wrong." Bees were stinging me inside my pants and top. I crawled along the logs toward him, my kneecaps aching.

He gradually turned to face me, sunlight on his wet cheeks, tears running into his beard.

"It's gone," he whispered.

"What's gone?" I asked softly. I wanted to be by his side. Damn, I was so slow.

"I got in the water and my wedding ring fell off," he choked out between gulps of air. His face was contorted. "It slipped off. I couldn't catch it."

It had fit just right the day we'd picked it out in Westville, Connecticut, a month before our wedding. His gold band, like my own, was engraved with our initials and wedding date. His ring had never been off his finger.

"Oh," I said, thankful that he wasn't physically hurt. When I reached him he leaned his head on my shoulder. His tears made me cry, too. This was the second time in two days that he'd lost something he cared about. They were material things that back home we would not sob over, but here they meant everything.

"Everything's being taken from us," he said, his voice muffled in my hair. He lifted his head to shout angrily again at the sky, but this time he stopped midsentence and began to weep. We held each other for a while, crying. It was better than words. The tears felt cleansing.

Then Fitz pulled himself from me, his eyes wild. "Is there nothing this goddamn river won't take? Is God going to take everything I care about?"

"We've still got each other," I reminded him quietly. Even though Fitz had fallen apart before, watching it happen continued to terrify me. I saw his shaken mind and collapsing body declining further as we continued to starve. I didn't think I could ever get used to my husband crumbling before my eyes.

He held out his left hand to show me where the ring had been, his fingers revealing the shape of every bone. He began to sob again.

I crooked my shoulder and arms around him, urging him to hear me, to feel some relief.

"Fitz, we'll get another ring," I told him. "We can have it engraved the same way."

"It won't be the real ring."

"No. It'll carry extra meaning because of all we've been through together. It'll be a true symbol of our love and perseverance."

He didn't say anything, but his shoulders relaxed into me.

We held each other as we sat on the edge of the raft, only inches above this offshoot of the Madre de Dios, our source of life, providing drinking water, but also the source of our wretchedness and the probable cause of our death. This ruthless river might win, but not yet. Not yet.

I reassured Fitz that we could make it home; we just had to get past this dreadful moment.

I'd only ever seen him cry once before, and that, too, had been here in this damned swamp.

We rested all morning in the tent, if such is rest, with the bees our constant companions. For all my momentary vigor to keep Fitz from despondency, I was floundering. I felt so lost that I couldn't even write in my journal. Once, when I was a child of eight or nine, I'd felt uncertainty when I heard my parents arguing. My mother was sobbing. My dad's normally soft voice was loud, and then he banged the door and left the house. I crept into the room. Our world seemed to be falling apart. I tried to console my mom, arms around her. When she calmed down, I'd felt that I'd helped. I was a lot more uncertain now. Now I wasn't sure if I could help at all.

Chapter 37

Tiny Frogs

MARCH 13

Twenty-third day trapped

The smell of bacon frying wafted down the hall, teased me awake, as did my mother's boisterous voice and Zelda's high-pitched bark. Pulling back the blanket, I sat up in my childhood bed.

Fitz's raucous laugh made me turn to see an indentation in his pillow. He was already in the kitchen, telling tales. The peals of laughter rose like musical notes, a cacophony of rhythms. I could hear the distinctive voices of the Conklins and the FitzGeralds. They'd all come to welcome us home.

They were seated at the oak table because I could hear it creak. Dad had replaced its original Victorian pedestal with steel legs, his idea of keeping current. The legs wobbled beneath the weight of the tabletop, even when leveled with slivers of wood. My shoulders and neck relaxed back into the pillows; I felt buoyed by the voices and smells of home. On the wall opposite my bed was the Henri Rousseau–type jungle mural I'd painted when I was seventeen. Friends thought it remarkable that my parents had allowed me to paint my walls any way I chose. I was so glad my parents hadn't painted over it in the years since I'd moved out.

It was still winter and cool as I rose, sliding on my slippers, jeans, and sweatshirt to hurry down the hall. I'd soon be filling myself with breakfast.

As I turned the corner into the kitchen, Mom was pulling steaming corn bread from the oven. "Here, darling." She handed me a piece then put her arms around me. I hugged her until I trembled.

Someone laughed from the kitchen table. "Hey, Hol, did that lady in Peru really serve you the rump of a guinea pig?"

"Oh, yes." I laughed, walking toward everyone. "Poor Fitz—he got the head." I doubled over, giggling. "He couldn't eat it then, but if we'd had it in the swamp we would have devoured it."

Salivating, I bit into the buttery corn bread then stuffed the rest into my mouth. I hugged Mom again. I hugged her until I couldn't breathe and tears came to my eyes.

As cotton candy dissolves at the touch of a tongue, so went my mother and the corn bread. My eyes snapped open to see the gauzy tomb of mosquito netting that cascaded from the tent peak to fold beneath our sleeping bag. Somehow bees had pushed past the tent flap and penetrated the *mosquitero*. They were buzzing, licking, swarming over me. I turned to see Fitz lying prostrate, covered in bees.

Overhead, a loud droning. Two large black insects that looked like hornets, each the length of my palm, dipped up and down inside the tent peak, carrying daubs of mud. They had begun to build their home just a few feet above us. It was as if we didn't exist. I closed my eyes, desperate to return to my dream.

The bees continued to crawl across my saggy, bug-bitten skin, fiercely determined to lick every drop of salty sweat. My fingernails were split from paddling and pulling bushes and vines, from clawing in rotten logs for grubs. My skinny legs were bruised from banging into rocks and roots, unseen in the muddy water. We were sleeping so much now that I knew we were near to sleeping forever.

The unrelenting hornets droned fitfully around the peak of the frame, just outside the mosquito netting, intent on their construction.

"They want their colony here," Fitz mumbled, his eyes half open. "They sense we won't be around for long."

My heart thumped as I fought off the sadness left in the wake of my dream. I wanted to tell Fitz, but I saw that his spirits were down. "Fitz, we're still here," I said. "We have to keep fighting, no matter what." I knew how frustratingly hollow I must have sounded. "Let's see if more snails grew on the logs."

The bees hovered over our skin as we lowered ourselves into the swamp. "We can't do this much longer," Fitz said, wiping his cheeks with mud.

I looked at his gaunt face and knew he was right. I wanted to speak, but I didn't know what to say. I felt on the edge of crying.

We slowly clambered back onto the deck to catch our breath. We were safe from the bees for a few minutes, as long as the water trickled down our skin and wiped the sweat away.

"But so far we've been lucky," I said, breathing heavily, trying to rally, to find optimism, as I watched the swirl of current around slick brown logs far out in the channel, my hand on Fitz's.

Fitz agreed but said that our raft was so close to the water that anything could happen.

I reached down the outermost log of the raft and felt for snails. "Here." I handed five to Fitz. I found five more along the raft's edge.

He looked between each log but had no luck. "There aren't enough to cook up. Let's just eat them raw."

Fitz's face glistened with perspiration, his eyes tightly shut as he forced the snails down.

"I love you," I said as my eyes welled. These had been tender days of quiet understanding between us.

I suggested we look for berries. We found twenty ripe ones where I'd seen none yesterday. Many had been picked over by the birds. Others were small and green, not yet edible.

We continued paddling. I caught sight of a three-inch-round frog under a leaf. "Fitz, a frog!" I mouthed, pointing to the spot. Fitz was in the stern and would drift by her after me. He lunged for it.

"I missed." His hands were still clasped together. "Wait. I feel something." He looked down to find the frog was pulsing in his hand. He immediately stabbed it with the knife so it wouldn't jump away.

We cooked it with the snails. The frog had considerable roe and a little meat on its legs that we tore with our teeth. Chewing felt good, like our jaws were doing what they were meant to do.

We ate the berries for dessert. This was our second-biggest meal. Feeling hopeful, Fitz went out after dinner to fish, putting the frog's head and intestines on the hook. Again no luck.

We lay down to sleep long before the sun set. While Fitz slept, I watched the shadows of the bees dip down and up along the outside of the tent. Something heavy smacked against the plastic. My body stiffened. I was too scared to look at what had hit the tent. Fitz looked so peaceful, a half smile on his face. I closed my eyes again and tried to picture Zelda waiting by the front door for her morning walk.

Chapter 38

Time Meshes

MARCH 14

Twenty-fourth day trapped

We slept about eighteen hours before waking to find the sun already high. Sitting at the stern of the Pink Palace, we watched two small birds building a nest in a bush that grew out of the water just six feet away. As usual, bees were crawling all over us.

"I'm getting used to them," Fitz said, as if being stung incessantly was somehow normal.

I nodded, aware of the bees' little feet on my neck. I tried to ignore them as I focused on the birds.

Despite my hungry impatience, the birds' antics entranced me. The female chirped at her mate constantly. I wondered if she was prodding him to hurry, or if she was telling him he wasn't placing twigs correctly. Perhaps she was cheering him on, though her tone sounded insistent. They were taking so long we began to wonder if they had another nest and were using this one as a decoy. I knew this was absurd thinking, but to us, so desperately hungry, they seemed intentionally slow.

"I don't think they'll ever finish," I sighed.

"They're outwitting us." As Fitz spoke he raised his hand unconsciously to whisk the bees from his ears.

We pulled the medium raft up against the Pink Palace so we could climb onto it. Then we dunked in the water so we could keep the bees off us while we paddled away. If we could get even ten yards from the Pink Palace before our skin dried, the bees wouldn't follow us.

Paddling along our quiet cove, we were surprised by two enormous birds, flapping into the air from the marsh.

"Look at those beauties!" I followed them with my eyes, my stomach not far behind.

"They might have a nest in there!" Fitz exclaimed, turning the raft in the direction of where they'd launched.

"Their eggs would be huge!" I threw my weight behind my paddle.

We maneuvered the medium raft down a narrow channel through the marsh until it could go no farther. Despite our feebleness, we secured the balsa and lowered ourselves into the mucky water. Fitz swam ahead, pulling himself deep into the reeds. He found two nests, but no eggs or young birds. They must have already hatched and flown away.

"Look!" he called out, pointing to a high pile of sticks. "That must be the goose nest!"

Adrenaline pushed me to catch up.

He reached the pile first. "Don't come," he said in a barely audible voice. "Just a bunch of dead branches."

I watched him pull himself back over the logs and through the grasses, swimming when he could, hardly able to raise his arms, kicking his legs to get back to the raft. It was excruciating to see him move so slowly. I felt so completely helpless, as if I were falling down an elevator shaft.

Spots whirled in front of my eyes. "I don't know what's wrong with me," I apologized after he arrived at my side.

"We're starving, Hol, we need to lie down." Fitz put his arm around me when we got back to the tent.

When I woke, Fitz was sitting next to me impishly grinning. "Look what I found while you were sleeping." He handed me the metal can. It was filled to the top with miniature frogs.

I stared at them in disbelief.

"The rain must have brought them out. There's about thirty in here!" His voice was ecstatic.

I gently embraced him. "Let's get the grill going."

Fitz sat beside me on the logs, trying to get comfortable. "After snails and frogs, I can't wait for some birds' eggs."

He placed twigs into the stove and lit them with pages torn from our paperbacks. Soon about a half inch of brown water was bubbling in the frying pan. He dumped the can of frogs into the hot water then covered the pan.

A minute later, I peered into the pan as Fitz held it away from the fire. "Fitz, they're wonderful."

Fitz quickly dropped a frog down his throat then pushed the pan closer to me. We alternated until only one was left. I gestured for Fitz to take the last one then we sat together, feeling almost full.

Fitz leaned toward me. "How do you feel now, Hol?" His voice was soft, his brow brooding.

"Much better." I kissed him on his bearded cheek. "Where's your mouth under that mustache?"

Fitz pushed his whiskers aside and kissed me.

"Do I taste like frogs?" I asked.

"Umm. Delicious."

MARCH 15

Twenty-fifth day trapped

"Fitz, come see," I whispered, peering out of the tent at four big birds that had appeared in the swamp. Neither of us had ever seen anything like them before. The largest bird was brown and yellow, with long, thin legs that she used to scamper across the disklike lily pads. Her three young were almost her size but were light tan in color. They teetered awkwardly, still learning to use their long, slender toes to balance.

They were such fun to watch that I almost forgot how good it would be to eat one. I inched silently out of the tent and sat on the raft to get a better view. The birds were only five feet away, but they ignored me, intent on pecking at minuscule bugs that I couldn't see on the lily pads. I asked Fitz if a slingshot would hit one of them, but he said it would take a lot of practice, and besides, we didn't have any stones. Soon the bird family pecked their way across the lily pads and around the bend, beyond our sight.

We'd slept all morning. Fitz complained of feeling very faint. Fortunately, I was doing better, so I went out to look for food. By the time I'd crawled onto the medium raft, Fitz was right behind me, assuring me that he felt well enough to help.

I found two dozen smooth black berries. We didn't wait to test them. They were mouthwatering. The clunky raft kept getting caught on vegetation waving in the murky swamp.

"This marsh is so beautiful now that spring is coming," I whispered, glancing at the green and yellow reeds against a backdrop of black branches in the marsh, and a brilliant blue sky above. I felt as if I were out of my body, detached from the young woman who was starving to death. A huge sun-yellow frog lay in the water in the reeds, staring right at me, at least five inches around. Fitz tried to net it but it jumped backward and got away.

"Tiny frogs!" Fitz yelped. "This is where I found them yesterday."

I leaned beyond the little raft toward a frog and plucked it from the swamp. Dozens of them were floating in the sun-drenched water, their spindly legs stretched out behind them. I grabbed any within my reach. Fitz did the same. We plopped them in the can and quickly covered it. My heart jumped at the thrill of filling the can.

"Forty-six frogs and one snail with a shell. It's the best catch so far." My heart was pounding as I looked over at Fitz.

He was still searching the water with fast-moving eyes. He relaxed and sat back as I spoke. Putting his hand on my shoulder, he kissed the nape of my neck.

"This is like the Garden of Eden. Food is springing up everywhere."

"Well, almost," Fitz cautioned.

We were always in sight of the Pink Palace, but now she seemed so far away as we tried to paddle back to her. I looked back at Fitz. He was having trouble, too. The sun bore down on us with such ferocity that it seemed like a personal attack. Sweat spilled down my back. I guzzled water then tried again.

Along the tree line I spotted a small fruit that looked like a cherry tomato. When Fitz reached for it, his shaking hand fell to his side. We waited for a minute, not saying anything. Then he reached again, pulled the fruit off the branch. The inside was brown. "Too risky," I concluded, dropping it into the water.

"We've got a great dinner coming up," Fitz said, sounding lighter than his slumped body showed. "Can't wait to put the fire on."

I plopped my paddle into the water, straining to push it forward. I envisioned filling my concave belly, if we could just make it to the raft.

After supper, as dusk descended and the mosquitoes made their appearance, we crawled into the tent.

"This was a good day," Fitz said, trying to hold up his head, his skeletal arms and legs slightly trembling as he eased down on the sleeping bag.

"Yes. Twenty-three baby frogs each. A feast!"

We were actually weaker than we had been before, as if the energy spent to find food exceeded the nutritional gain. I lay next to him as I pulled the snapshots of Zelda and Liza from the camera bag. The photos were worn and water-stained, but I could still see their little faces with the flashlight. I pressed the photos against my chest then shifted onto my side to put them back in the camera bag for safekeeping. When I turned to face Fitz he kissed me.

"I'm so lucky to have you, Monkey-face."

"I'm so lucky to have you, too, Jerry Julep. Good night," I whispered, touching his sunken cheek.

Chapter 39

Chasing the Monkey

MARCH 16

The twenty-sixth day

During the night I awoke to high-pitched, angry shrieks roaring back and forth. They seemed closer than ever. "Fitz," I whispered, but he was in a deep sleep. My muscles were taut rubber bands, ready to snap. For several minutes I didn't move, waiting, open-eyed in the dark.

After the screeches ceased, I didn't hear anything beyond Fitz's short, hard breaths. Then they stopped. "Fitz!" I listened to his chest. "Fitz!" I poked him.

He groaned and turned onto his side.

It was just a matter of time before animals found us. I was amazed they hadn't already. A loud splash outside the tent made my heart stop. I lay rigid, trying to picture my hand sinking into Zelda's thick ruff, warm and soft.

The bees again. Their thumping against the tent woke me in the morning. Parrots prattled like people, making me feel more alone than ever. I put my hand on Fitz's shoulder for assurance then began to trace his cheek with my fingers, feeling the bones beneath his beard, his jutting jaw. My love. Since we'd been trapped, I'd wondered every night if we'd wake up in the morning.

Fitz was so still. So quiet. I listened for his breathing. I couldn't hear it.

"Please, Fitz, wake up." I nudged him.

He didn't stir.

"Fitz!" I said, frightened. I shook him. His arm fell limp across his chest. My heart raced. Was he going to die in my arms? Was he already dead? I took in a deep breath. The Pink Palace felt like a double coffin. If we had to die, I wanted to go first.

"Fitz!" My voice was shaking. "We're going to make it out of here. I just know it." I kissed him. I didn't know at all.

He stirred, opening his blue eyes, grayed over, cloudy windows to a body consuming itself. "Hi," he whispered.

"Thank heavens!" I kissed him again. I wanted to squeeze him, but it would be too painful. Our rice-paper-thin skin hung over our bones with no layer of fat. I placed my hand gently on his ribs.

"I love you!"

He kissed my hair but said nothing.

I guessed it was around nine o'clock, but the heat and humidity inside the plastic were skyrocketing. I was sure it was 100 degrees. Our perspiration pooled onto the synthetic sleeping bag.

I fanned Fitz with the small parrot fan. It did nothing but move the stagnant air around.

"It's brutal, Fitz. I've got to open the flap."

His body stiffened but he nodded.

It took a few minutes to haul myself to my knees then push the netting aside and open the tent flap. A light breeze soothed us for barely a second before the bees invaded. The two hornets hovered at my face then flew to the tent peak to continue their mud construction.

I froze, waiting for the bees to land. Hundreds swarmed to Fitz's legs and arms, up his shorts, into his shirt sleeves. He lay motionless as they settled.

Sweat poured from my forehead and burned my eyes. Bees crawled over my cheeks to my eyelids and stung me as I inched back to the sleeping bag. "I've got to get in the water," I whimpered, turning toward the tent opening again.

The bees hovered above me as I immersed myself in the channel, clinging to the side of the raft, letting my legs float behind me. For these few moments of cool weightlessness I felt human again. My foot banged against something. I held my breath but nothing moved around me. Just a branch? Slithery bodies brushed my legs.

I tried to pull myself onto the Pink Palace but couldn't get a grip; I was even weaker than I'd been yesterday. A soft hum in the distance caught my ear. I looked up: a black dot in the sky was heading toward me, growing to glistening silver. "Fitz! It's a plane!" Leaning on the raft with my left arm, I tried to force my right arm up to wave but it refused to work.

The plane flew fifty yards to the right of me. I continued trying to wave until it disappeared. A few minutes later, two more planes flew overhead, one after another. My heart soared again. We hadn't seen a plane in weeks. Now three planes in one morning! This must be a sign.

I watched them bounce away over the trees, listening for them to circle back. They didn't.

In my heart I knew no one was looking for us. No one was coming. I hauled myself onto the raft and crept back to the tent, feeling more sorrow than I ever knew existed.

Fitz's eyes were closed. The bees covered his entire body, even his flaking lips.

"Fitz, I just saw three planes. They might . . ." I faltered, looking through the bees for my husband. I waved at them, they rose, and I took Fitz's hand.

He opened his eyes and gave me a wan smile. "I don't feel too well," he said.

"What hurts, Fitz?"

"I feel so weak, don't know if I can get up."

I tried to keep my voice steady, trying not to think of how strong he'd always been. "You need water, Fitz." Reaching for the canteen, I put it to his lips, carefully supporting his head. He sipped until he'd drunk it all.

"That helps," he mumbled, turning his face toward me. I had a second container by my side. He took a few sips from that bottle then grimaced.

"Pretend it's a cold beer," I urged, keeping it at his mouth.

Shaking his head, he finished off the bottle then closed his eyes and let his head fall back on my arm. His skin was gray.

"Fitz," I pleaded. "We've come this far . . ."

I felt tears. They trickled down onto my cheek then fell onto his, disappearing into his beard. I gripped his hand, as if that could keep me from losing him. Hand in hand, I remembered, we had often run downhill at Squantz Pond near our rental cottage, with Zelda zigzagging back and forth at our sides. We ran through grass, later through snow, laughing, falling, embracing. Zelda barking for us to get up.

The memory strengthened me. It seemed to generate a

kind of clarity, as if a dense fog had lifted to reveal mountains I'd never known were there.

Calmness settled inside me.

"Fitz, we've had enough." I kissed him. "God's taking us out of here, today."

He opened his eyes, looked up wildly at the hornets, then stared at me. "Where's he taking us?"

"Home." I glanced at the empty water containers. "I'll fill these up. You need more."

"No! I'll do it." He winced as he pushed himself to a sitting position. "I'm going in the water."

Bees flew all around us as Fitz got to his knees, haunches pushing through his sagging flesh.

"I'm going with you."

"I'm fine," he said firmly. He groaned, staggering toward the flap on all fours like a weakened, famished animal. He banged into the frame. I had to look away.

On my knees now, I smoothed the sleeping bag, plumped pillows of clothing, ignoring the remaining bees that hadn't followed Fitz. I listened, waiting to help Fitz climb out of the water. I doubted he could do it alone. I'd heard splashes when he'd gone in and his deep sigh of relief to be momentarily free of the bees.

Suddenly he screamed, "¡Socorro!" Then, louder, he yelled for help again, his voice stronger than it had been in weeks.

"What is it, what is it?" I edged toward the tent door, frantic to get out.

"Men! Give me my glasses! I thought it was a log, but it's going against the current! It's moving this way!" His voice was fast and trembling.

"Men?" I was afraid to believe.

"Yes, I think it's a boat. Hurry!"

I seized his glasses from beside the sleeping bag and thrust my head out of the tent. Fitz reached his hand up from the water to take them.

Staring down the channel, I saw two men in a dugout canoe paddling toward us. They were just seventy yards away, coming out of the flooded woods—the first human beings we'd seen in thirty-one days.

"Oh, Fitz, you're right. They're men!"

"*¡Socorro! ¡Socorro!*" Fitz shouted again.

"We're saved!" My heart was thundering in my chest.

Fitz didn't answer me. He was focused on the men.

As the canoe glided closer, I realized the men were Indians. Their short, straight black hair was swept back from their foreheads, their skin brown as cocoa. They stared intently at us as they paddled, never breaking rhythm.

Fitz called out again.

No response, but they kept coming. They seemed so grim.

"Why don't they answer?" Fitz didn't take his eyes off them.

"I don't know." I was riveted, too.

There was no sound except the paddles quietly dropping in and out of the water. Then I heard the men mumbling.

"Do you think they're friendly?" Fitz asked, grasping the side of the raft.

"I hope so."

"*¿Hablo español?*" we yelled repeatedly, thinking that we were asking the Indians if they spoke Spanish. Their continuing silence bewildered us. They were now close enough for me to see their high cheekbones and dark eyes. The front man was lean, his face narrow and his puckered mouth small. The man in the stern was muscular, with a broad chest and thick arms. His face was wide, his mouth a straight line.

I caught my breath when they were nearly upon us. Their paddles thrust the canoe forward, but the Indians' bodies, like stone carvings, did not move. The men gave no sign of communication, their unblinking eyes penetrating us like arrowheads.

"What if they pass us by?" I asked, panic rising. Then I saw a rifle lying across the bow. "They've got a gun. You don't think they'll hurt us?"

Fitz's mouth twisted downward. "The other guy's got a rifle, too. Holly, get back in the tent." He freed a hand from the edge of the raft, his eyes fixed on the men. "Hand me the knife!"

I ducked my head inside and fumbled in a box for the Girl Scout knife.

"Hurry!" Fitz pressed.

I dropped the knife into his palm. It looked small and useless in his unsteady hand. When I raised my eyes the men were perhaps twenty yards off. Modesty hit me. "I need clothes," I said, backing into the tent.

"Stay in there," Fitz insisted.

"I'm not leaving you. I'll be right out." I was afraid of the men, but I wanted to trust they would save us. "I'm sure they're going to help us," I called through the plastic wall as I knelt over my backpack and grabbed my purple dress.

"I've got to decide now before they reach the raft," Fitz whispered hoarsely. "Our only chance is surprise. I might be able to get their rifle."

"I know they'll help us," I repeated, searching for the dress's neck hole.

"Stay in there, Holly. They're here."

I dropped the polyester shift over my head and staggered to my feet. My rubbery legs surged forward, pitching me through the door with no control. I couldn't stop. I fell off the balsa and tumbled into the air. The bright blue sky spun above me. I saw the rifles. I saw the silent Indians grab the bow of the Pink Palace. I saw them watch me as I fell toward the deep, murky swamp. "*¡Socorro, por favor!*" I called out as I went under.

Chapter 40

Banana Chips

Gasping, I popped to the surface. An Indian's hand was reaching out to me. "*Oh, señora, pobre señora,*" the voice said gently. I lifted my hand from the water and he grasped it. I raised my other hand and let him pull me into his canoe.

As the Indian extended his hands to Fitz, I fell onto the roughly chiseled canoe bottom, gulping air, trying to take in the two men and the sudden prospect of rescue. Somehow Fitz crumpled next to me. We trembled, hugging each other. Overwhelmed with joy, we both began to cry.

"*Gracias, gracias,*" I repeated between sobs.

The men began to speak to each other in Quechua.

"I hope we can communicate with them," I said to Fitz.

He turned his head toward the Indian closest to him in the bow. "*¿Hablas español, señor?*"

The Indian nodded. His mouth opened but said nothing.

Using Spanish and his finger to point at himself and me, Fitz told them our names. Resting my hand on Fitz's back, I felt the effort it took for him to speak.

The men sat staring.

"What are your names?" I ventured, looking back and forth at each of them, hoping to give Fitz a moment to rest. "Roque," "Silverio," came their solemn replies.

Silverio, the man with the wider face who'd pulled us from the water, was seated at the stern. Up close, he looked Incan, his posture regally straight. His arms bulged like tree trunks from his white short-sleeved shirt. No taller than me, he was all muscle. His straight black hair was cut in bangs but fell to either side of his face, mostly under a bandanna. He looked blind in one eye. His good eye searched mine, but he said nothing. His soft *"pobre señora"* had soothed me, but now his solemn manner made me anxious. I couldn't tell if he was friend or foe. I looked for warmth in his good brown eye; his grayed eye didn't move.

Roque, slightly taller, had a slender face and physique. He had narrow cheekbones, a long nose, and arched eyebrows hinting at Spanish ancestry. His shirt was bright red, torn in the left shoulder. Patches covered the knees of his muddied khaki pants, and the big toe of his right foot burst from a hole in one boot.

"You're a miracle," I said in what I hoped was correct Spanish. "We've been here twenty-six days."

Roque blew air from his mouth so his cheeks puffed out, as if he were incredulous to see us. "Here there is no land, no people," he said in Spanish. He pointed to a tree that had dark green leaves grouped in fives, like fingers, converging to one stem. "In July, this lake dries. We can tap the rubber trees."

July's four months away, I thought. We would never have made it.

Once Roque started to speak, his Spanish grew loquacious. "We were on the Madre de Dios hunting turtles." He nodded to a dead turtle in the canoe. "We saw a monkey in a tree. Very good eating. We chased it through the flooded forest. When we got here, to Lago Santa Maria, we lost the monkey." He paused. "Then we saw you." He crossed himself. He still seemed amazed to see us.

I squeezed Fitz's hand. He sat in front of me, behind Roque. Fitz glanced at me, his eyes shadowy from hunger but glistening a little. When he put his arm around me, he was still trembling.

Lago Santa Maria. I wondered about such a beautiful name for a seasonal lake that could be so deadly. Roque's and Silverio's chiseled faces softened. Roque wanted to know how we ended up here.

Although weak, I was exhilarated and bursting to talk. Fitz joined in. Using rudimentary Spanish with lots of gesturing, we explained what had happened to us. The Indians' eyes widened as Fitz and I told our story.

At the end we were breathless. Looking around I saw we were still at the Pink Palace and wondered why we hadn't moved. The hunger gnawing in my stomach was an urgent need to escape. "Please, take us with you?" I pleaded.

"*Sí, sí, señora*," Silverio nodded, extending his hand but stopping short of touching me.

"*Oh, gracias.*" I wept, my shoulders shaking.

Fitz, his eyes ghostly again, asked if they had food: "*¿Tienes comida?*" He was so thin I thought he would blow away.

"*Sí*," Roque replied.

"Where?" asked Fitz, glancing wildly around the inside of the canoe.

"The *barraca*. Señora will feed you," Roque explained.

He looked beyond us and nodded to Silverio. They

still weren't moving the canoe. I became afraid they would change their minds and leave us here.

"What is '*barraca*'?" I asked.

"Downriver, a few hours from here," Roque replied.

I must have asked "where," not "what." The men began discussing something. What are they saying? I wondered.

Shifting my hand in the ten-foot dugout, I pressed down on something clammy behind me. I turned to look. My hand was on the head of a three-foot-long turtle wearing a grim smile. My hand shot back into my lap.

"She's dead," Roque beamed. He pointed to his friend and himself.

Rescuing us would cut short their hunting. Was that what they'd been discussing? I tapped Fitz. "What if they want to keep hunting? They might need this space in the boat for game."

Fitz pushed his hand through his hair. "They could be on a long expedition."

The canoe had been cut from a balsa tree by a machete. Besides the rifles and the turtle, I saw a green glass bottle and a small cloth bag. "They don't look like they have overnight supplies."

"Can we go with you?" Fitz asked again in Spanish.

"*Sí, sí,*" they both agreed. But still we did not move.

"*¿Ahora, por favor?*" I asked the men. Now, please?

"*Sí,*" said Silverio softly, but he didn't pick up his paddle.

"We were trying to get to Riberalta. How far is Riberalta?" I asked him.

The men conferred before Silverio replied, "Eight hours by boat."

We almost made it by ourselves, I thought. We were so close but for that abominable storm.

"*Comida*," Fitz pressed.

The late-morning glare on the hollows of his cheeks spotlighted his emaciated face, even with his beard.

"*Sí, sí*. Bring your things," Roque said.

"We can leave them." Fitz glanced at the Pink Palace. "You can have them. Just take us, please."

The men did not seem to be in a hurry. "Go." They gestured with their arms. What if they leave us the minute we climb out? I thought. I didn't want to budge.

Silverio smiled at us.

"Stay alert," Fitz warned me.

We crawled out of the canoe and into the tent. Peering out often, to make sure they were still there, we fumbled with fatigue as we tied our money belts around our waists and collected the black camera bag with the camera and film. I pushed my journal, thin budget notebook, and the parrot feather fan on top of the clothing into the bag. We couldn't think what else we would need.

We just wanted to climb back into the canoe before the men changed their minds.

We're going to get out of here; we're going to get home, I repeated to myself. I felt a spurt of energy from fear of being left behind as I dragged the black bag to the door. "Oh, Fitz. We've got to hurry. What else should we take?"

"Clothes," he mumbled, his eyes darting around our tiny home.

We stuffed clothes into the bag. None of our things mattered to me now. We emerged from the tent to see the men patiently waiting.

"More," they said when they saw how little we'd packed.

Reluctantly, we crept back under the plastic and dragged my orange backpack and Fitz's gray canvas bag outside. The Indians lifted them into the canoe.

"More!" Silverio held on to the Pink Palace with one hand.

"I'll get the woolen blankets and my typewriter then," Fitz said, half smiling.

We sat down on the Pink Palace and hauled ourselves into the canoe. "Please come back later for the rest. You can keep it all," I said.

The Indians leapt onto the raft. The canoe jumped away from the Pink Palace because Fitz and I weren't holding on to it. Fitz reached for a paddle and maneuvered the dugout close enough for me to grab the balsa. The men busily bundled the mosquito netting around the clothes we'd left in the tent. They grabbed the fishnet we'd made from Fitz's shirt, the hammocks we had planned to use on the boat we'd missed, the roll of extra plastic, rope, the pots and pans. They handed us the sleeping bag and Girl Scout kit.

Quickly the men ripped the faded plastic off the poles of the tent and yanked out the stakes. I wanted to cry out. No question, without the Pink Palace we wouldn't have stayed alive long enough for the Indians to find us. The men collected nails, pried the oilcan cookstove off the balsa, and placed them all in the canoe. Within minutes the Pink Palace was a bare raft again.

Our things were of considerable worth to the Indians. Fitz and I stared, openmouthed, as they began to pull up the tent's floorboards with pocket knives and their bare hands. Lago Santa Maria must not be close to their home, so they wanted to take everything now.

"Please," Fitz said, "will you come back for the boards later? We're so hungry."

"*Sí, comida, por favor.*" I had my hand at my stomach.

The men stopped to look at us then nodded to each

other. Silverio dropped the floorboard as Roque put his knife in his pocket.

"*Gracias*," we both said.

I don't know where they could have stacked the boards, anyway. The canoe was stuffed.

Their kindness brought tears to my eyes.

The Indians took their positions in the canoe. Roque, with good eyes, knelt in the bow.

Fitz sat behind him and I sat behind Fitz. Silverio took the stern to steer according to Roque's directions. He handed Fitz the green glass bottle. It was corked with a piece of corncob. "*Chicha*," said the Indian, indicating what we knew was fermented corn juice. We had tasted the mealy drink in Ecuador. The smell was distinctive.

Roque handed me a small cloth bag containing thin, circular pieces of fried plantain.

"Eat."

The preserved fruit was the first food we'd been offered in twenty-six days. My hands shook as I brought a chip to my mouth. They were hard and crunchy, like potato chips, but sweet.

At last the men began to paddle. As we pulled away from the raft, I listened for the jungle sounds behind me. No orchestrated birdsong farewell. No wing-flapping applause at our good fortune. Even the bees weren't around to witness our escape. The heat of midday had brought quiet to the animals. My body flinched as I heard a thin hum of bees in the marsh. A frog croaked, a tree creaked, there was a brief rustle in the canopy above, then sultry silence fell over us. I focused on the sound of the paddles slicing into the swamp. It was a paltry good-bye.

As we floated briskly away, I stared back at what remained.

A narrow row of balsa logs held only paperbacks scattered across the partly raised floorboards, the bones of our Palace. I would never return. Neither mourning nor wistful, I was serenely joyous, grateful beyond telling. I would need no lingering look to remember the Pink Palace forever.

Facing forward, I was curious to see how the Indians would find their way to the elusive river. The dugout rode the flooded lowlands much higher than our little balsas had. Sunlight glittered on the water, dancing in front of us. Like angels guiding us, I thought. "I wonder how they'll get out of here?" I asked Fitz. "I'm sure they can't go up against the current."

"I was wondering that, too," Fitz replied, his brow furrowing. "Probably the same way they came in."

The Indians crossed our bay to the opposite side of the swamp, about an eighth of a mile. The paddles plunged into the murky water, deep and smooth. We made good time. Roque called out obstacles, and Silverio steered around them. They headed directly through the flooded jungle, between the trees, occasionally hacking at brush with their knives.

Fitz and I grasped each other's hands and mumbled, "Thank you, thank you," to God, and to these two men. I was overwhelmed with emotion, my entire body shaking, tears filling my eyes. Silverio patted my head, moaning, "*Señora, señora.*"

Fitz's face and body unexpectedly tensed. His eyes darted around the dark forest. "Where are we going?"

I felt perfectly relaxed with these men, like a child with her parents. "Don't worry. They know what they're doing," I reassured Fitz. I had no doubt about them.

"How do we know where they're taking us?" Fitz asked.

"We're just going to have to trust them."

We ducked under branches as the canoe rode midway up the trees. The branches beneath the water level scraped and slowed us down. It was much cooler in the darkness, even without a breeze. A shiver passed through me. Looking up, I saw shafts of light falling between the trees, briefly illuminating us, like God's grace.

The Indians found a narrow opening into a canopy of taller trees, many of them palms, which we hadn't seen along the swamp. Once we were inside the canopy, the low horizontal vines weren't as numerous, allowing the canoe to glide easily over the calm water, well above the mud and bushes below. Tall, smooth trees and rough-barked palms rose from the water in silent witness to our liberation. The streaming light now changed to dappling splashes on the dark, swampy bayou.

"Where are we going?" I asked, turning to Silverio.

"*Barraca de Santo Domingo, señora*," Roque replied.

"Good news. We'll be there soon," I told Fitz, my hand resting on his shoulder. He nodded, his eyes suspiciously searching our surroundings.

"How long to get there?" I asked. "My stomach wants to know." I tried to make them laugh, and it was true, my stomach did want to know.

"Soon, soon," Roque chuckled.

"Will we get food?"

"*Sí. Comida.*"

I started naming foods in Spanish. "Oranges, rice, beans, bread."

"*Sí,*" they giggled.

As we skimmed into a wide pool of open water the Indians set their paddles across their laps. I felt sure there was quickmud below us. The men mumbled to each other as the canoe became still. A few minutes passed. I felt panic rising in my chest as Fitz's back stiffened. Are they lost? I wondered. Even if they were, I knew they would find their way again. This was their world.

"They could do away with us, right here," Fitz said, tension in his voice. "They've got guns, and we're too weak to fight back. They could shoot us and push us over the side."

I was alarmed. "Why would they do that?"

"We have things they might want."

For a moment, all turned black in my mind. I realized that if the Indians wanted to, they could easily kill us and leave. No one would ever know.

A scowl sat on Fitz's forehead. His jaw twitched under his stubble. "Be ready," he warned.

"Maybe they're just trying to find their way out."

"They know this area like we know Danbury. Why would they be lost?"

"Sometimes we get lost in Connecticut."

The Indians' mumbling stopped. The canoe started forward across the big span of dark water, toward eleven o'clock, then again entered a group of tight, interlocking trees.

I heard Fitz sigh.

After about an hour, perhaps two, we broke through the trees and glided toward a wide brown river.

"Madre de Dios?" Fitz asked.

"*Sí, señor*," Roque replied.

My breath came short.

We'd tried so hard and fought so long to reach the river. Now that we were here she flowed steadily, indifferently, pushing stolidly on toward Brazil. The river reflected the colors of everything she saw: abundant green trees, gray

Me with residents of *Barraca* Santo Domingo, an oasis on the banks of Rio Madre de Dios. With the depletion of the rubber market, the site has since been swallowed by the jungle.

At Santo Domingo with Roque and Silverio, the two heroes who came upon us just in time. Fitz is able to stand only by clutching Roque's trousers with his left hand. I am standing but barely.

Gregoria (*left*) holding a plate of the chicken given to us by Roque and his wife. Her nephew (*right*) who would take us downriver is with his family. His youngest daughter holds a string attached to her pet baby monkey at her side.

Barraca Santo Domingo, quite possibly what heaven looks like. I took this photo as we were leaving. I didn't want to leave it and the people; I didn't want to leave the land. I hated to go back on the river, but we had to look forward, take one more step toward home.

Our boat to Riberalta. We weren't strong enough to sit on the benches, so Fitz and I were told we could lie down on the enormous pile of Brazil nuts. We ate some as we went downriver, amusing fellow passengers, since the nuts were meant to be eaten by pigs, not people.

The wonderful nurses' aides at Hospital Riberalta, where we recuperated, who loved to braid my hair. They were fascinated by my blue-green eyes.

Fitz "fattened up" after seventeen days of three meals and two snacks daily. It was never enough food.

At the Plaza de Armas in Lima, Peru. We were a plane ride away from home, so grateful to be alive and together, and so anxious to be reunited with our loved ones.

Home! *Left to right*: me with my niece Liza; my mom; my sister, Mimi; and our dogs. My good friend Bejou made a necklace with a bell (not visible here) for me so that I could never again be lost. I'm wearing that turquoise necklace in this photograph.

clouds, slate sky. I leaned over the side of the dugout and scooped water into my hand. It looked clear compared to the swamp water we'd been drinking.

"I said I'd kiss her if I ever saw her again." I smiled at Fitz, touching my lips to the water.

She hadn't even noticed we were gone. I placed my hand on Fitz's back. He was still tense.

"Lago Santa Maria begins up there." Roque pointed behind us to a separate channel that led off the main river.

I stared at the entrance of our storm-driven turn toward disaster. Then I averted my eyes from that channel for the very last time. "How much longer?" I asked, desperate for food.

"Twenty minutes," Silverio said, moving his head back and forth.

We can make that, I thought, though the anticipation was excruciating. South American time ran slower than ours. Twenty minutes could mean hours, or even most of a day. No matter, I told myself. We will survive.

The mile-wide Madre was calm, unlike the night when she'd nearly killed me. The two men paddled hard to break into her main current, then we glided effortlessly downriver toward the place the Indians called home.

A red riverbank rose on the distant side. We had not seen solid earth in nearly a month.

"Land!"

"We're not there yet," Fitz replied.

Chapter 41

Barraca

Fitz was irritable. "They must have food at the *barraca*. I need to eat!"

"We're almost there." I tried to soothe him as I told myself, We've waited twenty-six days. We can wait a little longer.

Fitz hadn't been grouchy during our month of starvation, but now that we knew food was coming, his restraint had burst its dam. I understood how he felt. I wanted to devour oranges by the tree-load. I wanted land to cradle me. Like an infant, I wanted my needs taken care of, immediately.

"Will there be fruit?" I asked Roque.

"*Sí.*"

"Meat?" Fitz blurted.

"*Sí.*"

"Rice?"

"*Sí.*"

We needed constant assurance.

Nosing around a bend, we saw four small thatched roofs about fifty yards up an emerald hill carved out of the jungle.

"*¿Barraca?*" I asked.

"*Sí, señora. Es Santo Domingo.*"

Fitz and I squeezed each other's hands. We couldn't take our eyes off the row of wooden buildings and the long sweep of green grass rising to meet them. I took a deep breath. I knew I was going to cry.

The dugout struck the bank with a thump.

When the Indians helped us clamber out of the canoe, we collapsed onto solid ground. I stroked the soil, mesmerized by the sweet, moist earth, tears flowing off my chin.

Roque and Silverio practically carried us up to a tree near a house. Fitz and I dropped onto our backs in the tree's shade. The Indians trudged back to the canoe to collect our packs, leaving us alone with the unbearable anticipation of eating. My sharp bones pinched me as I sought to position my crumpled body. Within seconds, a few natives wandered over.

"*Buenos días. ¿Tienes comida?*"

"*Sí,*" they replied, but they offered us nothing.

A few chickens pecked in the grass nearby. Fitz eyed them hungrily but he didn't move.

The house on short stilts had a porch. A building to the right of us had no walls, just a steep roof that reached almost to the ground. The third building was another stilt house, and the last one looked like a barn with hay packed around its foundation. I glanced down the hill toward a black-and-pink mottled pig grunting along a worn dirt path toward us. Food, I thought, but my body refused to budge.

There were footsteps beside us. A woman in a white shirtwaist dress stood cradling the biggest orange I'd ever seen. A blue headband held her brown curly hair in place around her stern, flat face. She stared down. I stared at the orange.

A younger woman came with her small daughter. She

knelt and began to fan me with her hand. It felt exquisite in the stiff, hot air. The older woman handed us the orange. We peeled it, trembling. We devoured it instantly, sucking the bitter peel.

A crowd of ten to fifteen gathered around, staring as if we were exotic animals. Roque spoke Quechua to them, apparently telling our story, which he repeated to each new arrival. Silverio nodded and beamed.

"What's going to happen to us, Fitz? We can't even walk." I felt we were at the people's mercy, and no one seemed to be in charge.

"Are we going to get more to eat?" Fitz grimaced as he turned onto his side. His bones looked ready to puncture his skin.

I pulled myself up on my arms to lean against the trunk of the tree. "I hope so." My spine felt raw against the bark, but sitting up gave me a better view. I tried to see past the growing crowd.

Fitz raised his eyes to find Roque. "¿*Comida?*" he whispered.

"*Sí, señor.*"

The Indians and mestizos jostled for position, moving in closer to us. Unable to sit up any longer, I crumpled to the grass.

At that moment, a small plate of rice and fried plantain was passed through the crowd to us. We couldn't see who had brought it, but we ate it with our hands. Another peeled orange followed. We split it and put it to our lips.

I closed my eyes to savor the pulp melting in my mouth. There was so much juice it flowed like a stream down my chin.

Fitz placed his finger on my chin to catch the escaping juice, pushing it back up to my lips for me to drink.

Just then the crowd parted. A European-looking woman with short, curly silver-brown hair appeared. She wore slacks and a fitted top, like my mom. Hands on her hips, she scowled, snatching the orange from us and throwing it away. I watched the pieces roll down the hill. "Bad for you," she scolded, shaking her head. She was Bolivian and spoke Spanish. "You can't have acid. Stomach, stomach!" She rolled her hand in front of her abdomen. A concerned smile flickered across her face. "I am Gregoria Desdre." She turned to Roque and Silverio, directing them to take our belongings into her house.

We entered a small sitting room with a wood floor, reed walls, and red curtains tied back from screened windows. Four wooden chairs, two benches, a small table, a treadle sewing machine, and a torn hammock furnished the simple room. Roque guided me to a chair, but Fitz couldn't take another step and buckled to the floor.

I stood up to help him but fell back onto the seat, my legs also liquid.

He barely nodded. "I'm all right. I just need food."

A number of people were already sitting and standing around the room. With a sweep of her hand, Gregoria introduced us to her tiny white-haired mother and other family members.

"I'll make food," she announced before she disappeared through a dark doorway.

Someone hung a hammock from the roof for me. Someone else pushed two benches together for Fitz to lie on. One young girl entertained us with her baby pet monkey on a string. I smiled as the monkey scrambled up and down her arm. I thought of the monkey that had led the Indians to us. It was a friend, not food. Squealing children chased a ball that rolled under my hammock. Girls of different ages gathered around me, exclaiming excitedly over my colorful cloisonné ring. We'd given most of our belongings to Roque and Silverio, but now I wished we also had something for these people who'd taken us into their home.

Fitz remembered that in the black bag were two rings he'd given me, as well as ten straw rings I'd bought in Copacabana. I found them in a side pocket and handed them out to Gregoria's nieces and grandnieces. I also took two rings off my fingers and gave them away.

Sitting on a chair beside us, Roque explained that he didn't want our possessions.

"We want you to have them," I insisted.

"We want to give you more!" Fitz added.

Roque put his hand up. "No, no."

I looked at his toe poking out of his old, ripped shoes. These people deserved more than what they had.

Gregoria said that our beaded jewelry, sheets, pots and pans, mosquito netting, and other camping supplies would make the Indians wealthy by comparison with others on the *barraca*. They were, she explained, serfs to her brother, who owned Santo Domingo, the rubber tree plantation, along with the horses, pigs, cows, and chickens that we'd seen wandering on the lawn.

Though the Desdre family lived simply, their clothes weren't torn or ragged. They slept in beds rather than hammocks. Their home had a wooden floor, not packed dirt.

Gregoria gave us cups of what she called nestone. The hot, extremely sweet liquid cereal, made with a great deal of milk and sugar, went down so easily. Gregoria insisted on pacing the food portions. The gruel, later a bit of fish and rice, later a little more.

I was extremely warm, despite being inside the house and away from the pepper-hot sun. A girl pulled a chair near my hammock and began to fan me. Her name was Mercedes, she said shyly, her large eyes at half-mast.

Children tittered as they brought us sugarcane and a small yellow fruit with a large pit. It didn't have much meat but tasted delicious. I could hardly believe this wasn't a dream. A warm glow of tranquility suffused me.

"Let's celebrate this day every year," I suggested to Fitz. "March 16 will be our personal Thanksgiving for how fortunate we are."

Effusiveness overpowered my fatigue. I tried to raise myself in the hammock to look at him.

"I like it." He smiled from the bench-bed, where he looked peaceful. "Instead of eating the rich meals we dreamed of on the raft, we'll give thanks with food like we ate today."

Gregoria returned with a comb and sat beside me. She and Mercedes began to sort tangles from my hair. I'd assumed that if we ever escaped my long hair would have to be shorn, but these patient women proceeded to comb it smooth then wove a braid down my back. It felt so good to be spoiled by these strangers.

Gregoria gave me dry clothes to replace my damp ones.

Her nieces helped to shuffle us over to the little table. We ate roasted banana that was dry and hard to swallow. Gregoria joined us as we greedily slurped the hot soup, chicken, and rice.

When we'd finished we lay down again, deliriously satiated. My heart leapt wildly. I was intoxicated with being alive.

A few minutes later, men showed up with fresh fish. As the red sun set they wanted to hear our story. There were no lamps, but a three-quarter moon soon streamed soft blue light through the windows. We talked in the dark to their seated shadows.

They asked us where we would go next. "Riberalta," Fitz replied. They told us local boats traveled to Riberalta every couple of days to take produce to market. Like taxis, they stopped at *barracas* to pick up passengers. We would be able to catch a ride in the morning.

In response to Gregoria's demands that we see a doctor, we agreed to stop by the Maryknoll missionary hospital in Riberalta for a quick checkup before continuing our worldwide journey. Although we still couldn't walk without support, we were both so elated that we didn't doubt we could keep traveling.

The little house filled with the aroma of freshly cooked fish. One of Gregoria's nephews took my arm to guide me, by lantern light, to the tiny eating nook. Another one helped Fitz. The nook barely had room for the four-foot table and a bench on either side. I squeezed onto a bench then was startled by something rough and warm against my legs. I lifted the table cloth to find a big sow, snuffling for scraps.

"Fitz, look!" It seemed so incongruous, so magnificent.

Fitz smiled. "I bet you'd love one of those under our table at home."

"Yes!"

"Not for bacon," he promised, now that our stomachs were finally being filled.

The fish was served with a buttery sauce, and we inhaled every bite. The lantern light played on the walls and faces, casting an orange glow over the room.

"I'll never forget this day, or your kindness," I told Gregoria and the rest. "Thank you."

"*Sí, sí.*" They nodded. "*Es extraordinario.*"

Fitz looked exhausted, murmuring, "Thank you so much."

Marina, the niece, noticed our eyes drooping. "Come. You must be tired."

She made us a bed on the sitting-room floor with sheets, blankets, and our still-damp sleeping bag for padding. Many people sat around the edges of the dark, bare room, talking quietly as we lay down.

Drifting toward sleep, I heard a boat's engine cutting to silence at the Santo Domingo bank. Marina jumped up and ran out. We learned it was her husband returning from upriver with a boatload of Brazil nuts. He joined us in the sitting room, eager to hear our story. My eyes closed in the darkness, lulled toward blissful sleep by their lilting Spanish voices. He would take us to Riberalta in the morning.

"*¡Señora, señor!*" I was jolted awake by Gregoria as she led a man and woman through the front door. More people! She lifted her lantern to the man's face. It was Roque. He'd come to introduce us to his wife. She stepped forward and handed me three perfect white eggs; then a plastic bag of bananas was dropped onto our sleeping bag. "*Por señora.*" Roque placed a pure-white hen in my hands. It all happened so quickly. Tears flooded my eyes.

"We can't take these," I said.

"You must," Gregoria responded.

She explained that Roque and Silverio didn't feel right about accepting our gifts, so they'd come to give us one of their best chickens and three white eggs, a week's worth of wages. They, who had so little, gave so much. It was difficult to stop crying.

Eventually the Desdre family and friends went to bed. Fitz was lightly snoring, but I couldn't get back to sleep. It was stifling on the floor, and the mosquitoes had found their way in, despite the screens. I watched the hammock sway in the windows' breeze. It would be cooler than the sleeping bag. I climbed into it.

My spine curved to the rope cradle as I studied moon-lit patterns on the floorboards. Extending my arm into the moonlight's path, I watched my hand turn silver. The splendid moon's puckered face looked down at me as if we were the only ones awake in the world. Its beam seemed to wink approval that Fitz and I were safe. The last three-quarter moon had led us to the riverbank in Puerto Maldonado, for our very first night on the raft. It seemed so long ago.

Gratitude settled into my soul as I cherished this private moment with the moon. I'd savor each day, clear or stormy, for the rest of my life.

Chapter 42

Maryknoll

MARCH 17

I awoke in the darkness to voices down at the boat. Everyone was up but Fitz and me. Gregoria soon brought us nestone, bread, and coffee. I wanted to ask her if we could have Roque's eggs for breakfast but it seemed there was no time—Marina's husband was in a hurry to go.

"Ooh, I feel terrible," Fitz moaned, bending over with both hands on his stomach. He'd eaten too much last night, but there was no time to feel better.

"Can you make it?"

"Yeah, we can't miss this ride."

We gathered what wasn't already in our bags, leaving the eggs in the drawer where I'd placed them.

"What about my lovely chicken?" I asked Fitz. "Can we take it with us?"

Gregoria overheard me. She picked up the live chicken and said she'd cook it. I was heartened that she could cook a chicken when there seemed to be no time to cook eggs, but she was boss and people followed her lead. She must have decided the captain could wait. For a moment I was wistful about the fate of the chicken, almost wanting to keep it as a pet. Within twenty minutes, the chicken had been killed, plucked, cooked, and plated for us to take with us. As the sun rose behind the hill, somehow I managed enough strength to take photos of our rescuers together, one of Roque and his wife, and some of the Desdre clan. Then I showed a young man—who I don't believe had ever seen a camera before—where to press the button to photograph Roque and Silverio with Fitz and me.

The twenty-foot boat, piled high with Brazil nuts, was roofed from bow to stern. Fitz and I plopped down on top of the mountain of bumpy nuts. Gregoria handed us the chicken and hugged us. I photographed the well-wishers cascading down the hill to see us off. Silverio and Roque and his wife boarded briefly to say good-bye. We sat on the nuts, not able to rise easily. Eyes misty, we each hugged these men who had plucked us from certain death.

Lines were hauled, the engine roared, and the men pushed off. The trip would take about six hours.

Two girls, also passengers from the *barraca*, offered us Santo Domingo oranges. "The best on the river," one said.

"The best anywhere," I replied, and meant it.

We ate all of Roque's bananas as we talked, then extras were passed out. We ate some of those, too. Then we offered our chicken. Most travelers politely declined, saying it was ours to eat. It was our second dinner from Gregoria. I saved the wishbone for good luck.

It was Saint Patrick's Day. I would accept more of Fitz's Irish luck if it came. I'd never seen the serendipitous monkey, but I gave him thanks for guiding Roque and Silverio to us. I hoped that he'd have a blessed life.

"I don't think that monkey came by chance," I said to Fitz. "He could have been a spirit of good fortune sent to save us."

Fitz was looking out at the Madre, which was perfectly reflecting a bank of clouds and the never-ending jungle as we motored along. He turned his gaze to me. "I've been wondering about that myself." His voice was barely audible over the engine. "There's a monkey on my family's Irish coat of arms. It seems such a coincidence."

"A monkey?"

"Yeah. Supposedly it snatched a FitzGerald baby from its cradle and carried it out of a burning home."

"Amazing!"

Fitz nodded. "Doesn't it seem weird that a monkey has saved FitzGeralds again?"

I tried to fathom how the pieces came together. "Remember how I just knew we'd get out of the swamp yesterday? I felt so sure of it but didn't understand why. Perhaps it was divine intervention."

"Maybe so," Fitz replied, gazing at the riverbank.

Within the hour I felt urgently hungry. The cook on the small boat had boiled rice with some unknown meat and tossed baked bananas into it. After the others had eaten, one of the passengers shoveled a pile of rice into his bowl and handed it to me, along with his spoon. I grabbed the rice with my hands and gobbled it down. Fitz complained about stomach cramps and didn't eat the meal. He did crack open a few Brazil nuts, using a board as a hammer.

We became tranquilized by the breezes and scenery, forgetting that just a few hours earlier we could barely walk to the launch. We discussed continuing our trip, as if nothing had happened to impede us. Too happy to sleep, I relished the feeling of being safe.

Fitz dozed as the motor hummed. By midafternoon, Riberalta's waterfront appeared. Closer to the harbor I noticed circles of iridescent oil undulating on the surface. Small motorboats buzzed every which way. Long, flat-bowed riverboats, just like ours, floated near the worn clay bank with planks thrown to board or exit.

Hacked from the forest, Riberalta stood high up the bank, a jumble of structures with corrugated roofs and peeling stucco walls splattered with mud. I was transfixed as I watched the men moving about on the bank, loading and unloading boats.

"Wake up, Fitz. We're here!" I jiggled his shoulder and grabbed his hand.

Gregoria had told us to stay with her sister in Riberalta, but no one had mentioned that on the trip. As the captain steered the boat to shore, he asked us where we were going. Fitz and I looked at each other.

"The hospital," I said, and turned to Fitz. "Afterward we can go to a restaurant and get a huge meal."

The plank from the boat to the bank was narrow and long. My legs began to sway under the weight of my backpack and the camera bag. I tried to put one foot in front of the other without falling.

"Fitz, are you okay?" I called behind me. He didn't reply.

When I made it to shore I turned to see him trying to carry the typewriter and his bag down the plank. His eyes rolled upward as he began to teeter. I wanted to run to him, but I could barely stand myself. I wanted to yell at the captain, but I could only whisper, "Please help him." He didn't hear me. Incredibly, Fitz reached the riverbank.

Catching my breath, I called to the captain, "How can we get to the hospital?"

He pointed for us to walk up a high hill to the plaza, saying that we'd find a motorbike taxi. We knew Riberalta had few roads, all of them dirt. Motorbikes had arrived in town only within the past year. We stared up the hill, immobile. Finally, the captain beckoned to a young relative to carry some of our luggage.

Fitz stumbled, fragile as a feather, up the steep, red-mud slope, carrying the typewriter and the camera bag. I wobbled close behind him in case he fell. Pure grit got Fitz up that hill.

Two motorbike taxis pulled up next to us. Fitz struggled onto the first one; the second driver helped me onto his dusty seat. We clung to our drivers as the motorbikes swerved around mudholes and over bumps, then screeched to a stop at a low, white stucco building just a few minutes away.

A woman in a white uniform called from the porch in English, telling us to go to another entrance, before she disappeared. Now that we'd arrived at the hospital, my legs and arms refused to work. I slumped over the gate.

"Are they just going to leave us here?" I said to Fitz. "I can't take another step."

"If they don't come, we'll have to drop here and sleep on the ground," Fitz said softly. A nurse with snow-white hair came out the door and walked down the path toward us. A halo of sun sparkled around her and bounced off the gold cross at her neck. "I'm Sister Bernice, director of this hospital," she said, in a New England accent. She studied us with her piercing blue eyes under black eyebrows. "May I help you?"

"Yes, please." I could barely lift my voice.

"Speak up, please."

"Can't walk . . . need food."

She asked me how we got to the hospital—as if there were no urgency.

Fitz was too weak to talk. I couldn't stand it a moment longer. "My husband needs help! Please!"

"Come in," she said, finally taking charge and opening the gate.

Fitz and I willed ourselves to move. We leaned on each other as we walked the ten-yard cement path then staggered up the four stairs to a porch. A round-faced nun was drinking lemonade and eating cookies.

"We don't see many Americans in Riberalta." Cocking her head in the direction of the round-faced nun, she said, "This is Sister Patricia. Please, sit down."

Fitz and I slumped onto wooden chairs.

Sister Bernice gestured toward the blue tin of Danish cookies. "Help yourselves. I'll get you glasses for the lemonade."

"What are you doing out here, in the jungle?" I asked, before crunching a buttery cookie.

"We're Maryknoll sisters, based in New York," Sister Bernice replied. "The Maryknoll brothers asked us to help with health care along these rivers. We saw the need was great, so we started this hospital." She smiled as she set down two glasses and poured.

My hands shook as I lifted the lemonade to my mouth. Fitz and I gulped down four glasses each. The nuns stared at us but politely said nothing.

"I've called the doctor," Sister Bernice continued. "He doesn't live far from here. Where are you from?"

"Connecticut." I looked at Fitz, who was trying to get comfortable in the chair. He had a cookie waiting at his lips to replace the one he was chewing.

"So am I!" the nun replied.

Turns out her hometown was only a half hour from where I grew up. I shook my head. This day was surely strewn with stars. Reality seemed unhinged, as if we were sitting on porch chairs back in the States.

Despite the sugar boost, Fitz and I could not prop ourselves up. We were both flopped over when Dr. Vaca Diez arrived.

He was a portly, distinguished-looking man in his sixties with gray hair, and dressed in a gray summer suit. He first conferred with Sister Bernice then he examined Fitz and me.

"You've lost a great deal of weight," he said as he escorted me down the hall toward the scale. "You're both extremely dehydrated. Your husband's reflexes are imperceptible. How long have you been unable to walk unaided?"

"We've been crawling for weeks," I replied.

Dr. Vaca Diez told Sister Bernice to admit us to the hospital immediately.

"We have two beds you can have for a couple of days," she agreed.

I'd expected to be examined, given medication, and then sent off to a hotel. The doctor's verdict flooded me with relief. The luck of the Irish was with us still.

The nurses put Fitz to bed, drew blood, and hooked him up to an IV. I was disappointed to learn that patients were separated by gender, married or not, four to a room.

After Fitz fell asleep, Sister Bernice sat with me in a dark hallway with dim generator lighting. "Tell me how this happened." She slipped an IV into my arm.

"I don't know where to start." I began to shiver as our reality settled in.

"You're safe now," she said kindly, placing my hands in hers to quiet them.

My words spilled out like the flooding river. Sister Bernice listened in a warm and friendly way, her intelligent eyes locked onto mine. She looked overwhelmed by my story as she massaged my hands and sometimes closed her eyes, before quietly asking for more details.

I described the three phases, as I saw them, of survival that Fitz and I had gone through as we'd faced death on the raft. There was the initial action stage, when we'd tried to escape the swamp, fueled by our hope of getting out. Then came the talking and meditation stage, a period of acceptance that we were stranded, when we'd prayed, reasoned with, and questioned God.

Finally, we'd entered the single-focused hunt for food, no matter how small the morsel. These stages intertwined and overlapped, but they also felt like separate experiences because of the emotions that characterized each one.

I talked on and on. Now that we were safe, now that Fitz was safe, I wasn't afraid to face the truth. The relief was staggering.

My worst thoughts were confirmed when Sister Bernice said that she and Dr. Vaca Diez didn't think we could have survived beyond another day or two. The realization that we'd been so close to death, that Fitz was still too close, battered my mind. I began to cry.

Fears that I hadn't dared even to write in my journal were validated. Each night I had prayed that Fitz would wake in the morning. I hadn't feared not waking up myself. If I'd gone first, it would have been better than my waking up to find Fitz dead. Watching him deteriorate had been unbearable. Now I was free to feel it all.

"What would I have done with his body?" I asked Sister Bernice, shaking violently. "I don't think I could have pushed it into the swamp, or held him as he rotted in the sun."

She hugged me, silently, as we both shook with tears.

Chapter 43

Riberalta

It was midnight when Sister Bernice finally led me to a room. She dressed me in a clean pink-and-white-striped hospital gown, also called a johnny gown or johnny, and a pink floral cotton bathrobe. On the table that swung across my bed she placed a toothbrush, toothpaste, a bowl to spit into, and a mirror. "Tomorrow we'll give you a sponge bath. You're not ready to stand in a shower just yet."

I climbed between the crisp white sheets that smelled so fresh, felt so good against my skin. As I brushed my teeth, I examined my sunburned face in the little handheld mirror and told my bony self that I was the most fortunate woman on earth. Lying back on the bed, I sank into the pillow, breathing a deep, luxuriant sigh

That first night did not go well. I worried about Fitz being way down the hall. We'd been together through this whole ordeal. Half of me had been cut away. What if he needed help and no one was there?

During the night I sensed an enormous dark figure emerge from under my bed and move slowly up the footboard to hover over me. Even without opening my eyes I knew Death. Had he already taken Fitz? My heart was a jackhammer. I tried to calm myself, but my whole body was shaking. It took me a few minutes to find the courage to open my eyes to see that I was safe. I smelled an antiseptic hospital odor and saw light coming into the room through the opened door. Our rescue was real. I willed myself to relax into the sheets and smooth mattress until I eventually slipped into sleep.

I was confined to bed for several days, and so was Fitz. My arms ached to hug him. I wrote love notes and sent them to him through the nurses and their aides making rounds. Fitz sent me notes as well. I constantly asked the nurses for updates. His blood work showed that he had parasitic amoebas, which explained the cramps whenever he ate. No one could understand why I didn't have them, too. The doctor hypothesized the amoebas had been lying dormant in Fitz since Vietnam. He prescribed strychnine to rid Fitz of them. The poison gave him even worse cramps, but apparently that was the only way to kill the parasites.

I was constantly hungry. For the first two days at the hospital, we ate only soup. The doctor didn't want us to eat too much, too soon. Our stomachs had shrunk and would need time to expand. We were allowed a snack of crackers, fruit, and tea before lunch and dinner to hold us over.

It didn't take long to notice that my Bolivian roommates, two women and a little girl, received far bigger meals. When the food arrived from the kitchen I threw up my hands and said, in an exaggerated tone, "¡Que! ¿Nada?" to make them giggle. My tray came later, from the sisters' kitchen, with boiled, filtered water, and North American food. Playing to my audience, I'd stare at the single cup of soup then groan, "¡Que! ¿No mas?" This entertained them immensely.

Meals were markers of the day. When I wasn't eating, I was lying in bed reading or writing letters. Sometimes I'd write in my journal, or tell my roommates stories in poor Spanish. The nurses enjoyed listening to my stories and liked to tell stories, too. Sister Virginia, who had vibrant red hair and luminescent skin, couldn't understand how we'd survived in the swamp for so long. Eyes round with terror, she described poisonous spiders and boa constrictors dropping from trees.

"And the caimans," she emphasized, "they'll eat you in a minute! God's will kept you both alive. A miracle."

I marveled that we had never even seen a caiman.

Green geckos scampered up and down the wall behind my headboard.

"They're just catching bugs," Sister Virginia grinned. "It's tarantulas you have to watch out for in the shower—when you get well enough to take one."

Dr. Vaca Diez dropped by every day. The sisters boasted that he came from a pioneering Bolivian family for which the province was named. He explained that even though the hospital had just twenty beds, it was one of the finest in Bolivia. I looked out my window at the brown Rio Beni passing by the hospital grounds before it emptied into the Madre de Dios. This is the finest hospital on Earth, I thought.

After three or four days I was strong enough to walk down the hall to Fitz's room, pushing my IV cradle before me. Fitz wasn't ready to walk, so we played cards on his bed table and talked about the hospital, food, and home. He was ever ravenous and grouchy from his pain.

In our second week, we both began to receive normal-sized portions of food, though Fitz didn't believe it. One day he studied his breakfast tray of oatmeal, two eggs over easy, bacon, toast, and tea. He banged his hand on his tray and demanded of Sister Bernice, "When am I ever going to get a decent meal around here?"

I was stunned, but Sister Bernice understood that Fitz was not in his right mind.

Starvation made him feel like he was never going to get enough food, ever. "Your body is malnourished and craves food. It's normal to feel this isn't enough," she explained.

I held Fitz's hand. "Hang on, Fitz. We're lucky to be alive. And look at all this food—more breakfast than we dreamed of on the Pink Palace! It's a feast!" I tousled his hair. "Your stomach just hasn't caught up to your head."

"It's hard to believe this really is enough," he grumbled, simmering down.

I knew I was getting better when my yearning for food was replaced by a strong desire to talk to my parents. Brother Casmir, a ham radio operator, lived in a house next door to the nuns. He was able to patch us through to a ham radio operator in Rhode Island, Dick Canavan. Our parents hadn't known anything about our disappearance until Dick called them at home and explained where we were.

My heart soared at my mother's voice.

"Oh, darling," she cried. "We had no idea. You said you'd be off in the jungle and wouldn't send mail. We're so glad you're in such a wonderful hospital. How are you feeling? Are you getting plenty to eat?"

"We're having great food," I assured her, fighting back tears. "We're getting stronger by the minute. What are you and Dad up to? How's Zelda? How are Mimi and Brad and Liza?" I didn't dare talk about what we'd been through.

"The symphony is throwing a fund-raiser ball with a moon-walk theme." She giggled. "Dad has blown a twenty-foot-tall Styrofoam coating onto chicken wire and painted it mustard. It makes quite a mountain in the backyard."

I laughed. "I can't wait to see it."

"It's so big he's not sure how to get it to the ballroom. He may have to cut it into pieces."

My mother didn't touch on our time in the swamp, except to say, "It must have been awful." She may have been eager to hear our story but didn't want to push me in case I wasn't ready, perhaps recognizing that I just wanted news of home.

Dad got on the phone next. "A raft? How did it happen? How did you make it out?" They'd only heard rudiments from Dick, who didn't know the full story himself. I said something vague to Dad, sensing that he didn't want to upset me.

Mom got on again. "I love you, darling. We miss you. Come home as soon as you can. Dick will let us know when to pick you up at the airport."

I heard yearning in her voice. It matched my own longing to see her. I couldn't remember the last time she'd spoken cuddly words to me. My parents were reserved. Mom saying she loved me brought a lump to my throat. It was a gift that encouraged me. "I love you, too, Mom. I love you both. I can't tell you how much we thought of you on the raft. It helped us to keep going . . ."

I broke off as I choked up. The phone cut out.

In the afternoon of April 2, I put on my short floral skirt, white top, and brown sandal heels. I'd gained back most of my weight from 93 pounds and could fill my clothes. Not so with Fitz. His jeans were pinned in folds around him, but the doctor felt he was ready to travel. He'd been 124 pounds when he'd arrived at the hospital. He was still much too thin at 136 pounds, but his reflexes were back and he could walk without assistance. He was cleanly shaven except for his usual mustache. I could see his chiseled jaw, but his eyes were clear again behind his glasses, a brilliant sky blue.

Before leaving, we posed for photographs with several nuns and their aides, as well as one of my roommates. Sister Bernice had been called away to the river clinic. I was surprised how much I already missed her. I found myself wishing that the hospital staff wouldn't be so far away that I would never see them again.

A car waited for us as we thanked and hugged everyone good-bye. Fitz and I walked back through the gate we'd collapsed onto just sixteen days earlier.

I felt weak climbing onto the plane. We'd not flown since Sepa. There was so much to absorb from our experiences, but all I could think of was home.

Fitz and I held hands, a little more tightly than usual, as the plane took off. Once we were in the air, I looked down at the rivers that converged at Riberalta like liquid snakes. The plane dipped as it turned then leveled off, revealing a series of lakes that twinkled below us. It flew so quickly over this world of water that I realized the Pink Palace could not have been easy to spot from the air. I wouldn't have been able to see her even if we had flown right over Lago Santa Maria because we'd given the pink and blue plastic to Roque and Silverio. There was nothing to distinguish our raft now from any other pile of brown logs on the water.

Fitz squeezed my hand then looked out the window of the small craft. He turned his eyes to me, leaned close, and whispered, "I hope we prove to be as worthy as somebody up there thinks we are."

Within two days we arrived at JFK International Airport, at last safe in the arms of our families, with Zelda licking my knee for attention.

Epilogue

There is no hallmark card for Raft Day, but every year on March 16 Fitz and I replicate the meal Gregoria served us. The bits of orange, fish, and rice reflect the understatement of our rescue. No helicopters. No fanfare. No TV cameras. Our lives were saved by the decision of two men to turn their dugout canoe into the flooded jungle to chase a monkey.

Fitz and I spent that spring and summer recuperating, mostly at my parents' vacation home in Stowe, Vermont, where Fitz helped my dad and a friend build an addition onto the little house. Come October we were back on the road, off to pick grapes in France. In ensuing months, we explored Britain and Ireland, then flew to Jakarta, crossing Java to Bali for Christmas on the beach. We spent a month each in Malaysia and Thailand, then another trekking in Nepal, reaching India just in time to ride scooters around the burning vehicles, overturned trucks, and screaming mobs of the Patna bread riots. We traveled throughout the subcontinent then flew to Addis Ababa, Ethiopia, where Fitz was jumped in the dark twice, once by a guy with a knife. We hitchhiked across Kenya, camping one night in

Amboseli Game Reserve, where monkeys stole our supper, and in a rented VW bug we outran a charging mama rhino. In Tanzania we toured game parks. Turned away by the only hotel in one such park, and with no ride, we rather foolishly decided to walk to the highway at dusk. En route, a tribe of baboons encircled us aggressively. Somehow we broke through and ran back to the compound to sleep on a hotel worker's floor. We slept outdoors through sandstorms in Sudan and rode across the Nubian Desert from Khartoum to Egypt tied to the roof of a steam train. And we kept on traveling, wanting more and more.

But it is the jungle especially that remains with us. Sometimes, as I am just standing on a street corner waiting to cross, the swamp appears. I shiver until the light turns green and I realize that I am back at home. Our days are painted by our children and their families, our friends and meaningful work, our interests, and, sometimes, travel.

My life, like the Madre, is a running river: widening, moving forward, always changing. It is sometimes calm, sometimes raging, often joyously rippling. I am ever curious about what lies around the bend.

Acknowledgments

I have so many people to thank along the journey of writing this book. Beginning with my daughter, Megan, who picked up a brochure for a memoir class and told me, "You should do it!" The class was two hours once a week for four weeks. A small commitment it seemed. So although I was working and had just laid my mother to rest and couldn't really put my heart into a new project, I decided to try it.

Four weeks turned into years. Thank you to Kerry Egan, twice-published book author, who taught the course and continued with me far after the official class ended. She never stopped believing in me. Thank you, Trina Bigham, original classmate with unflagging interest and help, and Nicola Burnell, who carried on after Kerry moved away. Her assistance was tremendous. Thank you to all of you for the pleasure of your company.

My heart fills with gratitude for my perceptive readers and supporters. Thank you, Mary Leeson, Cheryl Stern, Marsha McCabe, Kathleen Peck, Frank Phillips, and Jackie O'Hara. Also, Kris Phelps, the late Richard Leeson, Sally Myers, Amanda Cook, Jane DeBarbieri, Jonathan Pogash, and Charlie Barmonde. Aiden, my daughter, an excellent writer and editor, pushed me to apply to the Bread Loaf Writers' Conference. We were both admitted as, I'm told, the first mother-daughter duo to attend. Huge thanks to the whole Bread Loaf team: to the instructors, the staff, and to my writers group.

Special thanks to author Damon DiMarco. I will never forget your generous advice, your delight in my manuscript, and for bringing it to the attention of Martha Kaplan.

Thank you, Martha Kaplan, my agent *grande* and enthusiastic promoter who believed *Ruthless River* would find the right home. To my astute, quick-witted editor, Vicky Wilson, who provided the right home; to her most helpful assistant, Ryan Smernoff, and to all the other dedicated staff at Vintage, my heartfelt thanks.

And most of all, to Jerry Julep, a star to me from the first time we met, I owe my deepest appreciation. He has been my number one champion and editor, as well as devoted husband. He fought by my side for our lives in the jungle. We've had a life filled with challenge and joy. I salute him for all that he does and all that he is, ever proud that he's my husband.